Edwin Muir: Uncollected Scottish Criticism

EDWIN MUIR: UNCOLLECTED SCOTTISH CRITICISM

edited and introduced by
Andrew Noble

VISION
and
BARNES & NOBLE

Vision Press Limited
11-14 Stanhope Mews West
London SW7 5RD

and

Barnes & Noble Books
81 Adams Drive
Totowa, NJ 07512

ISBN (UK) 0 85478 324 5
ISBN (US) 0 389 20202 9

Printed and bound in Great Britain
by Mansell Bookbinders Ltd.,
Witham, Essex
Typeset by Chromoset Limited,
Shepperton, Middlesex
MCMLXXXII

Contents

Acknowledgements

I am deeply grateful to Mr. Gavin Muir for granting the copyright to his father's writings included in this volume. Thanks for the copyright are also due to *The Glasgow Herald, The Listener, The New Statesman, The Observer, The Scots Magazine, The Scotsman* and *The Spectator.* I am also grateful to Honor Mulholland, Peter Gilmour and Kenneth Simpson for their helpful suggestions and assistance in preparing the manuscript, and Mrs. Jean Leithead and Mrs. Christine Cunningham, Department of English Studies, University of Strathclyde for typing it.

Introduction

"The inspired poet's tongue must have an echo in the state of
public feeling, or of involuntary belief, or it soon grows harsh or
mute."

Hazlitt

"For if it's no' by thocht that Poetry's wrocht
It's no by want o' thocht.
The verse that flatters ignorance maun seem
To ignorant folk supreme
Sin' nane can read the verse that disna
The damned thing bides as if it isna."

MacDiarmid

Towards the end of his life Edwin Muir was invited to deliver the
prestigious Charles Eliot Norton Lectures at Harvard. In these
lectures Muir brought to lucid consummation one of his central
preoccupations: the nature and fate of the poet as, in the
momentum and among the artefacts of cosmopolitan modern
society, he found himself increasingly deprived of an audience.
Unbeknown to his American hearers, Muir stood before them in
the immediate wake of what was to prove his last and perhaps
bitterest attempt to sustain a relationship with an audience
composed of his fellow countrymen. The visiting professor
ironically had just been declared inadequate and redundant by
central elements of the Scottish adult educational establishment.
Foreign recognition and native repudiation had, in fact, been
Muir's consistent fate and this last incident is simply more telling
in the degree of disparity between American enthusiasm for his
genius and Scottish apathy. In these Harvard lectures, whose
cogency was unaffected by failing health, it was natural, then,
that Muir should turn to the problem of the breakdown of the
vital relationship between poetry and community. Natural, too,
that in discussing such a breakdown Scotland should never be far
from his thoughts for Muir's personal experience as a creative
writer in Scotland and his interpretation of Scottish literature,
which was certainly influenced but not distorted by that
experience, was of a culture with perhaps unique powers to abuse
and resist the literary imagination. My purpose, then, has been
to demonstrate Muir's life as that of a modern writer of genius in

9

a Scottish society which did little to nourish him and much to thwart and impede. From this biographical account I have developed an account of Muir's historical vision of the misalliances between the Scottish writer and his society.

Like MacDiarmid, I consider Muir as "incomparably the finest critic Scotland has ever produced." All the pieces in this collection show the extraordinary lucidity of his prose, the formal elegance of his intelligence in the genre of occasional writing and his unswerving eye for the truth. In any healthy state of affairs such criticism would provide an impetus for an interest in and republication of Muir's other works and a recognition that he was not only a poet and critic of the highest order but a novelist and historian of ideas of great merit.[1]

Sadly, present trends do not seem to offer much encouragement to hopes of such a revaluation. Other than the highly commendable republication of *Scottish Journey* by Mainstream Press, recent critical comment on Muir has had an air of bland condescension which seems largely to mask a deep ignorance of the man and his age.[2] We tend to assume, perhaps too easily, the veracity of Dr. Johnson's belief that time itself delivers to us the true from the false in writing, the creator from the hack. Muir himslf was not at all certain that this was so. Writing about Burns, a poet who had also some harsh, incisive things to say about his native land, Muir remarked on how such dissent had been segregated and nullified:

> I think I have said enough to show that Burns has been unostentatiously but securely swallowed and digested by Holy Willie during the century and a bit since his death . . . Something has happened to him since his death, and it is what happens to all writers after their death, no matter what they have written. It may not be true that all writers reflect the economic ideology of the society in which they live—I do not think it is—but it does seem to be true that their writings are finally and in the long run made to reflect that ideology, by a process of elimination and transformation, until the most influential classes in society can finally put their seal on the result.[3]

While much of what has happened to the best Scottish writers undoubtedly corroborates this opinion, we should also remember that, like Kierkegaard, Muir's central preoccupation was with asserting the primacy of eternal truths over the false

10

certitudes, whims and fanaticisms of mere historicism. He believed that the creative imagination was the servant of such truths and that a human world was not only inconceivable without such a form of imagination but, like one of those fabulous, resilient animals from his poetry, it could survive the imperious beasts which persistently sought to devour it. Or, as he wrote to Herbert Read on the outbreak of the Second World War:

> As for where advancement (so far as there has been any) has come from, I suppose you would agree with me that before it could prevail it had to pass through the phase of anger, that it had to meet opposition and envy and fight against them; but I feel pretty certain, on the other hand, that the spring of advancement, the thing that always had to be fought for, did not come out of opposition or anger at all, though when it enters the world of action it rouses anger, until, when the anger has burned itself out, it emerges in a somewhat defaced but still positive and workable form.[4]

No statement could better illustrate the spirit of the man or the principal theme of this collection.

A Scottish Literary Life

In one of his last essays Edwin Muir wrote that "I feel to explain anyone is an attempt that should never be made."[5] Muir did not, of course mean that we should not attempt to understand one another. He meant that the individual's spiritual freedom, hence his capacity to bear truthful witness, should never be explained away by some finalised and thereby reductive act of the mind. Such a warning is particularly salutary with regard to understanding the nature of Muir's relationship with Scotland. Muir's personal experiences of Scotland were, with varying degrees of intensity, largely painful. Indeed the earlier ones can be strictly described as traumatic. We should not, however, as a consequence of this see him as some kind of case, an unrepresentative figure whose largely aberrant opinions are to be accounted for in terms of the individual distortions of an unfortunate and oversensitive man. Muir's life, I would contend, was not by choice but perhaps by some mysterious fate an exemplary Scottish one. No poetic extrovert, he did not, like Whitman, desire to make himself the touchstone of the national destiny, the locus through which all the varied strands pass. Such a burden was more imposed than sought and yet there was almost always truth and grace in the manner it was accepted. While there is an unstinting frankness, honesty and, at times a near savage wit, in Swift's sense, in his critique of his own nation there is also no pettiness. Muir's style is consistently marked by a charitable reticence of manner. Often bitterly attacked, especially by MacDiarmid and his camp followers, Muir displayed an arguably non-Scottish dislike of wearing such resentments and affronts on his sleeve. Even more importantly his constant ability both to perceive and confront the deeper implications of the many profoundly painful experiences of his life, a heroic intellectual antidote to self-pity, enabled him to maintain that marvellous equipoise of clarity and passion which is of the essence of both his creative and critical voice.

Muir's personal experience of Scotland had in both time and space a comprehensive spread. He spent his childhood in rural Orkney, his adolescence and early manhood in Glasgow and the industrial West, part of his middle-age in St. Andrews and Edinburgh and, approaching old age, at Newbattle Abbey near Dalkeith. His knowledge of Scotland was, however, far from limited by having experience of no other nation. Other forms of national experience were not only extensive but gave to his analysis of Scotland almost as wide a comparative basis as his reading in foriegn literatures gave to his criticism. Highly relevant to his understanding of Scotland is that he saw it relative to the nature of English and European life. He was in this fortunate because he lived in an age when the European cost of living and the income derived from the writing and translating of both his wife and himself were still compatible, thus allowing him to breathe, at least between the wars, what MacDiarmid described as the more invigorating "plein air" of Europe.[6]

In Muir's studies of social and ethnic contrast what emerges is a pained but objective sense of Scotland's deficiencies. In his experience of England he was aware of London as a capital with a genuine literary life, not like Edinburgh a city of hollow pretension, and also of a rural life imbued with a sense of tradition and continuity unlike the sadly uprooted conditions prevailing in Scotland. He found pre-war Prague even more stimulating. In Prague he was impressed by the intimacy and warmth with which Karl Čapek was greeted in the street and this led him to remark "this warm easy-going contact could only have been possible in a comparatively small town, and it was the first thing that made me wish that Edinburgh might become a similar place".[7] Muir drew an unhappy comparison between the vitality of Czech nationalism in the Twenties and that prevailing in Scotland. Since he was to have two spells of residence in Czechoslovakia and since he was to see its national spirit twice crushed, that country perhaps became his single most important standard by which to judge the vitality of Scotland's sense of nationhood. This was particularly so because Czechoslavakia's tragic fate was to demonstrate what the loss of authentic nationhood did to a people. In *Belonging*, Willa reports their appalled sense of the calculated destruction of the inner being of the Czech nation at the hands of variant forms of German and Russian genocidal ideology thus:

> The Germans had struck with instinctive sureness at the very heart of Czech life, at that invisible emanation, made up of beliefs and traditions, heroic legends, folklore, art, poetry, music and vernacular songs, which surrounds a people and sustains its sense of identity and self-respect, being all the more potent because it is invisible. Today we are becoming aware of its importance; we call it the 'public image' of a personality or a people, yet it seems to be more than the name implies, to be more effectively real than any material facts.[8]

While, then, Czechoslovakia held for Muir the stark lineaments of a national tragedy, a nation overwhelmed by external, bestial force, Scotland's plight, the emptiness at its heart, was both less explicable and, if less suffused with pathos, more perturbing. Thus in 1935 he was to write that "the unfortunate thing for Scotland is that it is not an obviously oppressed nation, as Ireland was, but only a visibly depressed one searching for the source of its depression".[9] Scotland, consequently, was for him less the occasion for a sense of tragedy, it was more the stuff of the bathos of half-hearted suicide. The destruction of its inner being he believed had been largely self-destruction so that, for example, the perverted heroism of Knox's reformation had degenerated into the complacent, stagnant mood of modern Scotland:

> Courage beyond the point and obdurate pride
> Made us a nation, robbed us of a nation.
> Defiance absolute and myriad-eyed
> That could not pluck the palm plucked our damnation.
> We with such courage and bitter wit
> To fell the ancient oak of loyalty
> And strip the peopled hill and the altar bare,
> And crush the poet with an iron text,
> How could we read our souls and learn to be?
> Here a dull drove of faces harsh and vexed,
> We watch our cities burning in their pit,
> To salve our souls grinding dull lucre out,
> We fanatics of the frustrate and the half,
> Who once set Purgatory Hill in doubt.[10]

Muir's analysis of the harm wrought in Scotland by Calvinism is complex and we shall have cause to return to it in some detail. Sufficient to say at the moment is that the sensuality he experienced in pre-War Mediterranean France was profoundly therapeutic in countering the disembodiment wrought on him by God-fearing, industrial Scotland. In post-War Italy this process of reintegration was taken a step further when in Rome he experienced a sense of Incarnation, of the saving relationship of flesh and spirit in Christ. Such European experience deeply impressed on him the malign consequences of a minatory spirituality which existed in Scotland and of a culture which sought the fission rather than the wholeness of its members. These elements fuse in his fine poem, "The Incarnate One":

> The windless northern surge, the sea-gulls' scream,
> And Calvin's kirk crowning the barren brae.
> I think of Giotto the Tuscan shepherd's dream,
> Christ, man and creature in their inner day.
> How could our race betray
> The image, and the Incarnate One unmake
> Who chose this form and fashion for our sake.[11]

14

If Muir's extensive travels in Eastern and Western Europe gave him a relative sense of nationalism and faith he also, unwillingly but fruitfully, possessed a temporal awareness of Scotland far outwith the individual's normal historical experience. He described this sense of history in his first version of his autobiography thus:

> I was born before the Industrial Revolution, and am now about two hundred years old. But I have skipped a hundred and fifty of them. I was really born in 1737, and till I was fourteen no time-accidents happened to me. Then in 1751 I set out from Orkney for Glasgow. When I arrived I found that it was not 1751, but 1901 . . . I was brought up in the midst of a life which was still co-operative, which still had the medieval communal feeling. We had heard and read of something called "competition" but it never came into our experience. Our life was an order. Since the Industrial Revolution there has not really been an order except in a few remote places . . . To be born outside your age and have to catch up and fit into it is a strain. Yet I would not for any price have missed my knowledge of that first pre-industrial order; for it taught me something that is inherent in every good order.[12]

Thus Muir's childhood experience of Orkney, not only emotionally but intellectually, left an abiding and vitally important impression on himself and his work. This brutal "time-accident" constantly evoked in his poetry the mythical resonances of the Fall. The child who had experienced life as sanctified ritual and who was torn from a world where "time still sat on the wrist of each day with its wings folded" and plunged into a mechanised, restive, historical flux stands at the centre of all his writing. Also, in highly compressed form, Muir personally enacted the national fate—the transition over the last two centuries from an agricultural to an industrial country. Muir's sense of Orkney thus provided him with a cultural standard which he subsequently employed in evaluating other elements of Scottish life. He never forgot what he considered to be its essential virtues and his awareness of the loss of these virtues created in him not only a sensibility both angry and elegiac but a belief that the forms of life which emerged in modern industrial society, where they were not sinister, disturbing mutations of an earlier humanity, had been

15

manufactured out of a quite unnecessarily cruel destruction of previously existing forms.

As well as granting him a unique perspective on Scottish industrial capitalism, Orkney added a partially ethnic dimension to Muir's thought. Paradoxically he saw Scotland the better for seeing it from its Norse periphery. The ambivalence of his feelings for Scotland could, in fact, on occasion lead him to express a desire to seek refuge from his Scottishness in an alternative Scandinavian national identify. An early letter to his brother-in-law regarding MacDiarmid's republican and socialist ambitions for a new Scotland precisely catches such a mixed mood.

> He thinks that if Scotland were a nation we would have Scottish literature, art, music, culture and everything that other nations seem to have and we haven't. I think that would probably be likely; but I feel rather detached. as I've often told Grieve, because after all I'm not Scotch, I'm an Orkney man, a good Scandinavian, and my true country is Norway, or Denmark, or Iceland, or some place like that. But this is nonsense, I'm afraid, though there is some sense in it, as Lizzie will agree . . .[13]

Here we have Muir's wry acknowledgement that there is to be no fanciful ethnic escape route. The cup will not pass. Given, too, the degree of opposition Scotland could provoke in Muir we must seek in his usage of detachment a more specialised meaning. Neither wholly a native, who tends to be oblivious to what he has always seen, nor a foreigner, who tends to see only strangeness to the point of caricature, Muir's detachment existed in occupying a particularly lucid point between these extremes. A man of passionate convictions he also had a remarkable sense of fairness and balance so that, unlike so many Scottish commentators on their nation, he never allowed the strength of his feelings to escape the test of his intelligence.

It is this unusual combination of detachment with the extreme degree of emotional and intellectual tension generated by this painful transition from rural Orkney to industrial Glasgow which is of such vital importance in not only understanding Muir's subsequent moral evaluation of modern society but also his penetrating analysis of the corruption present since the beginning of the Industrial Revolution in Scottish writing. It was not merely taste or aesthetic theory but the very facts of his own experience which provoked in Muir such outright opposition to the prevailing Scottish literary mores.

Two parallel and apparently contradictory strands run through Scottish writing since the Enlightenment. On the one hand there is an advocacy of material progress in society based on individual entrepreneurial skills and rationalised methods of work. Smith and Hume are the internationally celebrated founding fathers of such a movement and, in the nineteenth century, MacAulay is the most celebrated propagandist of what he believed were to be the inevitable, imperial triumphs of commercial and industrial civilization. On the other hand in literature and belle-lettres no country has been more preoccupied with retaining a maudlin, retarded and pastoral image of itself. Indeed no country has been more successful in promulgating such a self-image and thus colluding with the majority of its writers in taking advantage of a seeming near universal appetite for such escape to an allegedly safe past. Where there was imaginative opposition to such a sentimentally synthesised Scotland as in James Thomson's poem about Greenock, *City of Dreadful Night,* or in Thomas Carlyle's rage about the terrible slum wynds of Glasgow ("under the hideous coverlet of vapours, and putrefactions and unimaginable gases, what fermenting vat lies hid?") the dominant forces in the culture of nineteenth century Scotland had ample power to either censor or wholly repress it. Thus, since the latter part of the eighteenth century there has coexisted in seeming amity a Scotland of fact and a Scotland of fantasy. Muir, however, felt that these two life forms were less symbiotic than sinister since it was the task of the imagination to confront the facts of Scottish life and not deviously to evade them. He considered that in Scotland imagination had degenerated into mere fancy and that the purpose of that fancifulness was the intensification of false and often lachrymose feelings as a method of disguising the intellectually irreconcilable disparity between Scottish theories of progressive, social optimism and the actual facts of Scottish evolution which increasingly presented the picture of a debilitated, depopulated countryside

17

and a malign coagulation of the life in the urban areas. Thus when Muir came to discuss one of the most celebrated of Scottish literary theories, that named by Professor G. Gregory Smith as "the Caledonian Antisyzygy" and defined by him as the Scotsman's happy capacity to be equally at home in the world of the densely tangible and the fantastic, he reacted sharply. Gregory Smith had expressed his notion thus:

> The Scottish muse has another mood. Though she loved reality, sometimes to maudlin affection for the commonplace, she has loved not less the airier pleasures to be found in the confusion of the senses, in the fun of things thrown topsy-turvy, in the horns of elfland and the voices of the mountains . . . There is more in the Scottish antithesis of the real and the fantastic than is to be explained by the familiar rules of rhetoric. The sudden jostling of contraries seems to preclude any relationship by literary suggestion. The one invades the other without warning. They are the 'polar twins' of the Scottish muse.[14]

While Muir not only accepted but celebrated the dynamism of a singular Scottish imagination like MacDiarmid's, "varied with a clean contrair spirit", he wholly disagreed with Gregory Smith that this supposedly mysterious dualistic interconnection between the fantastic and the real was a healthy symptom in either Scottish letters or life. For Muir the action of the imagination was always to intensify our sense of reality, however painful that might be. Scottish fantasy, he felt, was a parody of imagination by way of corrupt avoidance:

> Gregory Smith sees in Scottish fantastic poetry a proof that Scotsmen are at ease in both rooms of life; but the place they actually reach through this kind of poetry is a sort of half-way-house between the two. Franz Kafka in one of his aphorisms pictures man as fastened by one collar to the earth, so that when he tries to fly too high he is pulled back again, and fastened by another to Heaven, so that when he sinks too low he is brought up in the opposite direction. Scottish fantastic poetry represents a mean latitude in which a man finds the maximum ease from these two predicaments. It is a spirited recoil from the earthly which does not take one into too inconvenient proximity to the heavenly; both collars lie easily around the poet's neck, and for the time being he can imagine, if he pleases, that there is no collar at all. Finally the drag of ordinary gravity pulls him back to earth

again, and to explanations which will satisfy the ordinary man: drink being the most natural of these.

. . . ever since Gregory Smith's famous generalization, this quality has been accorded an exaggerated importance; it has been exalted as a major attribute of Scottish poetry, instead of an occasional mood, a periodic holiday of the imagination. As a holiday it is above all things enjoyable; but as an antithesis to prosaic experience it is inadequate, for it consists either in a comic propitiation of terrible things . . . or in a tangential escape from the ordinary world. It does not ask for the voluntary suspension of disbelief which we bring to *Kubla Khan*. Indeed it does not ask for belief at all, for it is completely sceptical of itself. In it we find imagination pulling one way and the intellect the other so that neither can reach its end, and finally coming to rest in the half-way house I mentioned before. I think it is not extravagant to see in this kind of poetry the ideal expression of the dichotomy which has been Scotland's ruin both in politics and literature; not a salutary and creative factor, as is sometimes assumed, but an expression, fantastic, humorous and sometimes delightful, or a stationary disharmony, a standing frustration. For imagination and intellect do not reach a reconciliation in this poetry, but a comic deadlock. The result is not creation, but distortion. To exalt this kind of fantasy, therefore, as a major attribute of Scottish poetry, is a dangerous flattery.[15]

Thus Muir believed that rather than the existence of a dynamic polarity operating at the heart of the Scottish imagination and, from such a core radiating energy into all aspects of the national life, there really existed cowardly negation and hence paralysis. Muir is particularly acute in his understanding of how such fancifulness operates in the social and political dimensions; of how a nation deeply committed to greedy practicality pretends to worldly disinterest.

Gregory Smith found in this vein of fantasy the compensating quality which offset what he called the Scottish "maudlin affection for the commonplace", which we may regard as an expression of Scottish materialism. He had an uneasy feeling that the Scots are a materialistic people, as all intelligent Scotsmen must have; and he wished to prove that they are not so materialistic as they seem, indeed that they are absurdly impractical and irresponsible, gay and illogical flouters of the material world. He acknowledged, on the other hand, that they

19

often returned to that world after these excursions and explained their behaviour in terms perfectly acceptable to it; but he did not draw the obvious conclusion from this fact. A hundred years ago Heine saw that sentimentality was the other face of materialism; but materialism has many faces. Scottish fantastic poetry is the natural recoil from a "maudlin affection for the commonplace", but it has no particular virtue beyond its naturalness . . . To romanticize this reaction, to picture the Scotsman as making merry in a clash of strange worlds and moods (but contriving presumably to earn a living meantime) is mere sentimentality, and perpetuates an ancestral weakness of Scotland, the weakness which turned all its history into legend, mainly tawdry, and created such ludicrous misunderstandings as the myth of Bonnie Prince Charlie. The response of the Makars and the Balladists to experience was a whole response; the response of fantastic poetry is a joke followed by an explanation.[16]

For Muir, then, Scottish Romanticism was, quite unlike its English and German counterparts, which he saw as essential modes of social comprehension and which had a seminal influence on his thought and poetry, exclusively sentimental. At the core of this sentimentality lay an impotence which sought release in fantasy or, in life and letters, a decking itself out in the borrowed costumes, especially the wholly historically unsanctioned tartan ones, of a lost Scotland. For Muir this was both to have one's cake and eat it. The materially rewarding practices of modern economic individualism were allegedly happily compatible with the communal sentiments of traditional society. For Muir this was the final self-indulgence of a greed not brave enough to declare itself. Thus, inevitably, the early experiences of Muir's life led him not to disavow the Scottish literary preoccupation with traditional life but to enter, by way of bitter opposition, into an imaginative recreation and evaluation of it rather than participating in the native tradition of its exploitation. Muir, revealingly, could find no Scottish writer to act as a creative model of how the past might be placed in creative context to the present. The alleged exemplar of such a form, Walter Scott, finally always rang false to Muir and it is in his comments on the work of the Austrian writer, Hugo von Hofmannsthal, that we come closest to Muir's own literary genius.

Before the disaster came Hofmannsthal had preserved in his poetry and prose the old Austrian life, as if it were an infinitely precious thing which might be lost, as it was now; his love still suffused it with a tender radiance. His description of the Austrian farm in *Andreas*, an unfinished novel, is unlike anything else in modern literature in its union of reality and enchantment and a sense that everything is rooted deeply and tranquilly in time. He knew that peasant life in a traditional land flowers into its own magic, as the life of industrial towns and great cities cannot; for it is tradition that nurtures enchantment, and when it collapses the natural shrinks into the bald shape of what is called 'real life': a theme for the ordinary novel. Hofmannsthal lived in a world where that transformation had not yet taken place; he saw tradition still shaping life, and for that reason his characters and scenes too are shaped, not copied, and exist beyond the reach of art which concerns itself with those numb facts which, set down no matter how faithfully, tell us nothing more than what they are. He had faith in what he knew and loved, and held that "powerful imaginations are conservative". His poems and plays preserve a lost world and give it back to us as part of experience.[17]

Like Hofmannsthal Muir is also a poet of past enchantment; a magic, however, suffused with a tragic sense of loss. Nor is there any sentimentality in their vision of the past. Sentimentalists can never grant the past such tragic purity; emotional cannibals, they celebrate what they have killed by lachrymosely devouring it. Fellow Romantics, Muir and Hofmannsthal have an intense sense of the unnatural condition of the modern world since it potently manifests itself to them as a mainly terrifying contrast to a lost but not forgotten naturalness. For Muir part of this naturalness was, of course, similar to that of Wordsworth's belief that life should be lived in intimate proximity to natural rhythms, forms and creatures. Part of the shock of Glasgow was to be suddenly projected into an environment denuded of these conditions. The impact of that city on Muir cannot, however, be fully accounted for by this factor nor by its extreme public squalor nor by Muir's sense of pervasive self-seeking as opposed to communal help which had been the basis of Orkney's integrated moral and economic life. All these elements certainly struck him with enormous force and were experienced in combination with a terrible sequence of family deaths. The inevitable result of this was to drive Muir in on himself so that after the loss of his brothers he became an increasingly ill and shadowy figure haunting dingy, ill-smelling public libraries, unconsciously feeding his intellect but in all other respects deprived. All this makes quite understandable Muir's developing sense of being dead in the midst of morbid forms of life and of his fear of going insane. To go no further than perceiving the cause and effect of these forces on Muir is, however, to stop short of understanding the fullest and deepest implications of what happend to him in his early years in Glasgow. Muir, in his autobiography, referred to himself at this period in his life as a Displaced Person and it is only if we understand the *metaphysics* of that displacement that we come near to understanding the extraordinary shift Muir believed had taken place from the traditional world to the new one. Temporally and spatially man, for Muir, had been wrenched out of the spiritual context necessary to his existence as a human being and delivered over not to freedom but brutal licence. It was the impact of Glasgow on Muir that made him perceive this nightmare dilemma of the modern self and, while, as he grew older he grew fond of other elements of the city's somewhat distorted vitality and its compensating wit and warmth, what happened to him in it subsequently served as a model for understanding the greater horrors and terrors which were spreading like a plague across Europe. Whether or not we like what he saw in them, Muir saw Scottish phenomena not enshrouded in their usual parochial cosiness but as worthy of attention as the mores and politics of any other society. Far from believing Scotland lived in some backwater safe from the deadly currents of modern life he saw Scotland as a chief agent and expression of the dilemmas of the modern condition. Hence in *An Autobiography*, we have this discourse on one of his most horrific Glasgow experiences:

> Religion once supplied that knowledge, but our life is no longer ruled by religion. Yet we can know what we are only if we accept some of the hypotheses of religion. Human beings are understandable only as immortal spirits; they become natural then, as natural as young horses; they are absolutely unnatural if we try to think of them as a mere part of the natural world. They are immortal spirits distorted and corrupted in countless ways by the world into which they are born: bearing countless shapes,

22

beautiful, quaint, grotesque; living countless lives, trivial, sensational, dull; serving behind counters, going to greyhound races, playing billiards, preaching to savages in Africa, collecting stamps, stalking deer in the Highlands, adding up figures in an office for fifty years, ruining one another in business, inventing explosives which will destroy other men and women on a large scale, praying for the cessation of war, weeping over their sins, or trying to discover what sin really is: doing everything that is conceivable for human beings to do, and doing it in a different way at every stage of history. I do not have the power to prove that man is immortal and that the soul exists; but I know that there must be such a proof, and that compared with it every other demonstration is idle. It is true that human life without immortality would be inconceivable because if man is an animal by direct descent I can see human life only as a nightmare populated by animals wearing top-hats and kid gloves, painting their lips and touching up their cheeks and talking in heated rooms, rubbing their muzzles together in the moment of lust, and going through innumerable clever tricks, learning to make and listen to music, to gaze sentimentally at sunsets, to count, to acquire a sense of humour, to give their lives for some cause, or to pray.

This picture has always been in my mind since one summer evening in Glasgow in 1919. I did not believe in the immortality of the soul at that time; I was deep in the study of Nietzsche, and had cast off with a great sense of liberation all belief in any other life than the life we live here and now, as an imputation on the purity of immediate experience, which I had intellectually convinced myself was guiltless and beyond good and evil. I was returning in a tramcar from my work; the tramcar was full and very hot; the sun burned through the glass on backs of necks, shoulders, faces, trousers, skirts, hands, all stacked there impartially. Opposite me was sitting a man with a face like a pig's, and as I looked at him in the oppressive heat the words came into my mind, "That is an animal". I looked round me at the other people in the tramcar; I was conscious that something had fallen from them and from me; and with a sense of desolation I saw that they were all animals, some of them good, some evil, some charming, some sad, some happy, some sick, some well. the tramcar stopped and went on again, carrying its menagerie; my mind saw countless other tramcars where animals sat or got on or off with mechanical dexterity, as if they had been trained in a circus; and I realized that in all Glasgow, in all Scotland, in all

23

the world, there was nothing but millions of such creatures living an animal life and moving towards an animal death as towards a great slaughterhouse. I stared at the faces, trying to make them human again and to dispel the hallucination, but I could not. This experience was so terrifying that I dismissed it, deliberately forgot it by that perverse power which the mind has of obliterating itself. I felt as if I had lived for a few moments in Swift's world, for Swift's vision of humanity was the animal vision. I could not have endured it for more than a few minutes. I did not associate it at the time with Nietzsche. But I realized that I could not bear mankind as a swarming race of thinking animals, and that if there was not somewhere, it did not matter where—in a suburb of Glasgow or of Hong Kong or of Honolulu—a single living soul, life was a curious irrelevant desolation. I pushed away this realization for a time, but it returned again later, like the memory of my cowardice as a boy.

The animal world is a great impersonal order, without pathos in its suffering. Man is bound to it by necessity and guilt, and by the closer bond of life, for he breathes the same breath. But when man is swallowed up in nature nature is corrupted and man is corrupted. The sense of corruption in *King Lear* comes from the fact that Goneril, Regan and Cornwall are merely animals furnished with human faculties as with weapons which they can take up or lay down at will, faculties which they have stolen, not inherited. Words are their teeth and claws, and thought the technique of the deadly spring. They are so *unnatural* in belonging completely to nature that Gloucester can explain them only by "these late eclipses in the sun and moon".

The conflict in Lear is a conflict between the sacred tradition of human society, which is old, and nature, which is always new, for it has no background. As I sat in that tramcar in Glasgow I was in an unhistorical world; I was outside time without being in eternity; in the small, sensual, momentary world of a beast.[18]

For Muir, then, human nature is rooted in spirit and its growth is given sanctified form by tradition. The nature of his political vision is, indeed, very close to that of Coleridge. Society to survive had to be "bound together not by force and appetite; but by a sort of piety and human fitness, a natural piety".[19] Orkney had this quality, Calvinist Glasgow, in the grip of quite a different religious interpretation of life, postulated appetite in the form of *laissez-faire* economics and violence as the reality of the human condition. Deprived of a sanctified bonding in human relationships men are, triumphantly or despairingly, delivered over to defining themselves in terms only of their appetites. This leads to life as a form of unappeasable greed because no earthly limit can be seen to apply to such appetites since the soul, thwarted of its regulatory heavenly aspirations and overwhelmed by its creatureliness, cannot properly locate itself. Modern man had for Muir, by his megalomaniac self-assertion, lost sight of the boundaries between himself and the other dimensions of creation, the beasts and the angels, and as part of this terrible displacement had shrunk time to a sense not of a kind of spiritual fourth dimension which granted the individual his unique integrity but to that moment occupied by his immediate wants. Such an atypical model of what we now commonly conceive of as reality appeared to Muir in 1943, a time of bitter darkness when murderous force seemed wholly destructive of any form of order.

> I dreamed last night what must have been a symbolic pictorial representation of human life, with heaven above and hell beneath, angels ascending and descending, concentric beams of glory falling from the height, the animals in their places, and man in the centre. The picture did not present itself instantaneously, but grew detail by detail; the last detail, completing it, being a quaint little animal or sprite insinuated at the bottom of the right hand corner in the manner of an artist's signature (it looked very like one, except for the fact that it kept wriggling apologetically). This is all that remains clearly of the picture now. I think of it sometimes as a little fluffy dog sitting on its hind legs and fawning on an invisible master, and then as a neat, small, domesticated demon playing on a flute an air first learnt in hell but adapted a long time ago (perhaps in Eden) to the human ear and the human soul; the oldest music in the world. The little dog or demon or signature tune is all that remains. Yet I feel that if I found a propitious moment I could construct from that little hieroglyph the whole design, the glory and abasement, the summits and deeps, the light and darkness, the powers and dominations, and man himself in the centre.
>
> Thinking over this dream again, I do not feel so sure that I could reconstruct the picture; but that does not matter much, for what it has left behind is a sense of order, and that was the principle of the picture; the order was everywhere in it. Every complete vision of life—and by complete I do not mean including

everything merely, but including everything in its place—is a vision of life glorified. Where everything is included without order, we get a vision of life nullified. A vision of a few things arranged neatly in order, with all the rest left out, is a false vision. All three are worth having, since they are visions. But most of our lives we live without any vision at all, in our street, with our acquaintances, our habits, our worries, our comforts.[20]

Such dream visions of spiritual hierarchy can, of course, be seen as forms of regressive wish fulfilment. Muir, creatively unrelated to Scottish society and looking out onto a world suffused with the meaningless, destructive force of a war whose conclusion was by no means assured, was at a particularly low ebb when he wrote this. In Willa Muir's account of this central element in her husband's thoughts we can also see how easily we might sceptically disclaim the validity of such perceptions because of our allegedly more advanced viewpoint.

> Edwin had lived in an atmosphere saturated with legend, myth, ballads and Bible stories. There was some kind of accepted story to account for everything. It was natural for him to look for a great story, an all-encompassing myth, to explain the mystery of life as he later found it, especially in what seemed the chaos of Glasgow. Scottish Presbyterianism, Scottish argumentative rationality, confined him to criticism when he was searching literature for clues, but did not satisfy him; he was much closer to the Middle Ages than the people around him and he needed poetic myths.[21]

One can deduce from this that this compulsion of Muir's to look "for some great story, some cosmic pattern that would assign a place to every experience in life, relating it to an inclusive whole and justifying it" was either a form of spiritual, and consequently intellectual, maladjustment to the modern world or a stubborn honesty that would not accept the rationalism, causality and empiricism of science as the final criterion of reality. Again belonging to the Romantic tradition, Muir believed that the imagination had its own province and provenance and that the intrusion of scientific materialism into this sphere was innately destructive. He shared Yeat's historical belief that "the only thoughts that our age carries to their logical conclusions are deductions from the materialism of the seventeenth century; they fill the newspapers, books,

26

speeches; they are implicit in all that we do and think."
Consequently it is difficult to present our modern minds with
the kind of proof that would customarily convince them of the
truth content of Muir's vision. In Willa's perception of her
husband there may be, however, if not unbiased factuality, a
sense of a quality in him which bespeaks not only his capacity to
envision the spiritual forms of reality but how the very quality of
his being seemed to her a manifestation of a mysterious, often
subconscious, participation in such a reality.

> This true self of Edwin's was now the mainspring of his life.
> Having very human limitations, I used to think of it as reaching
> *down* into his feelings and imagination and reaching *up* into
> conscious lucid thinking. The 'down' and 'up' notion is rather
> absurd, and yet human feelings do seem to come up from the
> midriff and human thoughts to take shape higher up behind the
> eyes, so that one is easily misled into believing the administrative
> centre in one's head to be more important than the feelings moving
> down below. But in my thoughts I did not cut off Edwin's true self
> at either end, since for me the air around him seemed always
> quivering with something like electricity. I thought his true self,
> that elusive mystery, reached *down* beyond him into that other
> mystery, the unconscious, out of which we all arise, and that it
> reached *up* beyond him into the air; how far I could not tell, but far
> enough to catch invisible and inaudible radiation from goodness
> knew where. His true self, I was well aware, was a very sensitive
> and delicate instrument both for receiving and giving out
> radiations.[22]

This description, remarkably analogous to Coleridge's vision
of man's complex, difficult role as the link between the natural
and supernatural worlds, expresses Willa's belief that her
husband creatively stood at the mid-point of a vital continuum
flowing from matter to spirit. Indeed we can define Muir's poetry
as a profound meditation, perhaps even mediation, concerning
the boundary conditions of our humanity. Its concern is with
those areas where human consciousness impinges on brute
creation and on the higher levels of the mysteries of the spirit.
Again like Yeats, Muir conceived of lyric poetry as "the voice of
what metaphysicians call innate knowledge, that is to say, of
conscience, for it expresses the relation of the soul to eternal
beauty and truth as no other writing can express it".

27

Orkney provided Muir with a similar background to that which traditional Ireland gave to Yeats. His childhood was spent in a culture where his consciousness had relatively open access to both dimensions, the elemental and the spiritual. Hence the poet in him was nourished by both the local literature of myths, legends and fairy tales and by his proximity to the soil and the animal kingdom. Despite MacDiarmid's outrageously satirical account of the bestiary of Muir's poetic vision, one cannot but be aware of the impression made on him by the life of the farm animals he lived among as a child.[23] Further the compact of blood which existed between man and beast struck him with a particular force:

> My passion for animals comes partly from being brought up so close to them, in a place where people lived as they had lived for two hundred years; partly from I do not know where. Two hundred years ago the majority of people lived close to the animals by whose labour of flesh they existed. The fact that we live on these animals remains; but the personal relation is gone, and with it the very idea of necessity and guilt. The animals we eat are killed by thousands in slaughter houses which we never see. A rationalist would smile at the thought that there is any guilt at all: there is only necessity which is laid upon all carnivores, not on man only. But our dreams and ancestral memories speak a different language.[24]

It was, therefore, no accident that the nadir of Muir's experience of industrial Scotland took place in a bone processing yard in Greenock. It was not the frightful, writhing bloated maggots or the all pervasive stink, terrible as they were, which induced in Muir the degree of morbidity which became omnipresent for him. What he found most degrading was the desecration of the animal kingdom by mechanical profit seeking. In so treating the animals we wrought, Muir believed, an even more savage degradation on ourselves. Our guilt towards the animals declared redundant, Muir saw in that terrible place, with its malicious bureaucracy and its penny pinching, the quintessence of the evil of economic individualism. Animals and men had become means towards an allegedly higher good of profit. Men no longer ends in themselves became for Muir, as for Kant and Coleridge, deprived of their essential humanity. Everything was given over to a doctine of practicality which, while not without virtue, is not a virtue complete in itself. Detached from a higher vision, Muir saw it as having degenerated into a rapacious vice. Muir associated Calvinism's appearance in Scotland under the aegis of Knox with a kind of Fall and as initiating this kind of exploitative behaviour with its profound contempt for the powers and virtues of a mind higher than its own functional, power-seeking drives. Not for Knox a poetic attempt to "relate the soul to eternal beauty". This was a time-wasting pursuit and, even more dangerously, could involve one in forms of perception and value which might interfere with the operation of a prescriptive code given over to rigorously controlling men's behaviour and labour.

Muir's conception of the operation of Calvinism in Scottish life bit very deeply into him because what he experienced in the West of Scotland seemed to be a near total verification of the truth of a world so conceived. In the apparently quite unjustified and agonisingly drawn out deaths of two of his brothers, one of tuberculosis and the other of an even more tortuous and insidious brain tumour, he was tempted to perceive the malign, capricious workings of a God who indifferently divided the fallen from the elect. To such metaphysical speculation was also wedded the terrible guilt of the survivor on seeing the bitterness of his brothers as they saw their unlived lives receding from them. Almost inevitably, those dying young hate the life they see around because it speaks so penetratingly of all they cannot have. The very geography and demography of the city itself began to impose itself on Muir as a model of Calvinist truth. The suburbs of the elect stood opposed to the slums of the irretrievably fallen and Muir, unable and unwilling to join the safely prosperous and terrified of descending to the level of the damned poor, increasingly ghost-like, wandered between both worlds. His life in Glasgow is, of course, caught in his autobiography but is perhaps even more remarkably present in his novel, *Poor Tom*, where fiction allowed him to explore the terrible private and public pain of these times with a lack of reserve which, paradoxically, the autobiographical form did not grant.[25] Muir's was not, I think, an exaggerated vision of Glasgow. Writing about Muir, Archibald MacLeish returning to his parents' homeland in the Twenties remarked that it "was the most repulsive city of my young experience—and I had started from Chicago".[26] As well as the squalor, there was also the endemic violence of the street life of the slums. Muir associated Calvinism not with a theology of love but one of force and in the purposeless, sadistic strife around him Muir again saw the essence of Calvin's vision. Haunted by such a cruel dualism existing seemingly at the very heart of things, both loathing the stifling respectability of his social position as a petty clerk and clinging desperately to it, Muir began to become more and more perversely fascinated by the sheer squalor and depravity of much of what he saw. Losing faith in higher possibilities he moved towards a grudging, self-destructive acceptance of what seemed to be the sole nature of reality:

> The same attraction to squalor drew me to the football matches on Saturday afternoon. Crosshill was a respectable suburb, but there were vacant lots scattered about it, chance scraps of waste ground where the last blade of grass had died, so that in dry weather they were as hard as lava, and in wet weather a welter of mud. On these lots teams from the slum quarters of the south side played every Saturday afternoon with great skill and savage ferocity. Fouls were a matter of course, and each game turned into a complicated feud in which the ball itself was merely a means to an end which had no connexion with the game. Some of the teams had boxers among their supporters; these men stood bristling on the touchline and shouted intimidations at the opposing players. I first saw one of these games shortly after I came to Glasgow; a brown fog covered the ground, and a small, tomato-red sun, like jellyfish floating in the sky, appeared and disappeared as the air grew thicker or finer. I found later that more civilized football teams played in the Queen's Park recreation ground, and I began to attend them instead, and later still, when I was earning enough money to spare a sixpence on Saturday, I attended the matches of the Queen's Park Football Club. But there was a grimy fascination in watching the damned kicking a football in a tenth-rate hell.[27]

Transfixed by such visions of violence and squalor at the heart of life, sensually deprived, plagued by strange and often possibly psychosomatic illnesses, imaginatively repressed, all Muir's energy seems, in these grim Glasgow days, concentrated on his critical intellect. In one of the most astonishing feats of autodidacticism in literary history, Muir acquired, by voracious reading in public libraries and even in the office toilet, not simply a knowledge of the complex, difficult and innovative writing of Modernism but a degree of critical awareness which, as a relatively young man, was to give him publication in the best British and American journals and an international reputation. As rightly celebrated a figure as Allen Tate was soon to remark of him:

> Mr. Muir further articulates his philosophical requirements of literature by means of Arnold's criterion, "the criticism of life". He has a shrewdness not unlike Arnold's, and he has more than Arnold's sensitiveness to writing which philosophically perplexes him; for example, Virginia Woolf's classicism. However profoundly we may dissent from his main assumptions, he is the only critic who has succeeded in grasping the modern situation as a whole.[28]

It is a profound mystery that a creative intelligence could, in the midst of such other forms of malnutrition, so nourish itself. Certainly Muir could scarcely have fallen in with more stimulating works. Heine, Nietzsche and Dostoevsky made particularly heady, early literary companions. Their immediate influence on him was not, however, a healthy one. Dostoevsky's work held too much of the substance of things that were poisoning his own life to be therapeutic. Muir's Glasgow was too close for comfort to Raskolnikov's Petersburg and the temptation to revolt into atheism, so appealing to Dostoevsky's rebels, tempted Muir also. Unable, as yet, to respond to the Christian counterpoint of the Russian's vision, Muir sought refuge in the Germanic world of Heine and Nietzsche. Heine offered him a cloak of evasive irony, morbidity of mood and a Utopian radicalism which, combined with the native brand of socialism, allowed him to live in a fantasy akin to that state of blissful communality present in evangelical conversion and which was an inversion of the prevailing conditions of aggression and isolation. It was Nietzsche's stimulating but ultimately toxic intellect which, however, held most sway over him. The concept of the superman was attractive because it was such a compensatory model for all that Muir felt wrong with himself. By as early as 1924, however, Muir was able to diagnose the nature of his condition at the time of writing the epigrams of his first book, *We Moderns*. The degree of self-awareness is, as usual, acute:

> And in the English edition you will have a further shock; you will find an appendix of ill-natured couplets full of bumptious conceit, written I really cannot tell why, because I am not ill-natured, and have no ill-will, so far as I know, for anyone alive. Probably it was my profound unhappiness of that time coming out in this queer way; for I did not sting to wound, but I almost believe, like the scorpion in a kind of desperation, when he feels himself in a circle of fire.[29]

This image of the self as a scorpion which destroys itself in attempting its own defence is, arguably, analogous to the psychological concepts of another, later, Glasgow influenced writer, R.D. Laing. In *The Divided Self* Laing postulates that, when threatened by a hostile environment, we tend to manufacture alternative protective selves. This is, however, inevitably a system of false security since such selves are increasingly sterile and unreal. Thus, the more Muir cocooned himself in his vision of the superman the more ill he became. The occasional feeling he had experienced in Orkney as a child of having a terrifying sheet of glass between himself and the world became a constant sense of being cut off from real life. Not only was his earlier vision of a unified world displaced, he became aware of being displaced from himself and of going towards an abyss where the very nature of brute matter seemed to have the power to permeate and possess him. His marvellous understanding of *King Lear* was, in part, based on his sense that madness has to do with leaving the human dimension.[30] Latterly, in Greenock, his state was on the very brink of such a departure where spirit is wholly lost in matter:

> My state made me seek company with desperate eagerness; I was more sociable and more lonely than I had ever been before. I often woke in the night with this feeling of mingled longing and dread, and when I began to read Dante much later and came to the passage describing the souls approaching the river of Acheron I recognized my own state:
>
> > e pronti sono a trapassar lo rio,
> > chè la dinia guistizia li sprona

sì, che la tema si volge in disìo.

"And they are quick to cross the river, for Divine Justice spurs them on, so that dread is transformed to longing." But in my case it was longing that seemed to be transformed to dread: I stared at things for which I did not care a farthing, as if I wanted to attach myself to them for ever, to lose myself in a hill or a tiny gewgaw in a shop-window, creep into it, and be secure there. But at the same time dread raised its walls round me, cutting me off; for even while I yearned for these things I felt a hidden menace in them, so that the simplest object was dangerous and might destroy me. A memory of this state returns whenever I read Wordsworth's lines in *The Affliction of Margaret*:

My apprehension come in crowds;
I dread the rustling of the grass;
The very shadows of the clouds
Have power to shake me as they pass.

A jagged stone or a thistle seemed to be bursting with malice, as if they had been put in the world to cut and gash; the dashing of breakers on rocks terrified me, for I was both the wave and the rock; it was as though I were both too close to things and immeasurably distant from them.

I remember my great relief one day when for a few moments this obsession left me and I saw things without fear, as they were. I was crossing the Clyde on a train one Saturday afternoon; a soft west wind was blowing, and the river was yellow and swollen with rain. I could feel that great volume of water flowing through me, flooding my veins with its energy, sweeping the fear from my mind. I woke now and then to such realizations, like a drowning man coming up for air. But I lived for most of these years in a sort of submarine world of glassy lights and distorted shapes, enclosed in a diver's bell which had grown to my shoulders.[31]

Thus Muir's release from the foetid world of Greenock did not come a moment too soon. His marriage was a crucial turning point in his life and for the next fifteen years his life was to be lived outwith Scotland in Europe and England. In his letters written in the years close to his having left Scotland there is a quite understandable note of ambivalence concerning her national affairs. On the one hand, he approved MacDiarmid's plan for a socialist republic but, on the other, he had no real desire to become an active participant in such a cause. In 1926, however, reinvigorated by Europe and with fairly high hopes that Scotland would, at least, not diminish this sense of well being, he returned with his wife to her family home in Montrose. Willa's record of this visit shows how quickly their hopes were dashed:

> Edwin's conscious intellectual life at this time was strengthening and reaching out, so that he was very aware of his need for stimulation, and after the soaring discourses he had enjoyed with Sydney Schiff the flatness of people's minds in Montrose depressed him. He felt he had been pot-bound in Glasgow and was now afraid of becoming pot-bound again. His comments became barbed and his judgments sharper; he was no longer scrupulous in refraining from attack; he told Sydney that Scotland was "shut in, unresponsive, acridly resolved not to open out and live".[32]

Less introverted and more secure, this marks the beginning of Muir's direct confrontation with a Scotland which he had so far suffered in an unhealthy silence. He was not alone, of course, in his condemnation of a small town Scottish life. The notion that the small town was where the heart of Scotland achieved its soundest beat was one which had been carefully cultivated throughout the nineteenth century and reached its apogee in the writings of J.M. Barrie. The publication of George Douglas Brown's *The House with the Green Shutters* gave the lie to Barrie's vision and, to some extent, Muir's image of Montrose was influenced by his considerable admiration for Brown's novel. When he wrote *Scottish Journey* in 1935, Muir's feelings about such places had not, to say the least, been tempered by the passage of time.

> The window in Thrums which Sir James Barrie fitted so skilfully with stained glass is really, in its unendowed state, a horrific symbol of small-town Scottish life: there is nothing one feels, after listening to Thrums gossip in any place, that cannot be seen and is not seen through these destructive panes. The life of these towns, from top to bottom, is merely an aggregate of private lives under a microscope: private lives carried on with the greatest difficulty, forced indeed to become fantastically private beneath a reciprocal and insatiable scrutiny. This window with which the houses in the small towns of Scotland are fitted has the power both to enlarge and diminish everything that is seen through it; bad deeds swell and good deeds shrink; for its peculiar power is

that of reducing everything to the same common measure. Such a mode of existence is the expression of a frustration so deep that, while being revolted by it, one cannot help feeling sorry for those who endure it. Something resembling it can doubtless be found in any English small town; but the Scots are more thorough than the English, especially in small things, and it is this thoroughness which makes life in a Scottish small town so insect-like. This uniform chronicle of smallness is broken at rare intervals by some violent episode, when a black sheep of the flock goes resoundingly to the devil. But even such portents are quickly reduced to proportion by the indispensable window, and the reign of law is again vindicated.[33]

By one of the most extraordinary of tragi-comic ironies Montrose was during Muir's sojourn there blessed or, it might consider itself, doubly cursed by a figure whose sense of intellectual and creative claustrophobia was, if anything, even more severe. MacDiarmid's marvellous "Frae Anither Window in Thrums" catches all the terrible frustration of this period when he was caught between having to make a living in provincial journalism and being simultaneously in the furious grip of the muse.

> Here in the hauf licht hoo I've grown!
> Seconds but centuries hae flown
> Sin I was a reporter here
> Chroniclin' the toon's sma' beer
> Tinin' the maist o' life to get
> The means to hain the least we bit.[34]

Denied his Herculean task of revitalising the Scottish poetic intelligence, MacDiarmid threatened to become a small town Samson attempting to pull down the temple of Scottish philistinism. Brought together by accident, their early friendship was based on more than an alliance against the common, provincial enemy, of irresistible forces opposing an immoveable object. Their intimacy extended, in practical terms, to Muir having to climb through MacDiarmid's bathroom window to rescue the sleeping incumbent lying naked and well-oiled in his empty tub. There was, however, never perhaps a genuine proximity of spirit between them. In many ways they were opposites who did not attract.

35

Leaving Scotland in 1926, Muir was not to return till 1935 when he took up residence in St. Andrews. In part the decision to move to St. Andrews was taken on the basis of a first class literary review having been set up there under the editorship of J.H. Whyte. When, however, Whyte wrote to Muir in 1931 in the hope of bringing North a by now internationally famous literary critic to help in his programme for the resurgence of Scottish letters by way of his magazine, *The Modern Scot*, Muir answered more than a little sceptically. Muir's letter is remarkable not simply for its expression of his personal doubts about being able to locate himself profitably as a creative writer in Scottish society but also for the seminal content of his feelings about the general Scottish scene. These remarks contain the seeds of all Muir's important writing on Scotland which he was to undertake over the next decade.

> I did not think that there was much immediate hope of an economically self-supporting Scottish literature—and it may be that there isn't ever any ultimate hope of it. You are on the spot, and far more in touch with things than I am; and your findings— with which I can do nothing but agree—are pretty hopeless. But if there is no ultimate hope of such a consummation—or even no hope of it in our life-time—I think I am clear too on this further point; that Scottish literature as such will disappear, and that London will become quite literally the capital of the British Isles in a sense that it has never yet quite been; that, in other words, it will become our national capital in just as real a sense as it is the capital of an ordinary English man to-day. How long it will take for this to happen it is impossible to say—a few centuries, or only one, what does it matter? 'Hugh MacDiarmid' will become a figure like Burns—an exceptional case, that is to say—an arbitrary apparition of the national genius, robbed of his legitimate effect because there will be no literary tradition to perpetuate it. Scottish literature will continue to be sporadic— and being sporadic, it will be denied the name of a literature, and it seems to me rightly so. But for myself I feel so detached, when I look at this possibility objectively, that I cannot even quite exclude the thought that this resolution of the Scottish spirit, its disappearance finally into a larger spiritual group, to which it would inevitably contribute much, may be a consummation to be hoped for. At any rate, all things seem to me to be working for it: the fact that Scottish energy has gone mainly into international

forms of activity, finance, industry, engineering, philosophy, science—forms of activity where one's nationality is irrelevant; the fact Scotsmen have helped to shape the industries of so many other countries and neglected their own: their almost complete blindness or indifference to the forms of activity in which the spirit of a nation most essentially expresses itself—poetry, literature, art in general: all this, looked at from outside might almost make us imagine that Scotland's historical destiny is to eliminate itself in reality, as it has already wellnigh eliminated itself from history and literature—the forms in which a nation survives. But the really awful phase is the present one: we are neither quite alive nor quite dead; we are neither quite Scottish (we can't be, for there's no Scotland in the same sense that there is an England and a France), nor are we quite delivered from our Scottishness, and free to integrate ourselves in a culture of our choice. It was some such dim feeling as this that made me take up the question. The very words 'a Scottish writer' have a slightly unconvincing ring to me: what they come down to (I except Grieve, who is an exception to all rules) is a writer of Scottish birth. But when we talk of an English writer we do not think of a writer of English birth: we hardly think of such things at all. A Scottish writer is in a false position, because Scotland is in a false position. Yes that's what it comes down to; and now that I think of it, that is what fills me with such a strong desire to see Scottish Literature visibly integrated in a Scottish group living in Scotland for that would make the position unequivocal, or at least would be a first step towards doing it; it would not merely be a gesture, or an expedient, but a definite act, and therefore with a symbolical value. England can't digest us at the present stage, and besides one does not want to be digested—it is a shameful process—one wants to be there. And there is no there for Scotsmen. And the idea that there might be is, I feel sure, a dream. Like Scottish Nationalism and the great digestive act, Scotland will probably linger in limbo as long as the British Empire lasts. It seems inevitable.

All the same, at suitable opportunities, and when I feel like it, I am going to have a shot at advocating an indigenous Scottish school of literature in Scotland. I'm glad that you are thinking of writing an editorial about it. I think it should be pressed in the B.B.C. Don't you occasionally speak for them? The weekly review I pin little faith to: it would be inadequate for the purpose in any case. And I don't know why I brought the matter up at all except as a protest. It will have no effect in my own life, which

will go on pretty much as it has gone, except for the possible
accident that I may manage yet to write something better than
I've written so far. Which is quite a praiseworthy wish.[35]

To the wider issues of this provocative and fecund analysis of
Scotland we shall have cause to return. What is immediately
important is that, despite Muir's expressions of reserve and
detachment, he did come to live in St. Andrews five years later.
There were practical reasons for this. His son, Gavin, had been
involved in a serious road accident in London and medical
opinion suggested a quieter, traffic free environment would be
beneficial. Further Willa had happy memories of
undergraduate life there. Also, although they always achieved
near perfect creative balance, Muir's heart, in practical affairs,
often ruled his head. Post-Jacobite rhetoric to the contrary, it is
not, arguably, a Scottish characteristic.

St. Andrews was, however, to prove a deep disappointment.
In *Belonging* Willa records that she found it a town sadly
changed from her student days and memories. Indeed she
developed an increasing sense of guilt for being instrumental in
bringing them back to such a creatively inhospitable
environment. There is no doubt that Muir saw in St. Andrews'
lack of responsiveness and its sterile inner divisions a
microcosm of that deprived Scottish communality which was to
stand at the centre of his critiques of Scotland in his later poems,
articles and books. St. Andrews was a town stratified by class
groups and further divided by the gulf between the native
population and the academics. The level of imaginative
response among the natives appeared similar to that prevailing
in Montrose. Any hope that the academic community might be
an antidote to this was quickly dashed. With the exception of
the odd maverick European don, the university, especially the
English Department, reacted with that sort of vulgarity of
judgement, endemic in British arts faculties, where snobbery is
confused with imaginative discrimination. Muir was dismissed
not only as a modern writer but, much worse, one "who wrote
for the papers". Writing in *The Modern Scot* at this time, Duncan
Carswell had postulated that the Scottish Universities had
debilitated themselves by disseminating themselves too widely
and not concentrating their energies in evolving a major

European centre of learning in St. Andrews.[36] Rather than producing a worthy Scottish rival for Oxbridge, however, what had come into existence was a kind of parody of English values where, in line with the Anglicisation of Scottish middle-class life, all the Southern virtues were mainly excluded and all its vices incorporated. Muir had enjoyed life in Hampstead. He had had there the company of creative Scots like the Carswells and George Malcolm Thomson. Even MacDiarmid made passing visits. On one occasion, "his yellow hair fizzed up; he was radiant with sheer daftness", he came to attempt the theft of the Stone of Destiny.[37] No similar native company could, however, be found in one of Scotland's premier intellectual centres. Muir, increasingly aware of the coming European holocaust, found no private warmth to compensate for his prescient public fears.

To this personal deprivation were added serious money worries. Although Whyte's *The Modern Scot* proved to be, by any standards, a quite excellent magazine it was not economically viable in Scotland. It closed almost as soon as Muir had returned. His only regular literary income came from his brilliant fiction reviewing in *The Listener* which was initiated by a Scotswoman, Janet Adam Smith, but came from outwith Scotland. Thus, the grave doubts about the possibility for a life for the man of letters lived in Scotland expressed by Muir in his 1931 letter to Whyte became a sad personal experience. In that same year Muir had written an article in the *Evening News*— Glasgow popular journalism is not what it was—analysing the economic situation of the Scottish writer. This article can now be seen as a prophetic utterance on his own fate and also a consummate account of the enormous difficulties facing the serious, creative writer in Scotland.

Muir's article had been triggered by his irritation with the recent, accusatory prognostications of a Mr. Norman Bruce on Scottish writers who chose to live outwith Scotland. Muir's response was both succinct and tart.

> I fancy that almost every other country in the world gives its writers a chance to live in it; Scotland does not. I fancy that hardly any other country in the world objects when a few of its writers chooses to live elsewhere; Scotland does.[36]

This precision of tone and controlled acerbity of style was to become characteristic of Muir's analyses of Scotland. He believed that there was no need to add to the national surfeit of fustian rhetoric. Muir went on to argue that the Scottish literary expatriate was not a recent phenomenon nor was the degree of Scotland's culpability in relation to these exiles:

> From the tone of his articles one might imagine that he regards Scottish literary absenteeism as a contemporary innovation which must be dealt with at once, summarily and publicly. Yet this, of course, is by no means the case. The custom among Scottish literary men of residing mainly abroad in England or elsewhere, is one which goes back not merely for the century or so since the railway was invented, and not merely for the two hundred odd years since the Union (from which it is fashionable to derive so many of our indigenous vices); it is a custom which reaches back at least to Knox's time.
>
> Nothing is more certain than that since the time of Dunbar, Scotland has never been a country for literary men. Knox himself, who was no mean writer, was only driven to Scotland finally by the express command of his superior, Calvin, and by the threat of persecution in France. "The cause of my stop" he admitted later, "do I not to this day clearly understand." Burns himself was almost chased out of Scotland, and only illusive promises, which later disastrously deceived him, kept him back. Buchanan, Scotland's greatest Latinist, did not return to reside among his countrymen until he was fifty-five. Sir Thomas Urquhart, probably Scotland's greatest master of prose, spent a good deal of his time in England and elsewhere. Thomson, of "The Seasons", Smollett and Boswell were definitely Anglo-Scots. They have been followed up to our own time by Carlyle, John Davidson, the other James Thomson, Sir James Barrie and quite a number more whom it would be tedious to enumerate.[39]

Muir, then, saw the drift of writers from Scotland as part of a general drift of men and resources away from Scotland. Muir was haunted by the idea of the nation bleeding uncheckably to death at a rate which made it imperceptible to the victim. The loss of its best talents was central to this debilitation:

> But if Mr. Bruce or anyone else wishes to acquire an adequate notion of the number and variety of the talented men whose services Scotland has lost during the last five centuries, then he should read *The Scot Abroad*, by John Hill Burton, a dull book,

unfortunately, but an edifying one.[40]

Muir, of course, was not alone in noting this chronic and perhaps fatal decline. Writing a year later, Eric Linklater put forward a defence of the necessity for the Scottish writer to seek an English market which seems to be almost exactly like Muir's:

> The Anglo-Scots authors went south—or their fathers went south—for several reasons . . . They were loyal, as they had been taught to be loyal, to the sovereign image of Britannia. They knew that all was not gold that glittered, but felt they could be reasonably sure of what was properly milled round the edges. Nor, in this economic civilisation, can anyone blame them. They are doubly absolved from blame because in England the ground was truly more suitable for their work—and trebly are they free from culpability since Scotland offered them no inducement to remain, neither a handful of silver nor the riband for their coats.[41]

While both Orkadians address themselves to the same problem of economic solvency for the Scottish writer and the necessity to go South in order to achieve this, there is a distinct and revealing change of tone and emphasis between them on the subject. Linklater's fatal flaw as a writer is a capacity for verbal flippancy and pastiche which undermines the power of his intended irony. Here his allusions to literary apostasy, Browning's attack on the older, established Wordsworth, seem both unintentionally and extremely unfortunate in a passage where he is trying to establish the innocence of motives in Scottish writers with regard to allying themselves with England, their need for cash and their desertion of Scotland because it did not make tangible its esteem. Linklater's allusiveness, in fact, betrays an underlying sense of confusion between the harsh economic necessity imposed on the serious, creative writer and the world of the Scottish hack on the make, a type noted by Coleridge as having manifested itself on the London scene in considerable and growing numbers almost immediately after the Union.[42]

Thus, unlike Linklater, Muir made a radical distinction between those writers who had been forced into exile to support themselves and those others who had considered the profit motive as their chief end and their writing as a mere means to this end. Historically, from James MacPherson onwards, Muir was aware that an extraordinary number of Scottish writers had achieved fortunes based on their best-selling capacity. For many Scottish writers, then, the English market was not so much a sad alternative but a kind of promised land which would bountifully reward them for the images of a fantasy Scotland which they purveyed.

Sharing Eliot's deep reservations about the meretricious power of the best seller, a power he knew more intimately because to survive he had, ironically, to review so many of them, Muir was particularly suspicious of the Scottish version of that genre. He felt that too often these books depended on an international taste for a fantasy Scotland, most frequently a concoction of Celtic melancholia and militarism. He also saw in literary Scots an all too common desire to use their talent as a means to profit and power. They seemed to Muir not so much committed writers as thwarted men of action. Historically Muir explained this as one of the many by-products of Calvinism. Calvinism with its stress on the potent, practical man tends to dismiss the artist as a dreamer or, at best, tolerate him as an entertainer. In such a culture, therefore, the artist is constantly exposed to the pressure of a public opinion that has no respect for his gifts. There is, therefore, an obvious temptation for the artist to compensate for this by succeeding in the values esteemed by that culture—that is in terms of worldly success whose most tangible manifestation is hard cash.

Muir, then, unlike Linklater makes a radical distinction between two sorts of Scottish writer who went South. To distinguish these groups he, in attacking Bruce's resentful diatribe against the emigrés, addressed to himself the following question:

> I said that Mr. Bruce's articles raised an interesting and important question; but in fact they raise two. The first is this: Might not the constant exodus of talent over such a long period of time be attributed at least partly to Scotland? Has that exodus been a voluntary withdrawal or a banishment?[43]

Muir's answer to this question is that the truly creative writers were often driven out of Scotland since they could scarcely retain their integrity at home. In MacDiarmid's words:

Fu' weel I ken I would mak' verses which
'Ud notably enrich
'Oor Scots tradition'—in the minds
O' ministers and hinds;
And fain I'd keep as faur frae that
As Proust frae Johnnie Gibb—that's flat![44]

A more populous tribe, however, with James MacPherson as
its patriach, went there to exploit its false literary Scottishness
as a means of inserting itself into the London establishment. As
we shall see, Muir conceived of much of Scottish writing in the
nineteenth century belonging to this world of middlebrow
populism. In his own time, however, he thought the archetypal
figure was not so much that of William Black as that of Grassic
Gibbon. Most of his contemporaries, at least, had not so much
chosen exile as had it forced upon them.

Given this background, it is easy to understand the extent to
which Muir was provoked by Bruce's allegation that two recent
Scottish novels, Neil Gunn's *Morning Tide* and A.J. Cronin's
Hatter's Castle, owed their achievement and fame to the fact that
their authors had stayed at home. In the first place, Muir
pointed out that these two men could afford to stay at home
because they had non-literary professional incomes.

> The essential point, however, which Mr. Bruce quite misses, is
> that both these writers depend for their livelihood, not on
> writing, but on something else. Mr. Gunn is a civil servant. Mr.
> Cronin is a doctor. It is quite possible for them, therefore, to live
> in Scotland, but Cronin now lives in England.[45]

In the second place, *Hatter's Castle* was an absurd example of
what transpires when one sets up "a geographical standard of
literary criticism". Utterly unlike *Morning Tide*, *Hatter's Castle*
displayed the worst melodramtic vices of "oor Scots tradition".
Muir saw in it the near impossibility of a Scottish popular taste
evolving which had any real sense of both literature as such and
the Scottish literary tradition in particular. Sentimentality was
not only that public's essential diet but it was a particularly
exportable brand of the same. In a review article written
slightly later in the same year Muir returned to this problem of
these two books being celebrated and compared for the non-
literary reasons of locale and economic achievement. He

considered that no works could have been better chosen to demonstrate the disastrous gulf between Scottish popular taste and its genuine, original imaginative powers.

Mr. Neil Gunn's "Morning Tide" is a work of great beauty, steeped in atmosphere, subtle in its evocation of natural moods, and combining sensitiveness with power. It has faults: the women in it are romanticised, and there is often a tendency to strain the emotion, to maintain a mood of continuous intensity where a touch of nature, or even bathos, would have brought the relief of proportion. But on the other side the atmosphere of childhood is evoked with almost magical vividness, so that the boy hero seems to be embedded in layer after layer of it; and the power that could execute such a feat is a genuinely poetic power, for which one can only be thankful. The book is by far the most mature that Mr. Gunn has yet written, and one looks forward to the time when he will give us a work as sensitive and strong, and at the same time of wide scope.

It is inexplicable that the society which chose Mr. Gunn's book should also have chosen "Hatter's Castle," or it would be if one did not remember that another of its selections was a book called, I believe, "Red Ike." The success of Mr. Cronin's story is quite understandable; its literary success, on the other hand—its success with the critics—is both astonishing and a little disquieting. Disquieting, for it cannot be for the good of literature that such a book should be so inordinately praised. Astonishing, for what has been called its power is really a total incapacity for invention. One example will suffice: the scene where the father discovers his daughter's dishonour. Now, when Mr. Cronin makes him drive the poor girl out, he is already passively following the conventions of melodrama; but when he makes him drive her out, firstly in the night, and secondly in a snowstorm, the effect is not that of piling on the agony, but rather surrendering hypnotically to the suggestive power of a cliché. Dishonour, homelessness, night snow; this is not invention, but merely following the line or least resistance. After all, irate Scottish parents do not invariably discover their daughters' moral errors late at night, and in snowstorms. Had Mr. Cronin made the father kick the girl out on a Saturday afternoon when the crowds were returning from the local football match, with a thick fog, if necessary, for gloom—that would not prevent a football match in Scotland—one might have believed in the human probability of the act; but at midnight, and in a snowstorm, no. If my memory has unconsciously singled out this scene, I am sorry, but the whole book is made up of such material. Another such success will be perilous for Scottish letters.[46]

Thus, for Muir, the situation for the serious writer in Scotland was a parlous one. Such a writer was neither adequately rewarded nor recognized and aware of the corrupt popular sentimental tradition he was always tempted to sell out to it:

> But what I canna account for's no'
> Being' able to gie folk hokum.
> I can joke'em and sock 'em and choke 'em
> But the a'e thing needfu' is hokum.
> —I wish I was Neil Munro.
>
> It isna fair to my wife and weans,
> It isna fair to mysel'.
> The day's lang by when gaels gaed oot
> To battle and aye fell.
> I wish I was Harry Lauder,
> Will Fyffe or J.J. Bell,
> —Or Lauchlan MacLean Watt
> For the maitter o' that!
> —Dae I Hell![47]

The Scottish writer was further aware that such selling, as in the case of Cronin, could, in an international context, be extraordinarily lucrative. Cronin, true to his type, quickly disabused Bruce's notions of his literary patriotism by transporting himself to sunnier climes which suggests that the power of his fiction did not depend on thrusting of his roots ever deeper into his native soil. Even granting that Cronin was the last major example of the profitability of Scottish melodrama, Muir did not consider that his demise would herald a just recognition of native worth. MacDiarmid's genius, Muir felt, would be distorted by operating in a near vacuum. Nor would a context be created which would allow the vital integration of a group of Scottish writers working in co-operation and healthy conflict. Looking back into Scottish history Muir could not discern any remotely recent and comforting model of such a situation:

45

It was possible for the eighteenth century literary group whose headquarters was in Edinburgh for that group consisted mainly of professors, lawyers, ministers, librarians and gentlemen of private means and with no skill in any other profession; it has never been possible to live in Scotland since the Scottish Stewart dynasty began to lose power; since the death of James the Fifth in other words. Without extraneous aid it is impossible for a writer to make his living in Scotland to-day.[48]

As we have already seen, Muir's sense of Scotland's past refusal of her literary responsibilities boded ill for her present relationship with regard to the writers of the Scottish Rennaissance. Muir felt that the potential of this group was simply to be dissipated because the economic conditions necessary for its survival were not present:

> A national literary revival cannot be carried on entirely by *emigrés*, with the occasional writer so fortunately circumstanced as Mr. Gunn: yet nothing is more certain than that if Scotland cannot or will not support its writers, they will go to some more hospitable country than starve.[49]

Having elucidated Scotland's sorry literary past and her querulous, unsatisfactory present, Muir turned his attention to what might be done to redeem the present and lay sound foundations for the future. His second question addressed to Bruce was what practical means could be found to support Scottish writers in Scotland. He then made these eminently sensible and subsequently largely unheeded proposals:

> The second question, and the more important is how means can be found to support Scottish writers in Scotland. And those means exist just as plainly and indubitably there as anywhere else in the world. It is not a matter of inaugurating any vast scheme of charity; it is merely a matter of using machinery which is already in existence. There are the universities, the libraries and the newspapers, and there are many rich people sufficiently interested in literary things to start a weekly review.
>
> Now these simple means are the main support in other countries of writers whose work in itself is not remunerative enough to support them.
>
> I have nothing to say against professors, librarians and journalists; but I am certain that the universities, the libraries and the newspapers would not lose, but rather gain, by the

46

inclusion of an occasional outsider who is trying to add to the sum of literature.

Other countries recognise this; I think it is urgent that Scotland should do so too—if it is not to lose all its writers, and finally, along with the last of them, in a century or so, every national literary standard. For the measures I am recommending do not touch merely the present evil: they touch the whole future of Scottish literature.

It may be objected, of course, that the making of a livelihood is the writer's own job, and nobody else's. But the more civilised a nation is the less it will insist on such a purely economic consideration, knowing that the best work in literature is rarely the most remunerative. It would be the easiest thing in the world, without suffering the loss of a farthing, for Scotland to domicile a round dozen of its writers in Glasgow or Edinburgh. That this would be immensely salutary I am as certain as Mr. Bruce; daily contact, common aims, reciprocal rivalry, the sense that they were in their own country and represented something more than themselves as individual units, might well lead to a general activity.

Scotland has the power to do all this by merely lifting a finger, and if she has the power to do it, then she cannot escape the responsibility for the present melancholy state of things.[50]

After taking up residence in St. Andrews four years after writing this article Muir's ability to diagnose this melancholy state became more bitter and acute because it was more personal. It was, of course, a particularly bad time to be resident in a nation which, at best, is not given to generosity towards its creative artists. Industrial Scotland, having not properly recovered from the aftermath of the First World War, sank into the quagmire of the Depression. When war broke out in 1939, although it tended to reintegrate social life in St. Andrews, it did not quickly provide Muir with any improved economic opportunities. Over this period his career and MacDiarmid's ran a sorry and exemplary parallel with, in fact, MacDiarmid, definably much more the national bard, living at subsistence level in the Shetlands during the Thirties and then being put to work in heavy engineering on Clydeside during the war.[57] While the Muirs did not come to the pass of living off mackerel, MacDiarmid was given occasional buckets of the throw-away scavenger by the Shetland fisherman, they survived only by virtue of Willa working in a poorly paid teaching post. By the early years of the war both were quite seriously ill; Edwin with chest pains which his doctor said were symptomatic of imminent heart failure if he did not rest. Working as a minor civil servant in the Food Office in Dundee Edwin wrote in 1941:

> I found that my lack of an academic degree is a most astonishing obstacle: in Scotland nothing but a certificate of some kind seems to be recognised as really meritorious—a curious example of the preference of faith to works, for surely by this time I've done some work that should count.[52]

While Muir was aware of a frankness and vitality in the Scottish personality, especially in its West of Scotland manifestations, he was always more aware of its capacity for dourly sticking to the letter rather than the spirit. Such a rigid attitude is ruinous for creativity which is concerned with growth and change. Writing in *The Modern Scot* in response to Muir's newspaper article, Whyte further articulated this self-destructive division between creativity and the institutions which were allegedly the medium by which it should be both conserved and transmitted.

> Mr. Muir suggested in his article that places might be found within the present framework of Scottish life for those modern creative writers and artists who at present leave Scotland, as librarians, on the staffs of the Scottish Universities, and by giving them such sinecures as men of letters usually enjoy in other countries. But to secure such posts requires the sympathy and co-operation of the Government, the Carnegie Trust, and the Senatuses—and we frankly do not see the likelihood of such bodies as they are at present constituted inclining a favourable ear to writers whose only claim to such posts is their ability to create literature. This attitude prevails throughout the intellectual life of Scotland. Scotsmen for too long have been onlookers at the creative work of Europe—that is, scholarly commentators—and perhaps in the cultural life of no other European country has the antiquarian, the "disinterested scholar", such a prominence. The educated Scotsman is, in many cases, one of the best-informed students of modern literatures, but he has a vital interest in none, least of all in Scottish literature, because the creative genius of the country is

being stifled and Scotland has recently practically ceased to have a lot or parcel in the intellectual life of the Continent. Practically the whole bent of the nation is towards the scholastic, and if England has been with some justice called a nation of shopkeepers, the Carnegie Trustees, and every other learned body from one end of the country to the other, are going to see to it that we become a nation of teachers. We must at all costs put a premium on creative endeavour, and it is up to the Universities to lead the way.[53]

The degree to which St. Andrews was prepared to incorporate a creative energy such as Muir's into its academic structure appears, however, not to have been exceeded by her sister universities. Mr. John Speirs who, along with David Daiches, represented the only Scottish academic criticism comparable and compatible with his Renaissance contemporaries and who, again like Daiches, was not employed or to be employed by a Scottish university, was even more specific than Whyte in suggesting change. Writing about the Scottish situation in *Scrutiny* in 1936 in a review of recent Scottish books including, most importantly, *Scottish Journey*, he wholly agreed with Muir's analysis that the implosive pressure of cosmopolitan industrialism was depriving Scotland of the little of the authentic national life which still existed. Speirs was particularly hostile to the Scottish educational establishment at both school and university level. He considered that the very structures which should be conserving and vitalising the national literary sense were, at best, impotent and, in fact, often harmful. His proposal for healthy change at university level was, in the face of the Scottish establishment, nothing if not radical.

As might have been expected of so sensitive a critic, Mr. Muir shows himself, in *Scottish Journey*, especially in his chapter on Edinburgh, one of the very few Sctosmen who are conscious of what is happening. It seems a pity that the recent opportunity of having Mr. Muir placed in such a central position as that of the Chair of English at Edinburgh has been missed. One of the things which seems to be most needed in Scotland at the moment is a school of criticism, provided it would be astringent enough; there is now so much ground that would have to be cleared before the mind could be freed again for creation.[54]

When Muir did make a belated entry into the teaching profession it was, of course, not quite at this level. It was in Edinburgh but not at the university but in a British Council post offered him in 1942 by Harvey Wood and, characteristically, his responsive audience was mainly composed not of Scots but of allied troops, mainly Poles. This job led to a fairly long and highly fruitful connection with the Council. Immediately after the war he travelled across a devastated Europe to take charge of its Prague centre and, subsequent to the Communist coup, he was transferred to Rome. Muir was not only a marvellous teacher but, given communities compatible with his imaginative, natural warmth, a much loved figure. Willa describes him as having in these offices,

> a gift of permeating the space around him, giving out an unassertive sense of benevolence which was appreciated by his students, who also much enjoyed his improvised lectures.
>
> ... That marked, I suppose, the difference between an authoritarian and a poet, the one looking for rods to beat students with, the other trying to encourage the growth of a living mind.[55]

With such a record of both international recognition and achieved pedagogic excellence, Muir seemed the perfect candidate for the Wardenship of Newbattle Abbey which had been set up to educate mature students who had not received the benefit of a full secondary school education. Muir and his wife were delighted with the job and also with the opportunity, as they approached old age, to put down what they hoped were final roots in Scotland. The initial period went splendidly; some of the students were remarkably talented and the atmosphere did have "some faint air of Eden about it".[56] From such a scene the Scottish serpent of meddling resentment could not long absent itself. That characteristic idiom of the Calvinist mind, the reductive one, came into play. Far from honouring such a teacher and writer in their midst, malicious gossip about Muir as a pretentious figure abusing his position soon began to circulate. Trade union tribunes of the people and middle-class bureaucrats combined to attempt to turn the college into a day-release institution with a Knoxian stress on practical education which was mainly a rationalisation of their deeper malice towards a man who some of them had known and been allegedly friendly with over many years. In a sense the whole sorry affair proved the veracity of Blake's dictum that the real political struggle in modern society is not the material war between the classes but the spiritual one between the creative and the non-creative. In a poem written by one of the students of those days we can share in his glimpses of Muir's power of such spiritual illumination:

> Up to the window's edge the sand-hued stone,
> Sun-lanterned through the leaves, affirmative of the light.
> . . . Shadows flickered his face, as the soft voice spoke on
> To the room's chiaroscuro, half-day and tenebrous night.
>
> Some chafed at those hesitant lips, impatient of pause,
> Untutored to join that eye, illimitably seeing,
> While the poet groped meekly for words to give hint of the cause
> Which shone like light on the leaf, more light in his being.[57]

Such a man and teacher provokes strong passions. Unintentionally, his effect is a polarising one. To some he is both a light and a challenge to what is best in themselves. To others he is a constant dark reminder of what they either do not possess or what they have destructively repressed. Inevitably trouble accrues to such a figure and in Scotland, where repression of creative spiritual activity, with its belief in embodying spirit in aesthetic form, is a long preserved tradition, he is more endangered than in most cultures.

Willa, true to form, paints in *Belonging* a direct picture of as much of these squalid events as was legally permissible. With a strong grasp of the tradition of Scottish "flyting" and a caricaturist's eye, libel was always for her a potential danger. Edwin was more reticent, but in his series of poems, "Effigies", we can perceive how darkly he viewed these events in this poetry of maimed, power-seeking figures involved in the methodical destruction of Judas-like betrayal.

> Pity the poor betrayer in the maze
> That closed about him when he set the trap
> To catch his friend. Now he is there alone,
> The envied and beloved quarry fled
> Long since for death and freedom.[58]

Muir was, indeed soon to leave. In the midst of this Scottish chorus of resentment—Douglas Brown's "bodies" do go marching on—an invitation came from Harvard. The final change was only a few years away. Perhaps nothing Scotland had done to Muir did her more dishonour than his manner of leaving and, indeed, was more symptomatic of the very ills he had so lucidly diagnosed.

Edwin Muir and the Tradition of Scottish Literature

Edwin Muir's third and final book on Scotland, *Scott and Scotland: The Predicament of the Scottish Writer*, was written in 1936 as a contribution to the Routledge series, *The Voice of Scotland*. Leslie Mitchell and MacDiarmid has been given editorial charge of the project which, in the latter's case, was to be doubly ironic since his own contribution on the Red Clyde was found unacceptable for inclusion and his response to Muir's book was to be one of sustained outrage. Willa was also commissioned to write a book and this resulted in *Mrs. Grundy in Scotland*. She considered the nature of the enterprise to be one of witty provocation but the tone, nature and consequence of *Scott and Scotland* were to turn out somewhat differently. As she tells us in *Belonging*:

> In that spirit I wrote my Grundy book, more or less to entertain Leslie Mitchell, and it was a slap dash performance. But when Edwin sat down to do *Scott and Scotland* something of a very different nature emerged, with an undertone of personal exasperation in it, to be found in no other book of Edwin's. The emptiness in Scottish life which he had been aware of during his Journey and was now aware of in St. Andrews, a hiatus caused, he felt by the lack of an organic society with an alive centre, seemed to have crippled Walter Scott in spite of his genius and was bound to cripple any writer still trying to produce Scottish literature or any critic trying to assess it. The personal feeling comes through in quietly devastating remarks like this: 'Scott spent most of his days in a hiatus, in a country, that is to say, which was neither a nation nor a province, and had, instead of a centre, a blank, an Edinburgh, in the middle of it'. Or in contemptuous comment like this: 'Such is Scottish criticism; without standards, sensibility, or even common sense; more like a disease of literature than a corrective. I have tried to analyse

some of its causes and thus explain it. To justify it would be beyond the skill of any writer.'[59]

While the growing creative claustrophobia of Scotland provoked in Muir a fear of the waste of his talent and a consequent uncharacteristic acerbity in his prose style, it would be wrong to consider this element either excessively or damagingly present in the book. Janet Adam Smith, in reviewing the book, was wholly accurate when she wrote of it that it was "far and away the most sensitive and fundamental critique of Scottish literature that has appeared for years, marked by none of that spleen and personal prejudice with which Scots usually write about each other".[60] There is certainly a steely quality in the style of *Scott and Scotland* but this is a style which, while giving it a sharp cutting edge, bespeaks a clarity and lucidity of thought. Another early reviewer, Neil Gunn, caught its tone and that of Muir's customary critical voice perfectly when he wrote:

> Literary criticism of the quality of Mr Muir's is rare in any country; in Scotland even its tradition seems to have got lost. In saying as much, I am not concerned with particular attributes of penetration or insight, with individual gifts of paradox or brilliant exposition, but with that rare power of lifting criticism on to a plane where its observations and judgments combine in a synthesis that induces in the mind a state of harmony. His writing has, in fact, no tricks at all. It is quiet and lucid, and eschews colour and personal whim to the point of seeming cold. Nor is this the clarity of intellect alone. Metaphysicians are common enough. Behind Mr Muir's assessments is not only a fine intellect but an imagination of a very pure kind, and it is with the help of this imagination (or in its light) that his intellect is able to select all important factors (an intellect that included everything would describe nothing) and to combine them with the same sort of satisfying or harmonious effect as is achieved by any truly creative work. Whether his intellect is powerful or his imagination profound does not arise here. It is enough that his literary criticism is of this creative kind, because in Scotland we had almost forgotten that real criticism was anything but a collieshangie or a fight.[61]

With the exception of MacDiarmid, Muir's major contemporaries saw the book as of seminal importance.

Catherine Carswell and William Soutar were as enthusiastic as Janet Adam Smith and Gunn. If there was steel in the book it was akin to that, such was the compression of its thought, present in a spring, the release of which they felt would energise subsequent Scottish critical writing. While neither Gunn nor Soutar found acceptable Muir's social solution to Scottish ills, what they conceived of as the external *deus ex machina* of Douglasite economics, they were both profoundly impressed by the book's central thesis. Thus though Soutar felt the Douglasite system was akin to attempting "to heal the social cancer by the application of a poultice", he had no doubt of the book's ultimate value.

> But a repudiation of Mr. Muir's prognosis in no way invalidates the excellence of his dissection upon the broken corpus of the Scottish language; an investigation which makes his book not only one of the most valuable contributions to contemporary Scottish studies, but also a challenge to every Scottish writer.[62]

While *Scott and Scotland* made, for good and ill, a profound impression on Muir's peers, its general impact on Scottish literary culture was not strong. Ironically, its reception wholly validated one of its central theses which was that of the impoverished state of Scottish literary criticism. Living again in Scotland had confirmed Muir's worst fears about both the academic and more popular forms of Scottish criticism. The indifference of St. Andrews could indeed have been predicted from Muir's review in 1933 of an Edinburgh University publication, *Edinburgh Essays on Scots Literature: Being a Course of Lectures delivered in the University of Edinburgh by Members of the English Department and Others:*

> The course of lectures collected in this volume was initiated by Dr. J.C. Smith during the time when he temporarily filled Professor Grierson's chair at Edinburgh University. Apart from Mr. Mackay Mackenzie's paper on Dunbar, the only satisfactory reading matter in the book is contained in Professor Grierson's short preface (an apologia for the neglect of Scottish literature in Scottish universities and a plea for the institution of a Scottish chair or lectureship), which sets the level that might be expected in a volume issued by a great seat of learning.

Professor Grierson's case is that Scottish literature should not be treated as a part of English literature; he states it courteously, but with great force; and there is no valid argument against it. But the lecturers who follow him make a very ragged show, and tempt one to wish that Scottish literature might have been neglected a little longer. Mr. Mackay Mackenzie, the learned editor of Dunbar, says what he has to say with authority. Of the other six four know their subjects: Mr. Harvey Wood has already given us an admirable edition of Henryson; Mr. John D. Westwood is scholarly on "Scots Theological and Proverbial Literature" in the seventeenth century, and the same may be said of Dr. Oliver on "The Eighteenth Century Revival," and Dr. Kitchin on John Galt. Yet what they actually say is uninteresting and trivial. One would think that the audiences they spoke to had never heard of Scottish literature before, and were composed entirely of enquiring Bulgars or Turks.

The last two papers, "Modern Scots Poetry," by Mr. Ian A. Gordon, and "Modern Scots Novelists," by Mr. Angus Macdonald, are least satisfactory of all, for both lecturers suffer, like most of the rest of their collaborators, from a strange lack of critical capacity, and they have the additional misfortune of dealing with recent work which has still to be estimated. It is after reading them that one realizes what is wrong with the book: it shows only the faintest inkling of the existence of literary standards. It would be better for Scottish literature to languish in its time-honoured neglect, if this is the only publicity it can secure.[63]

While, of course, we are all aware how gloriously such academic shortcomings in the study of Scottish literature have been subsequently put to rights, what Muir considered the real deficiency of pre-war Scottish criticism was not so much its lack of comparative literary standards but its wilful parochialism so that, by keeping Scottish literature out of the turbulent mainstream of the radical developments in European Modernism, Scotland was, by implication, also to be kept out of the even greater turbulence of the political, social and economic change which followed the First World War. Thus, when Muir described Scottish criticism as "more like a disease of literature than a corrective", he was attacking not simply Scottish literary deficiencies but a state of mind which determinedly sought to praise a false, sentimental Scotland while denying the modern intelligence access to a nation fraught with profound problems stemming from an uncertainty about an already tenuous identity greatly increased by the growth of national feeling after the First World War; the doubts about a continuing degree of security provided by participation in British Imperialism and wracked by the economic problems of decay in both its rural and heavy industrial economies. An outstanding example of the kind of critical parochialism which provoked Muir's book is provided by a review by William Power, one of the better Scottish newspaper writers of the day, called "Harp of the North—Is the Scots Poetic Renaissance a Reality?". Power concluded that it was, but the terms of his acceptance were, in fact, a contradiction of everything that Muir and the Scottish Renaissance group stood for. Power wrote:

> It is true that practically none of the poets here represented has devised or adopted startlingly new forms, or produced anything that an old fashioned critic would stigmatise as "merely eccentric". Few of them psycho-analyse or dodge conception to the bourn of heaven, or pinnacle themselves dim in the intense inane. Scots poets, like Scots painters, are suspicious of new movements in which the immediate and sensuous appeal is overborne by mere cerebral complexity. Their canon in this matter has been immortally set forth by Lewis Spence in his "Bride or Handmaiden?"—
>
> Beauty ever was designed
> To thrill the heart and not the mind,
> To speak to the immediate blood,
> But never to the pensive mood.
>
> And when I hear one say that thought
> Has been to him by Beauty brought,
> I know that Beauty in his house
> Has dwelt as servant, not as spouse.
>
> That is not to say that the pensive mood is barred. Far from it. But the pensive mood, mere reflection, must be ancillary to the beauty that can alone justify the poem's existence. It is just because the Scots are metaphysical folk that they eschew the errors of Donne and Crashaw, of Browning and Meredith, and keep metaphysics and mere cerebration in its place where poetry is concerned.[64]

Such attitudes are so directly antipathetic to those prevailing in *Scott and Scotland* that one is tempted to think that, like the grit in the oyster which produces the pearl, this 1929 article had stuck in Muir's mind. It is not simply the monstrous complacency of the prowess of Scottish "common-sense", the "omnitude" MacDiarmid so loathed; that sinister severance of beauty and intelligence whose imbecilic corollary is the inadequacies of a mere English poet like Donne; that belittlement of the depth-seeking modern consciousness, but, perhaps above all else, the assumption of a vital Scottish literary tradition, which entails a vital Scotland, that is so extraordinary. It is far beyond the scope of the present essay to explore the matter fully, but one of the most remarkable of Scottish phenomena is the degree to which the Scottish literati have for almost three centuries manufactured a kind of ersatz Scottish identity to make up for the national surrender of 1707. Like MacDiarmid, Muir believed that such minds found "compensation in a 'romantic nationalism'"—sedulously disassociated from politics and practical realities of every kind" and that much Scottish art had been devised as escapism from the dire nature of the Scottish predicament.[65] Thus, for example, Muir wrote:

> The Kailyard school of literature was thus really a by-product of Scotland's economic history. All the songs and stories of Scottish country life after the Industrial Revolution got into its stride were for a long time dreams of comfort and escape. To anyone living in Glasgow or Dundee even the Kailyard must have seemed heaven. George Douglas Brown assailed this dream in *The House with the Green Shutters*, and that was the reason he was attacked with such bitterness. Before the Industrial Revolution the Scottish writer described country scenes vigorously and realistically: there are scathing domestic interiors in Burns himself, though he marked the deterioration of the tradition, as in *The House with the Green Shutters*. It was the increasing bestiality of industrial Scotland that turned the countryside of fiction into a Schlaraffen land and made Scottish literature for a time mainly a literature written by sentimental ministers.[66]

Such Scottish sentimentality should never, however, be seen as the mere by-product of national enervation. If the common people used sentimentality as they used alcohol, as a pain killer, there is little doubt that the Scottish establishment, assiduously and rewardingly served by the majority of eighteenth- and nineteenth-century Scottish writers, promulgated such a vision as a highly successful method of distracting attention from the real nature of Scottish problems and as a way of providing a series of flattering practical, militaristic and pastoral stereotypes designed to promote passivity. It is for this reason that *Scott and Scotland* is not simply a book of fundamental importance regarding the Scottish literary tradition, but it is an account of how much Scottish writing was perverted into a corrupt form of social consciousness. What in fact Muir and his creative contemporaries of the Scottish Renaissance group were involved in was as much a political as an aesthetic battle. The proof of this is the degree to which they were opposed. Thus, in an article which seems almost a parody of a certain kind of condescending, institutionalized authoritarian Scottishness, "This Scottish Tongue: The Renascence and the Vernacular" by one Gordon Leslie Rayne, we see the vicious resistance of this establishment to any attempt to awaken Scotland to the real nature of both herself and the world she now inhabited. Not Muir, but an unnamed MacDiarmid, is the central target of Mr. Rayne's thesis that no literary renaissance was taking place and that the writers were merely the somewhat inferior heirs of their immediate predecessors. It does, however, precisely articulate he kind of attitudes which *Scott and Scotland* sought to destroy:

> But is all this a Renascence? And is it all a Scottish Renascence? Though I have not yet quite attained the Psalmist's three score years and ten, I have known the literary giants of both this and some preceding generations, and I cannot altogether detect a change of tone or temperament that would justify the implication that those earlier days were times of darkness and unaccomplishment from which our emergence deserves to be hailed as a revival. Of course, the phrase may be a personal puff and a personal and unsupported judgment and no more, as though these trumpeting harbingers of dawn were proclaiming themselves the British Israel of literature, the veritable children of the inky ghetto. Yet let us not scorn their pretensions or deride their claims. Let us have information and a clearing up of the mooted and muddied problem: has Scotland really renasced or is

she (to employ a word admitted of the Academy) renascent? Is anything new to-day, fresh, original and purposeful, that the Edwardian or Victorian generations did not have? For my part, I am not convinced there is.

For, after all, the Scotland of the last fifty years did have its mighty journalists, editors, novelists, essayists, historians, biographers. In their own way and their own field I must pay homage to the Robertson Nicolls, the Andrew Langs, Crocketts, Barries, Ian Maclarens, Stevensons, to name only a few, who were hardly voices in the wilderness or pelicans in a Caledonian desert. They, too, were home-seekers and home-singers, from whose inkpots came many a paean of praise from the hills of home, the corries and the wee glens, the quiet broadcloth life of the hamlets, the mysterious, frowning streets of old Edinburgh, and the placid, sun-browned dales of the Border lands. When my mind roves back over the pages of theirs that I absorbed in my young days, I have a kind of echo of all the multitudinous call of Scotland in my heart still. They, too, used the vernacular and embodied in their amber little snatches of lore and language that even since then have withered and died out. Crowds of them there were: I cannot find it in me to be aught but grateful for the thrill of John Buchan's earlier work, even for the homely manliness of the "Surfaceman." Did they not minister to an illimitable public, mostly just plain folk, who knew life even if they had never heard of literature? Was their day one of such pitchy darkness that we had to emerge from it as from a tunnel and greet a brighter time? Continuity I can see; change of method and of mood I most willingly admit and demand; but "revival," "re-birth," "renascence," those condemnatory and laudatory labels I must regretfully refuse, until further proof is lead, to endorse or accept.[67]

If whisky and freedom do not always necessarily go together in Scotland, there is absolutely no doubt that sentimentality and authoritarianism, pretentiousness and populism do. Mr. Rayne, in fact, writes a particularly debased form of that critical genre initiated in the early nineteenth century by Jeffrey and Cockburn which stressed a private, local Scotland, frequently a land of childhood memories, to which one had transitory, sentimental access as a refuge from the real world of practical, mature action. The key which unlocked this world was always a self-conscious lapsing into vernacular speech so that one "embodied . . . in amber little snatches of lore and language."

The whole thing was a vast fraud. Behind this allegedly tremulous sensitivity lay a rigid political vision which did its utmost to prevent mature, creative intelligence from accurately interpreting Scottish society as one which was undergoing historical changes at least as deep and painful as other early industrializing nations. The extraordinary thing about Rayne, in particular, and Scottish society, as a whole, is that he and it attempted to sustain this notion of Scotland's divine dispensation to be an untroubled backwater not during the flood tide of Victorian optimism but in the blood tinged ebb of the First World War. There is a token attempt by him to accept the spirit of his age. While modern Scottish writers are so "desperately sober-sided," they do belong to a period "which has inherited an excessive load of woe."[68] On the other hand, while "they have one and all revolted in a certain measure from the standards and ideals of the past ... that revolt is not peculiarly Scottish, it is essentially modern and current throughout Europe."[69] Rayne, in fact, simultaneously attempts to perceive the Renaissance as both a kind of aping of a dubious European fashion and a denial of the true Scottish verities of the Crocketts, Barries and Maclarens. Mr. Rayne concluded his piece with a call to a true but undefined patriotism so that the new men might set aside the acerbic mood which, after all, was so uncharacteristic of the national genius or, at least, of one particular national genius. Thus he wrote:

> They have set aside a great portion, though not all, of that warmth of emotion and that melancholy douceness and repression that were supposedly the hallmark of our race two generations ago. But emotion is a two handed sword: it means readiness to laughter as well as a facility in tears. The genius of Sir Harry Lauder is part and parcel of the kailyard tradition, and since then our younger people have lost the gift of eliciting the deep chuckle and provoking the postponed, but persisting, grin of inner merriment.[70]

We will not, I think, fully understand Muir or MacDiarmid until we understand how hard they had to struggle against this kind of pervasive nonsense and how they understood it not as simply the silliness of provincial, fifth-rate minds but as a sinister form of control. They would have wholly agreed with

Saul Bellow's assessment of Collingwood's vision of the role of the artist in society:

> The artist, as Collingwood tells us, must be a prophet, "not in the sense that he foretells things to come, but that he tells the audience, at risk of their displeasure, the secrets of their own hearts." That is why he exists. He is spokesman of his community. This account of the artist's business is old, much older than Collingwood, very old, but in modern times this truth, which we all feel, is seldom expressed. ". . . no community altogether knows its own heart: and by failing in this knowledge a community deceives itself on the one subject concerning which ignorance means death . . . The remedy is the poem itself. Art is the community's medicine for the worst disease of mind, the corruption of consciousness."[71]

Despite this Muir himself saw the book as a challenge to a creative national effort and not an offering placed either on the altar of Scottish indifference or to become the object of rancorous dismissal. As he wrote in his conclusion:

> I began this essay by asking certain questions touching the present state of literature in Scotland. In trying to answer these questions I found myself involved in three main lines of inquiry: into the Scots language as a vehicle for literature, into the Scots literary tradition, and into the political and social state of Scotland. I reluctantly came to the conclusion that all three were unsatisfactory as bases for genuinely autonomous literature.
> The conclusion is negative, and an inquiry such as the present might be expected to produce a positive one. It appears to me, however, that it is the task of my readers to supply that for themselves, if they are sufficiently interested in Scottish literature; for a general evil can only be remedied by co-operative thought and co-operative will: all that any individual can offer is suggestions. So my main concern has been to describe the actual state of Scottish literature, not to show how I think it can be cured; for in doing the one I could expect some measure of agreement and in doing the other I could expect none. The first thing needful is obviously to see the position as it is.[72]

Scott and Scotland is not, in fact, as negative an image as it is presented here. While it is as concerned as *Scottish Journey* with a vision of Scotland disintegrated into discrete, unco-operative parts there is a historical sense not present in the earlier book that it was not always thus and, by enquiring into what once had been, a degree of hope that modern Scotland might savingly be reconnected with its unitary past. "That Scotish life is split in two," Muir wrote, "is certain; it is my main argument in this essay. But that it has always been split in two is false."[73] Muir's hope, however, that he might initiate a genuine debate among his fellow countrymen as to how to accomplish this task has, at least as yet, come to little. In part this is because the number and quality of Scots capable of involving themselves in the level of discussion normal to Muir has perhaps never gone higher than the number MacDiarmid felt to be available in 1925. Discussing the then prevailing state of literary culture and the possibility of Muir's contribution to it, MacDiarmid had written:

> Muir's critical apparatus is not designed for the spade-work that has yet to be done. Infants cannot profitably be sent direct to the Universities: and, relatively speaking, interest in literature in Scotland is infantile, while Muir is a Pan-European intervening in the world-debate on its highest plane. The number of readers in Scotland capable of following his arguments is extremely limited—proportionally to population much smaller than any country in Europe, or in the United States.[74]

Several of Muir's comments in *Scott and Scotland* certainly incisively corroborate MacDiarmid's belief in the thinness on the ground and poor quality of Scotland's literary men. Muir was, however, not so much concerned with writing a polemic against contemporary vices but with the difficult task of evolving a philosophic and aesthetic account of the breakdown of the Scottish mind, which he believed to have been engendered in the early sixteenth century, to the degree that, like its poetry, it contained "no principle of progress". Muir's sense of the central, vital role of dialectical thought, and the dire consequences of its Scottish absence, pervades *Scott and Scotland*. His sense of the dialectical is, however, not that of Marx's materialism but is deeply akin to the spirituality present in Blake's creative use of that form when he writes that:

> Negations are not Contraries; Contraries mutually Exist;
> But Negations Exist not.

In the direct tradition of English and German Romanticism, Muir saw at life's creative heart the dualistic operation of complementary forces, Blake's "Contraries", which by their activity create higher states of consciousness. The philosophical spine which binds *Scott and Scotland* together, then, is an account of the creative operation of these dualisms and hence the quality and value of the higher moral and spiritual states of self-awareness which stem from their synthesising activity. Thus Muir writes:

> For the major forms of poetry rise from a collision between emotion and intellect on the plane where both meet on equal terms.

and

> The greatest passages in English poetry [are] those in which we no longer seek for the idea or the feelings expressed, but for something transcending them.[75]

Poetry for Muir is the zenith of literary creativity and it arises out of the fusion and subsequent equipoise of thought and feeling:

> Poetry is not spontaneous in that it is restricted to the expression of simple and spontaneous feelings, but rather that in the sense that it reconciles the antitheses of feeling and thought into a harmony, achieving with apparent effortlessness a resolution of subject-matter which to the ratiocinative mind is known only as a difficulty to be overcome by intense effort. It was something like this that Schiller must have meant when he said that all art takes the form of play.[76]

Such play is, however, not an arty game played within the circumscribed safety of aesthetic forms and conventions. This balance of thought and feeling achieved in great poetry is for Muir central to the mature self-awareness of the morally good life and the empathetic, active engagement of such a life in society. The achieved harmony of poetry is for him not simply a model of such a life nor the by-product of it but its primary cause. He believed that Scotland had, at one time, such an integrated poetry. He discerned it in the Ballads, in Dunbar's high art speech, in the coherence and gentleness of Henryson's world picture and in the lyric poetry, some of it anonymous,

63

written in Scotland prior to Flodden and the onset of Calvinism. Much of the substance of his case in *Scott and Scotland* is, in fact, derived from this late fifteenth-century lyric poetry, which he saw as supplying the necessary preconditions for a quality of poetry comparable to that which was to flourish subsequently in English dramatic and metaphysical poetry but which was not to develop in Scotland. What struck Muir as particularly remarkable about this poetry, especially given the subsequent torments of the Scottish psyche, was its reconcilation of nature and religion, flesh and spirit. It had for him a quality of transcendent eroticism which Scottish poetry was never again, even in Burns's songs, to achieve. Such poetry, Muir believed, "had a philosophy of life and following from that a philosophy of love, sensual, romantic and spiritual, so that all three could be given their due force in one poem with perfect balance and propriety."[77] It is this quality of a self-regulating intelligence based on a coherent, comprehensive intellectual vision that Muir felt almost all subsequent Scottish poetry lacked. With the disintegration of a homogeneous national language and its replacement by unstable and decaying dialect forms, this vital core was not only perhaps irretrievably lost but more than a national poetry departed with it. Also the vacuum left by its departure was abhorrently filled:

> We never have this union of passion and reflection in folk poetry, or so far as I know, in dialect poetry; partly because poor and hard-working people have no leisure for it, and partly because dialect is not capable of the more exalted forms of reflection, expressing as it does everyday and local needs. Dialect and folk-poetry is rich enough in general reflections of the proverbial kind, that is reflections *on* experience; but what the poetry I have just quoted gives us is reflection that deals in the most intimate way with experience from inside, decisively modifying and enriching it. The enrichment of experience is as good a criterion of civilization as one could find; and by the evidence of Alexander Scott's poetry it is clear that the most sensitive and intelligent classes in Scotland were far more civilized four hundred years ago than they are now. For this kind of poetry must have had a contemporary audience which understood it and appreciated it; and that means that for some time towards the end of the pre-Reformation Age there must have existed in Scotland a high culture of the feelings

64

as well as the mind: a concord which was destroyed by the rigours of Calvinism, so that hardly a trace of it has been left. What took place was either simple irresponsible feeling side by side with arid intellect, or else that reciprocally destructive confrontation of both for which Gregory Smith found the name of "the Caledonian Antisyzygy": a recognition that they are unreconcilable, and that Scottish life is split in two beyond remedy.[79]

Leaving aside for the moment the vexed and crucial question as to whether language represents a form of life or *is* that form of life, Muir saw in the loss of a genuine native language, the "uniting and overarching principle", as both the main symptom and the cause of the degeneration of Scottish life, letters and mind into either discrete or fractious compartments. From the primary division of the language into disparate modes for thought and feeling, principally manifest by the split between the use of English for prose and demotic dialect for poetry, Muir believed that a consequent series of other destructive lesions took place dividing poetry from criticism and fact from imagination so that such aesthetic disruptions both prefigured and caused the subsequent disruptions in the Scottish body politic. In Blakean terms, Scottish life at all levels became increasingly morbid because rather than being energised by "Contraries", whose vitality derives from their binary function, it lapsed into "Negations".

Some of Muir's harshest comments in *Scott and Scotland* are reserved for the use and abuse of dialect Scots. He perceived it not merely as an irritating, cloying form of sentimentality but as something with deeply sinister political implications not simply in terms of its ability to suppress intelligent radical thought but as a screen used to disguise from its proponents the nature of their social and political actions. Thus he wrote:

> The loss of civilization is bound up with the loss of language; for no civilization can exist without a speech in which it can express both its thought and passion: without an adult tongue, for there can be no maturity except through a working relation between feeling and thought. Dialect is to a homogeneous language what the babbling of children is to the speech of grown men and women; it is blessedly ignorant of the wider spheres of thought and passion, and when it touches upon them its response

is as irresponsible as that of the irremediably immature. Anyone, indeed, who chose to enter into this problem of Scottish dialect poetry from the psychological side, could make out a good case for the thesis that Scottish dialect poetry is a regression to childhood, an escape from the responsibility of the whole nation to the simplicity and irresponsibility of the infant mind.[80]

Childhood, in Muir's thought, is a profoundly ambiguous moral and spiritual dimension. In part, like all the Romatics, he saw its retention as the spontaneous fountainhead of adult creativity. He would certainly have agreed with Coleridge's remark about Burns that "to carry on the feelings of childhood into the powers of manhood . . . is the character and privilege of genius, and one of the marks which distinguish genius from talents".[81] Equally Muir had a sense, derived from what he had seen in the nihilistic self-indulgences of Europe in the Twenties, that the immature person was not so much a biological malfunction as the creation of a perverted act of will. While the psychological regression present in Scottish life was neither as exotic or demonic as the manifestations Muir perceived in Europe before and after the War, Muir saw its willed immaturity as not only corrosive but corrupting. Such immaturity attempts to dispense with the critical intelligence and this dispensation is greatly facilitated by lapsing into an infantile dialect. The activity of the critical intelligence was for Muir that vital function which by its constant activity of testing what was real and authentic for the life of the individual or the nation established the basis of its choices and thereby its freedom. Without this inner consciousness, this conscience, Scotland had rejected freedom and abandoned itself to licence. The forms of Scottish licence were only apparently contradictory. On the one hand, it was a kind of arrested development, the Peter Pan syndrome of J.M. Barrie against which and whom MacDiarmid raged, where things remained eternally unchanged or it was a world of that form of brutal, direct activity which Freud informs us is the prerogative of solipsistic, infantile desire; the greedy appetite which must have immediate gratification. For Muir these elements were, however, different symptoms of the same chronic, licentious disease. Wilfully denying mature self-analysis Scotland wildly oscillated between a state of limbo with "its emotions untouched by thought, it sanctioned irresponsibility and endless false hopes", a false, fantastic freedom since such "freedom is not real freedom but the rejection of choice", and a form of uncontrolled, self-destructive action.[82] To choose not to grow up inevitably extracts a terrible price; its temporary compensations turn inevitably to toxic addictions. Scottish alcoholism kills many pains. For Muir there was a terrible abyss between Scottish consciousness and Scottish action so that the schizoid rhythm of its life swung from the catatonic to the hebephrenic.

> A nation in which the mind is divorced from the feelings will act with hot savagery at times, and with chill insensibility at others; and the loss of Scottish civilisation, of Scottish unity, is the only thing that can explain the peculiarly brutal form which the Industrial Revolution took in Scotland, where its chief agents are only conceivable as thoughtless or perverted children.[83]

In certain respects Muir's thesis of the split between thought and feeling is analogous to Eliot's celebrated concept of the "disassociation of sensibility" which he believed had taken place in English poetry after Donne and the other Metaphysical poets. What characterises the Scottish breach, however, is not only that it was more severe in its occurrence and its effects but that it took place signficantly earlier. Scotland did not, therefore, achieve the polyphonic forms of dramatic poetry or the "dialogue of one" present in metaphysical poetry. Muir believed that this lack of complexity of form entailed a lack of complexity of consciousness both concerning other men and ourselves and that a fall in the level of consciousness is directly proportional to the degree of freedom present in a society. For Muir genuine culture and totalitarianism were incompatible. Throughout *Scott and Scotland* Muir argues that the aesthetic forms present in a society are expressions of what the social and political forms of that society will permit. After the early sixteenth century Muir conceived a ruthless repression of aesthetic form taking place. Thus lacking a dramatic form Scotland did not merely lack a theatre but also a model for that kind of social and political dialogue whereby a society works towards a balance of its contending, conflicting forces where the sum is more than the parts and the end result is more than mere compromise. For Muir, then, Scotland's inability to move beyond Sir David Lyndsay's *Ane pleasant Satyre of the Three Estaitis* was symptomatic of a truncation both of literary and political development.

> The historical importance of poetic tragedy is ... that it confronts the poet immediately with a typical human situation, and compels him to work it out to an end. That situation is, by the very terms of poetic tragedy, a conflict, either a simple conflict between two definite opposing powers, or a complex one into which several powers enter; and the poet has to take every side in turn and state each with the utmost force and objectivity. This is never a cold and judicial act; it is much more like "a sustained passion of self-obliteration, through identification with the creatures of the imagination", to quote from Mr. Middleton Murry's book on Shakespeare. That is to define the dramatic process too violently, however; but it is at least a process in which the mind and the imagination are put to their utmost stretch in an objectivization of all the conflicting powers of the poet, not in peace or suspension, but in intense action. The result is a unique act of selfconsciousness, perhaps the most comprehensive act of self-consciousness possible to the human mind outside mystical contemplation. An act such as this changes the point of gravity of poetry; that is no longer the simple lyrical point, but rather a point determined by a balance between several contending orbits, each of which may be regarded as lyrical, each as a partial expression of the imagination, but given its place and value in an action working towards an end.[84]

If the debate with others was curtailed so was the inner conversation with ourselves. Scottish poetry did not go beyond the lyrical to the metaphysical and so participate in "all forms of poetry in which feeling is set against feeling and intellect enters as a comparative or critical factor".[85] Despite some marvellous early poetry which combined the religious and the erotic, Scotland did not attain to the metaphysical level with its impassioned and rancorous aspiration of the flesh to become spirit and of its awareness of the struggle of good and evil within the self. Her creative life became divided and contradictory, akin to that of Donne's sad alternative:

> So must pure lovers soules descend
> > T'affections, and to faculties,
> Which sense may reach and apprehend,

Else a great Prince in prison lies.

While it is not so anarchic in its tendencies as MacDiarmid's beliefs,

> A' men's institutions and maist men's thochts
> Are tryin' for aye to bring to an end
> The insatiable thocht, the beautiful violent will,
> The restless spirit of man . . .[88]

there is in Muir a comparable sense that literature is a form of free consciousness indispensable to the human struggle against tyranny. At the historical and intellectual centre of *Scott and Scotland*, then, exists, an account of precisely such a struggle and, tragically, of the defeat of the free Scottish consciousness. In the early sixteenth century Scottish freedom was assaulted from without and within. The external assault which culminated in the military and cultural disaster of Flodden is, as William Soutar has remarked, surprisingly and arguably unfairly not mentioned by Muir. The internal assult, that of Calvinism, is, as in all Muir's Scottish writings, omnipresent. In his earlier book *John Knox*, Muir had written of the cultural depredations of Calvinism's onslaught on Scotland. We need to recall these before we can pass to the complex, underlying reasons for Calvinism's hatred for high culture in general and imaginiative literature in particular. In his bitterly ironic conclusion to *Knox* Muir had written that:

> But here I shall accept the almost unanimous opinion of the historians, for it is unlikely that they should all be wrong. Their opinion briefly is that Knox, the reformers, and the Covenanters have made Scotland what it is; and they give the chief credit to Knox himself. Now if this is true, Knox's influence would be most clearly seen in the hundred years or so after his death. What did Calvinist Scotland produce during that time? In politics a long and wearisome series of civil conflicts; in theology 'The Causes of the Lord's Wrath,' 'The Poor Man's Cup of Cold Water ministered to the Saints and Sufferers for Christ in Scotland,' and 'Lex Rex'; in literature the charming diary of James Melville, the letters of Samuel Rutherford with their queer mixture of religious feeling and Freudian symbolism, and the Scottish version of the psalms; in philosophy, profane poetry, the drama, music, painting, architecture, nothing. Whatever was

done in literature during this time came from the opponents of Calvinism or from men out of sympathy with it; Drummond of Hawthornden's poetry and his still nobler prose work, *A Cypress Grove*, some fine verses by Montrose, and Sir Thomas Urquhart's great translation of Rabelais. Yet, during the same hundred years the nearest-lying country could show Shakespeare, Spenser, Jonson, Marlowe, Donne, Milton, in poetry and the drama; Bacon, Hooker, Browne, Taylor, Clarendon, in prose; the beginnings of modern science; and music, architecture, philosophy, theology, oratory in abundance. Was it the influence of Calvinism which preserved Scotland from that infection? There are reasonable grounds, I think, for believing so. Calvinism, in the first place, was a faith which insisted with exclusive force on certain human interests, and banned all the rest. It lopped off from religion music, painting and sculpture, and pruned architecture to a minimum; it frowned on all prose and poetry which was not sacred. For its imaginative literature it was confined more and more to the Old Testament, and though the Old Testament contains some splendid poetry, it has at all times been over-praised at the expense of greater works. Calvinism, in short, was a narrowly specialized kind of religion, but it was also a peculiar religion—a religion which outraged the imagination, and no doubt helped, therefore, to produce that captivity of the imagination in Scotland which was only broken in the eighteenth century. For this religion laid down that God had elected certain men for His approval from the beginning of time, and it was impossible to believe this His choice showed discrimination. Looking down on the Island of Great Britain in the century which followed Knox's death, the Almighty, it seemed had rejected Shakespeare, Spenser, and Donne, and chosen Andrew Melville, Donald Cargill and Sandy Peden. And if His choice was restricted to the godly, it was equally strange, for He liked the translators of the Scots version of the Psalms, and rejected Herbert, Vaughan, and Crashaw. Passing over the cacophonous:

> I saw Eternity the other night,
> Like a great ring of pure and endless light,
> All calm, as it was bright,

He listened with rapture to the more truly Calvinistic music of

> But loved be God which doth us safely keep,
> From bloody teeth and their most cruel voice,
> Which as a prey to eat us would rejoice.

70

This, then, was the strange belief which prevailed in Scotland for so long as a consequence, if the historians are right, of Knox's labours. How could the country have avoided its fate of becoming for over a century an object-lesson in savage provincialism? Hume, Burns, and men like them, it is true, lifted it from its isolation for a time during the next hundred years.

What Knox really did was to rob Scotland of all the benefits of the Renaissance. Scotland never enjoyed these as England did, and no doubt the lack of that immense advantage has had a permanent effect. It can be felt, I imagine, even at the present day.[87]

For Muir, then, Calvinism broke the continuity of Scottish culture. The poetic imagination in particular was deprived of both its traditional roots and the enormous energising creativity which other cultures had experienced by participating in the Renaissance. Thus, though Muir admired Burns, it was admiration qualified by a sense of the decline apparent to him in the art of the Ayrshire poet as to that of which, for example, Dunbar was capable. Further, desperately hard as Burns fought against the powerful Calvinist elements in Scottish culture, Muir considered these elements to be so strong that even a poet as great as Burns was limited, flawed even, by them. Thus he wrote of Burns in *Scottish Journey*:

> Burns is a very Protestant poet. Even in his remoulding of old folk songs he never goes back in sentiment past the Reformation. He certainly had no affection for the God of Knox, yet he himself had no other, except an eighteenth century abstraction. His ribaldry, blasphemy, libertinism and sentimentality are all Protestant, and quite narrowly so. The ballads are without this local Lowland Scots limitation. In their view of life they are older than Protestantism; and it is this depth of inspiration which is their distinctive quality.[88]

Poetry as a literary form predating Calvinism was disrupted by it. Muir, however, argued that even the fiction which appeared in eighteenth-century Scotland suffered a repressed, debilitated and even perverted development because of Calvinism's continuing grip on Scottish culture. While the savage iconoclasm of the sixteenth century was not obviously present in later Scottish culture, Muir believed that these anti-creative values had not so much moderated as metamorphosed

71

into covert but almost equaly strong forms of control of the provenenace of literature. Calvinism disbelieved in literature both because it was impractical and because theology was the only instrument of true knowledge. Muir believed that these fundamental attitudes to literature remained unchanged in Scottish society but, partly due to the increase in prosperity after the Union and the greater, if often questionable, receptivity to English values, literature, for the growing Scottish middle class, became a mode of instruction in the social graces and a form of entertainment. Thus literature as amusement became more acceptable, especially if through sales it could pass the acid test of high profitability, but unacceptable as soon as it dared to move from such immature activities to either a mature self-awareness or a critique of the actual interests of power. Barrie, as the best selling author of books about arrested development, is perhaps the summit of both his ambitions and achievements. In a splendid revaluation of Stevenson and his sometimes heroic struggles against the ambience in which he found himself, Muir cogently demonstrated the persistent and pervasive influence of Scottish culture on its writers:

Stevenson died in 1894 in his forty-fourth year. That is to say, he was still, for a novelist, a young man. Moreover he was younger than his years, for he had spent his childhood and youth in a country where everything combined to prevent an imaginative writer from coming to maturity. After three centuries of a culture almost exclusively theological, imaginative literature in Scotland in Stevenson's time was tolerated, where it was tolerated at all, only as an idle toy. That a novel should influence the character or humanize the emotions was an un-Scottish idea; and if Stevenson's relatives and advisers had contemplated such a secular operation it would have seemed to them illegitimate and insidious; for by its working morality, which should come uncontaminated from its pure source in religion or philosphy, it entered the character by clandestine ways, indeed stole past the conscience by lulling it to sleep, and took the soul by carnal wiles.

So one of the earliest ideas which must have been implanted in Stevenson's mind by universal suggestion was that story-telling was an idle occupation, and could be tolerated only as long as it remained so. He had before him, moreover, the example of his countryman, Scott, and he was probably too young, and too securely enclosed in national literary prejudice, to see that Scott's immense powers too were made idle by the general expectation of his countrymen that they should be idle. His fate indeed was typical of the fate of all Scottish imaginative writers since the Reformation who have not been, like Carlyle, directly and loudly concerned with ethics. In a country whose culture is almost exclusively religious, conscience finally becomes a matter concerned with only two spheres, the theological and the crudely material. There is no soil on which an artistic or imaginative conscience can grow, and no function for the novelist therefore except that of a public entertainer. If he refuses to accept the *role* he can, it is true, hit back at his audience as George Douglas did so savagely in *The House with the Green Shutters*. But that, though an exhiliarating, is an unprofitable exercise, and for criticism at once serious and urbane, the civilizing delineation of Fielding or Thackeray, there was hardly any scope in Scotland in Stevenson's day. So one may account in great measure for the tragedies of Scott, Stevenson and Sir James Barrie, all of them writers of genius, and all of them stultified. What distinguishes Stevenson from the other novelists of his race, however, is that he was not eagerly ready to be stultified; he suffered under his annulment and struggled against it; he strove to become the writer he was by endowment; he persistently aspired to be something more than a purveyor of light relaxation for serious church-goers; and there is little doubt that had he lived he would have been the first Scottish novelist in the full humanistic tradition.[89]

In *Scott and Scotland* which followed closely in the wake of this article on Stevenson, Muir explored more fully this problem of creative deprivation of tradition and audience in Scottish fiction with particular regard to Sir Walter Scott. In this account of Scott, Muir saw him as very much a victim of his circumstances; he was a great writer deprived of his means and his proper response because "he lived in an imperfectly integrated society where many aspects of life were ignored, and sensibility was an imported product."[90] Muir felt in Scott what he felt in Scotland, "a very curious emptiness' and this moved him to so define Scott's predicament:

> I was forced to account for the hiatus in Scott's endowment by considering the environment in which he lived, by invoking the

fact—if the reader will agree it is one—that he spent most of his days in a hiatus, in a country, that is to say, which was neither a nation nor a province, and had, instead of a centre, a blank, and Edinburgh in the middle of it. But this Nothing in which Scott wrote was not merely a spatial one; it was a temporal Nothing as well, dotted with a few disconnected figures arranged at abrupt intervals: Henryson, Dunbar, Allan Ramsay, Burns, with a rude buttress of ballads and folk songs to shore them up and keep them from falling. Scott in other words, lived in a community which was not a community, and set himself to carry on a tradition which was not a tradition; and the result was that his work was an exact reflection of his predicament. His picture of life had no centre, because the environment in which he lived had no centre. What traditional virtue his work possessed was at second hand, and derived mainly from English literature, which he knew intimately but which was a semi-foreign literature to him. Scotland did not have enough life of its own to nourish a writer of his scope; it had neither a real community to foster him nor a tradition to direct him; for the anonymous ballad tradition was not sufficient for his genius. So that my inquiry into what Scotland did for Scott came down finally to what it did not do for Scott. What it did not do, or what it could not do. Considered historically these alternatives are difficult to separate.[91]

In his other accounts of Scott, Muir was less inclined to see the emptiness at the heart of his work as merely the result of his being the victim of circumstances to the extent that his work could be no more than the sum of his nation's deficiences. The vision of Scott in Muir's poetry is, for example, much less charitable but, given the nature of the medium, perhaps nearer the truth of what Muir felt about him. Thus he and Burns are described as "sham bards of a sham nation" and, even more tellingly for the question of the Scottish literary tradition, the loss of the oral potency of the Ballads is attributed to that point when—

> . . . Scott and Hogg, the robbers, came
> And nailed the singing tragedies down
> In dumb letters under a name
> And led the bothy to the town.[92]

Such cultural breaks are, of course, never so clean cut, dramatic or perhaps so directly attributable. Muir, however, did see Scott as a principal adulterer of the

Scottish literary tradition. He was by no means alone among his major contemporaries in so perceiving him. Unlike present day academic enthusiasts for Scott, all the major writers of the Scottish Renaissance were aware of his, at best, discontinuous place in a Scottish tradition.[93] To an Anglophobe like MacDiarmid the nature of this discontinuity was directly the result of Scott's consent to the Union in 1707. For MacDiarmid this incorporation of English values, especially literary values, could not but bring harm. Muir also saw Scott at a point of confluence between the Scottish and English traditions. As he wrote:

> When one tries to relate Scott to tradition and see how he affected it and was affected by it, one discovers that there are two problems to deal with, two traditions to take into account. For Scott is both an English and a Scottish writer; he is related as closely on the one side to the line of English novelists whose greatest representative is Fielding as he is on the other to the anonymous ballads of his own country which he collected so lovingly and watered down so conscientiously. He derived from both those traditions, and in turn he influenced both.[94]

Where MacDiarmid, however, would argue that any attempt at procreation between Scottish and English creativity would lead to either abortion or degenerate offspring, Muir saw what happened in Scott's case as more complex. For him Scott failed to produce a virile hybrid because he brought to bear on his assimilation of both traditions the same Calvinist inspired vice of gentility and subjected them both to a form of social censorship which severely diluted both their powers. He described this process thus:

> The eighteenth-century English novel was a criticism of society, manners and life. It set out to amuse, but it had a serious intention; its criticism, however wittily expressed, was sincere, and being sincere it made for more civilized manners and a more sensitive understanding of human life. Scott marks a definite degeneration of that tradition: after him certain qualities are lost to the novel which are not recovered for a long time. The novel becomes the idlest of all forms of literary art, and by a natural consequence the most popular. Instead of providing an intelligent criticism of life it is content to enunciate moral platitudes, and it does this all the more confidently because such

75

platitudes are certain to be agreeable to the reader. It skims over every aspect of experience that could be obnoxious to the most tender or prudish feelings, and in fact renounces both freedom and responsibility. Scott, it seems to me, was largely instrumental in bringing the novel to that pass; with his enormous prestige he helped to establish the mediocre and the trivial.

How much of the moral responsibility for this rests on him, and how much on his age, which was awakening to gentility, it is probably impossible to determine. The fact remains that all that Scott wrote is disfigured by the main vice of gentility: its inveterate indifference to truth, its inability to recognize that truth is valuable in itself. No doubt there have been countless genteel writers in the history of English literature. But Scott was the first writer of really great powers to bow his knee unquestioningly to gentility and abrogate his responsibility. As a result the tradition of English prose fiction was devitalized for more than half a century.

When we turn to his influence on Scottish literature we find the same story. There were not many genteel Scottish writers before Scott; there have not been many ungenteel ones since. His gentility can be seen in his *Border Minstrelsy* which he loved and yet could not but Bowdlerize. But the difference he introduced into Scottish poetry can be seen most clearly by comparing his own poems in the ballad form with the old ballads themselves. It is pretty nearly the difference between

> I lighted down my sword to draw,
>   I hacked him in pieces sma',

and

> "Charge, Chester, charge! On, Stanley, on!"
> Were the last words of Marmion,

the difference between a writer fully conscious that he is dealing with dreadful things and one who must make even carnage pleasing and picturesque.

Scott was a man of great native genius and of enormous inventive powers. But has any other writer of equal rank ever misused his gifts and indefatigably lowered the standards of literature with quite such a clean conscience?[95]

What most disconcerted Muir about Scott and his vast influence on Scottish writing throughout the nineteenth century was not simply that such literary gentility was antithetical to traditional Scottish writing's capacity for the direct utterance of stark passions and facts but that this writing was such a surrender to and mere manifestation of the values of a genteel society. While Muir did not, like MacDiarmid, see canniness and respectability as undiluted evils, evils furthermore imposed on the passionate, eccentric Scottish spirit by the English hegemony, he did agree with him that literature's role was never that of the reflection or corroboration of a society devoted to such values. In a discussion with V.S. Pritchett he made this point in a manner which has considerable relevance to his critique of the "Anglo-Scottish" writing of the nineteenth and early twentieth century:

> You seemed to me, while you were talking, to identify the writer and the public much too closely.
> You said that the writer is the interpreter of the public to itself, but this describes only part of the writer's work and it gives him far too passive a role. What makes a writer different from the public is the capacity to think about the public's thinking and to feel about the public's feelings in a way which sets them in a new relation. It may be true that the writer helps to establish a connection between us, but what matters is the level on which the connection is made. It is not simply the level on which the public thinks, feels, wishes, loves and hates; it is a level on which their thoughts, feelings, wishes, loves and hates are translated so that they stand out in relief for us, so that they can see whether they are false or true, and not only enter into them but judge them too.
> I do not agree that each successive public as it rises to power simply imposes its own values on its writers. The rich manufacturers in the reign of Victoria did, I grant you, bring their values to bear on the Victorian writers, yet many of these writers were rebelling violently against them. The writer who is dictated to by the public and swallows its values blindly is the bad writer, the facile best-seller, for whom you have as little use as I have.[95]

The enormous popularity of Scottish writing from the latter part of the eighteenth century up to the beginning of the twentieth century was, in fact, due to its passive response to the needs of a new kind of middle class mass literarcy. Thus Scott's fictionalization of his native history within the safe if rather down at heel conventions of Augustan comic fiction, Byron's wittily rhymed versification of the Calvinist inspired gloom and guilt of the anguished lost soul and the extraordinary critical dominance of Jeffrey in *The Edinburgh Review* and later Lockhart and Wilson in *Blackwood's*. Nor was it the case that this kind of writing was a mere naive reflection of market trends. Scottish writing knowingly cashed in on romantic sentimentality but when, what Morse Peckham describes as High Romanticism appeared, the Scots either did not understand or were deeply antagonistic towards this English form of anti-sentimental critique of the dominant economic, utilitarian and mechanistic trends of the time. Provincially clinging to eighteenth century English modes, the Scots, with the eccentric exception of James Hogg, saw the innovative work of the new English movement as conducive not only to literary but social disorder. If the religious pressure of Calvinism debarred Scots from participating in the Renaissance, the social pressure of middle class gentility performed the same task with regard to Romanticism. It is far beyond the scope of the present essay to explore fully the Scottish misappropriation of Romanticism but Muir's insights lead to the perceptive conclusions of Tom Nairn who wrote:

Here was the second of the dreams still implanted in the subsoil of Scottish consciousness. European history shows a general relationship between Romanticism and the nationalism of the 19th century, not entirely unlike that between the Reformation and capitalism which we have already looked at. But again, Scotland was a drastic exception to whatever generalities hold in this field. There, the new freedom of expression and the discovery of folk-culture could scarcely be the precursors or the supports of a new nation in the making (as in Italy, Hungary, Germany), nor the accompaniment of triumphant nationality (as in England and America). The Scottish nationality was dead. Scotland was once more severed from those real conditions which should have lent meaning to her culture. No revolution against the humiliations of the Union, no Scottish 1848, was to furnish a historical counterpoint to Robert Burns and Sir Walter Scott. The romantic consciousness too, therefore, could only be an absolute dream to the Scots. Unable to function as ideology, as a moving spirit of history, it too was bound to become a possessing demon. Elsewhere, the revelation of the romantic past and the soul of the people informed some real future—in the Scottish limbo, they *were* the nation's reality. Romanticism provided—as the Enlightenment could not, for all its brilliance—a surrogate identity.[97]

Thus the level at which most Scottish writing connected with its vast not only British but European audience from James MacPherson to the degenerate elements in R.L. Stevenson was, while not lacking in complexity, not that of creating the moral perspective Muir describes as the essential role of creative writing. The complexity exists in the fact that the Scots did not only pander to the declared, public conventions of bourgeois respectability and its wordly-wisdom but rather fed the fantasy life which was a necessary compensatory part of these repressive conventions. As opposed to its practical, commercial energies which were thrown into colonial and industrial exploitation, the sensibility of middle class Europe after Rousseau was orientated towards a sentimental endorsement of noble savages and untamed landscapes. One might almost say that if the Scottish Highlands had not conveniently existed, European sentimentality would have had to invent them. Indeed, given the discrepancy between the facts and the fictions of writers like MacPherson and Scott, it was invented.[98] Consequently the Highlanders were the closest psychological and geographical approximation to the figures of fantasy sought by middle class Europe to allay the boredom of the practical, rational, respectable life it had prosperously fashioned for itself. It was only too easy for Scottish writing to cash in on the gross appetites of bourgeois Europe's greed for, at a safe, fictive remove, atavistic passion, violent militarism, supernaturalism, nostalgia and maudlin lament. It is not the least of the dark ironies of Scottish life and letters that, while experiencing culturally destructive economic and political restraints, the Highlanders, within the safe conventions of the best seller, should be made exemplary figures of that extraordinary unreal freedom derived from enacting the fantasies which such a public had repressed in its own behaviour and, to an even more extreme degree, in its own self-consciousness. Muir's acute understanding of the mechanics of this kind of Victorian best-seller is seen most comically and incisively in his account of a now forgotten Scottish author, William Black. Unlike Scott, who specialised in the more machismo fantasies of his age—as Anthony Burgess has recently suggested, "it is best to see Scott as providing his age with an image of aristocratic militarism of spurious pedigree for the new nabobs"—Black dealt with passions to which imperial Britain could give less scope.[99] Black, in fact, dealt with the titillations of the erotic and with both provoking and soothing the guilt and anxieties of the respectable consciousness. Muir saw in him a debased Wordsworthian purity of vision:

> A best-seller is generally a story in which the author both has his cake and eats it; but it can also be one in which he goes on swallowing two cakes that violently disagree with each other without suffering any discomfort, indeed with complete enjoyment. Black's books belong to the latter class. The two things that he swallowed and flourished on were, first, Victorian respectability which, granting all its merits, was an oppressively narrow affair; and secondly, a wayward freedom which was in some undefined way exempt from the trammels of that respectability and never infringed or violated it. The strictest convention had to be vindicated, the most irresponsible liberty allowed. Perhaps the simplest way of achieving such a thing was the best. So Black introduced into most of his books some foreigner, generally of the female sex, in whom waywardness is both more graceful and more excusable. He introduced French girls and Italian girls and Greek girls, above all, Highland girls. He planted them in the middle of respectable English life; he described, with that somewhat fictitious sympathy which we give to people who are not so fortunate or unfortunate as to live within the conventions which encase ourselves, their delightful blunders, their justifiable, indeed righteous aberrations. He described these not only with sympathy but with delight, the pathetic delight of a schoolboy dreaming of truancy while he is listening to the droning voice of his master and knows that there is no escape. His sympathy holds out even when his heroine pushes freedom past all permissible bounds, when she decides, for example, like the French heroine of *A Daughter of Heth*, to run away with a married lord. But the delights of truancy cease there; he firmly prevents the transgression; he sends a threatening sunset, and when that fails follows it up with a terrific tempest in which the recalcitrant heroine is struck down, and her lover's yacht, waiting impatiently outside Saltcoats, founders with the loss of all hands

but one—not the lover. Yet the victim retains our sympathy, as an indigenous Victorian heroine would not have done; she has an excuse, the excuse of a freedom which, while delightful, is inevitably punished if it is pushed too far.[100]

Thus in Muir's view the enormous and sustained commercial success of Scottish writing was in inverse proportion to its authenticity to its own traditional powers. Corrupted by the Calvinistic ethic of profitability and genteel respectability, creating a pastoral, sentimental Scotland both for home consumption and export which simultaneously entertained the middle classes and reassured their deep political anxieties about industrial proletarian unrest, almost wholly lacking that critique of imperial and utilitarian mores which is so powerfully present in the great English writers of the nineteenth century, Muir would have found little comfort in laudatory remarks like that of William Power's concerning the fact that literature stood only second to golf as a national activity.[101] Muir's diagnosis is, in fact, almost that pertaining to the terminal stage of the Scottish imagination.

That death did not take place, at least at that point in time, was due to the appearance of a remarkable creative generation of which Muir was part. Acknowledged by his contemporaries as a critic of the first order, Muir was wholly aware of the revivification that was taking place and, while he was always pessimistic as to the ability of this new group to connect with a native audience, he saw in them both elements of traditional Scottish literary virtues and a capacity not to surrender literature to the values of Kailyard Scotland. Thus in an essay "New Paths in Fiction: Scottish Novel Since the War", he cogently demonstrated how this new fiction broke radically away from what preceded it:

> The best way to get a fairly clear idea of the Scottish novel since the War is to compare it with the Scottish novel in the decade or so before the War. The best-known Scottish novelist at that time was J.M. (Now Sir James) Barrie. Neil Munro was writing his less popular descriptions of Highland life. Mr. John Buchan was beginning to make a name for his romantic stories of adventure. "Ian Hay" had had his first popular success. "Annie S. Swan" was steadily turning out her pictures of middle-class Scottish life for a grateful public. George Douglas Brown was dead, and "The House with the Green Shutters," having survived its phase of scandalous notoriety, had passed into a

81

cheap edition. Leaving aside Douglas Brown, who was a discordant voice in the happy chorus of Scottish fiction, and who had no successors of importance, the typical Scottish novel before the War was thus what we would now call the best seller.

It was sentimental, and it was written with one eye on the market, except, I think, for the novels of Neil Munro and "Annie S. Swan," which seem to me to be an honest expression of their authors' temperament. It was cut off from the influences which were remoulding the novel in England, where the most admired novelists of the time were Henry James, Joseph Conrad, Arnold Bennett, John Galsworthy, and Mr. H.G. Wells. It closed its eyes to or was unaware of the problems, both of thought and technique, which were agitating these transmontane writers. Its ideas were the ideas of the comfortable middle class, its technique the technique of the magazine serial.

That, I think, is a fair picture of the Scottish novel before the war. In that concert of best-sellers the voices of Barrie and Munro were by far the most distinguished and original. But all of those voices, from the most refined to the most pawky, had an inflection which would have been recognised and appreciated by constant readers of the "People's Friend." Now that cannot be said by any stretch of fancy about the characteristically post-war Scottish novelists—about Mr. Eric Linklater, or Mr. Neil Gunn, or Mr Lewis Grassic Gibbon, or Mrs Willa Muir, or Miss E. Brysson Morrison. Nor can it be said even about Mr. A.J. Cronin, who has written one of the most popular best-sellers of the day, a book that has been absurdly over-praised and unjustly under-valued.

The Scottish novel, then, has changed since the war; it has become less friendly to the people, less popular, less sentimental, less Scottish in the old sense, and less commercial. It has also grown more responsible, in as far as it shows an appreciation of the fact that truth and art in fiction have a value of their own, apart from their use in selling a story. It is more outspoken and consequently more sensitive, for suppression of feeling finally leads to obtuseness and sentimentality, which is a technique for whipping up feeling and convincing the author and the reader that it is actually. If one reads Mr. Neil Gunn, and then turns to Barrie or Neil Munro, one can feel very clearly this mingled insensitiveness and mawkishness in their work, caused, I think mainly by a stuffy convention of middle-class decorum, which was essentially as barbarous as a taboo.

One of the things then that has happened to the Scottish

novel is that fresh air has been let into it. In other words, it is no longer parochial, no longer contentedly accepts the second best as its ideal, or is satisfied to be judged by a standard which would be considered provincial or commercial in other countries. The curse of commerciality has weighed on Scottish fiction ever since Scott; why, it is hard to say. Perhaps because to the Scots, brought up in Calvinism, that which could not pay, and pay well, either in this world or the next, could not be really of much importance. The influence of Calvinism on the Scottish novel has never been seriously gone into. All the five novelists I have mentioned are more or less explicity anti-Calvinist, and none of them is touched with the commercial taint which spoiled the work even of such a fine writer as Stevenson. I do not pretend to draw any conclusion from this, but let the fact stand.

The outspokenness which the Scottish novel has won for itself since the war has not been won without scandal. The public was never indignantly enraged by the sentimentality of Sir J.M. Barrie: no shocked letters were written to the papers about "The Little Minister." But when Mr. Eric Linklater drew a faithful picture of island life in "White Maa's Saga," a picture, in my opinion, quite without offence, there was an outcry which has not yet died down. The same thing happened to Mr. Lewis Grassic Gibbon, when "Sunset Song" appeared. Yet this kind of objection, which before the war would have been sufficiently strong to damn a book (Stevenson lived in terror of it), is now, though unpleasant enough, fortunately ineffectual. A Scottish novelist has now freedom to say what he wishes to say.[102]

While Muir felt a renewed faith in Scottish fiction, correctly seeing Gunn and Grasic Gibbon as of particular importance, the figure who most impressed him was MacDiarmid. In reviewing *Circumjack Cencrastus* Muir was not only rightly struck by the extraordinary modern power of this poem but by the manner in which this power was stimulated and derived from a formal and linguistic quality he felt to be particularly Scottish. He described it thus:

Scottish poetry at its best has never run to sweetness or magnificence like English, but to a sort of wild play with imagination and technique, coming from an excess of energy which expends itself both recklessly and surely. It is seen at its most characteristic in Dunbar, the greatest craftsmen in Scottish poetry, but it is seen in Burns too, though he was only an apprentice in his art compared with the older poet. It is

83

displayed in Dunbar's almost endless and yet effortless surplus of internal rhymes, his 'showing-off', and in such grotesque fantasies as 'The Seven Deidly Sins' with their wild but extremely skilful mixture of the coarse and the terrible. This kind of poetry by a natural twist, a 'thrawnness', combines the most violently opposed elements out of an intellectual relish in the contrast. 'Hugh MacDiarmid's' poetry is of this kind; for though there are passages in the present volume where he rises to magnificence, they are always broken into by some deliberate incongruity reminding us that he is simultaneously dealing with the greatest and the meanest things.[103]

Given Muir's awareness of MacDiarmid's achievement his later judgement that Lallans would not become the general language of Scottish creativity did not come easily to him. His openmindedness about such problems can be seen in an essay he wrote on the state of Scottish poetry prior to writing *Scott and Scotland*. Here he remarked that:

A more pressing question is whether the language in which he writes is actually, as it claims to be, a language able to sustain all the forms and degrees of poetry; for on the answer to that question depends one's hopes for the future of Scots poetry. MacDiarmid himself has shown that he can use this language, and that in his hands it is capable of astonishing force and variety. It would be too much to say that he uses it with sureness; the language is too young. But I think he has shown with good fortune, that is with assistance from other poet's present and future, it can be consolidated and win a place for itself. If something like that does not happen, then it is hard to see any future for Scots poetry; for the old folk-tradition cannot linger on for ever, since Scotland is not exclusively a country of cottars' houses and towns like Kirriemuir. Scots poetry was moribund; Hugh M'Diarmid has wakened some hope for it; and that, apart from his intrinsic poetic gifts, makes him a uniquely important figure in contemporary Scottish literature.[104]

By the time he wrote *Scott and Scotland*, however, Muir was convinced that MacDiarmid would have no successors other than those who used Scottish dialect as a mode of sentimental evasion and who, rather than seeking "intellectual relish" by way of violent contrast, were intent on the use of disparate entities to curb the intelligence by promulgating a world where fact was undermind by fantasy. Thus, while MacDiarmid's initial response to Muir was as warm and perceptive as the latter's had been to him, the publication of *Scott and Scotland* which announced—MacDiarmid's achievement apart—the abuse and consequent exhaustion of certain traditional Scottish modes and also an endorsement of English, was for him a declaration of war and he was never a man to avoid a fight. While Willa cannot be considered an unpartisan witness, her assessment of the cause and severity of the breach is, as reported in *Belonging*, a fair one. She wrote of her husband that:

> He deduces that 'a Scottish writer who wishes to achieve some approximation to completeness has no choice except to absorb the English tradition', since in Scotland he will find 'neither an organic community to round off his conceptions, nor a major literary tradition to support him, nor even a faith among the people themselves that a Scottish literature is possible or desirable, nor any opportunity, finally, of making a livelihood by his work'. All these provocative statements occur in the Introduction, which finishes by saying that the problem cannot be solved by writing poems in Scots.
>
> Nothing in the rest of the book could make up to Christopher Grieve for that flat denial of the gospel according to Hugh MacDiarmid, neither the delicate discrimination with which Edwin compared Scottish poetry before the Reformation with that produced after it, nor the candour of this tribute: 'a really original poet like Hugh MacDiarmid has never received in Scotland any criticism of his more ambitious poems which can be of the slightest use to him'. For Christopher, Edwin now became The Enemy, and his fighting blood, like that of a Border cateran, prompted a literary vendetta against Edwin Muir which went on for years, during which he published many vituperative polemics to which Edwin made no answer of any kind. I think Edwin's indifference to all this invective was genuine, although he regretted the rupture of friendly relations; these attacks on himself seemed a small issue compared to what was happening in the world at large.[105]

What Willa did not perhaps realise, or take seriously, was that an essential part of the violent intensity of MacDiarmid's response was that he did not see his argument with Muir as an insignificant side-show, an artistic storm in a tea cup, as the world lurched towards and into war. By the time of the publication of his autobiography, *Lucky Poet*, in 1942, MacDiarmid was of the opinion that the triumph of Churchill's British Empire constituted a greater threat to Scotland than Hitler's Nazi Germany (a comparison of the nature of Pound and MacDiarmid's political vision would be not without interest) so that Muir's suggestions that Scottish literature had to adopt wholly the English language and that its inheritance was strongly derived from the English tradition was seen not so much as an act of literary criticism as an act of unpardonable political treachery. The treatment of Muir in *Lucky Poet* has, then, little of the flyting, outrageous wit of Scottish satire but is mainly demeaning and ugly. Muir is seen as belonging to the treacherous hegemony of Anglo-Scots who have kept Scotland in thrall to England. Unlike the eternally rebellious MacDiarmid, he is presented as an establishment man "whose prose has a marked resemblance to Ramsay MacDonalid's.[106] From such singular infelicities of stylistic assessment, MacDiarmid proceeds to even more grandiose misreadings not only of the political nature of *Scott and Scotland* but also *John Knox*. With a certain crazy logic everything is twisted to prove Muir's subversive intentions as an agent of the English. Thus MacDiarmid wrote:

> Muir by his refusal to meet the case of the Scots Renaissance *ipso acto* gives away the reactionary aim of his book—the continuance of the nineteenth-century traitor attitude of Scots Literature and of Scott's prestige (all of which is implicit and simply taken for granted as axiomatic to all right-thinking and, above all, well-bred people in Sir Herbert Grierson's biography, not explicit as in Muir's book). *Scott and Scotland* is an attempt to recall the literary public in Scotland to its allegiance to its former idols. The dangerous thing in it is not its confused theorizing, which is of the 'swindling catchword' Fascist-Imperialist order and is not expected to be taken seriously, but its glorification of Scott. Scott's novels are the great source of the paralysing ideology of defeatism in Scotland, the spread of which is responsible at once for the acceptance of the Union and the low standard of nineteenth-century Scots literature except in the hands of men like the Gaelic poet, William Livingston (1808-70), who were consciously anti-English—a defeatism as profitable financially to its exponents (Scott, Stevenson, Tweedsmuir, &c.) as it is welcome to English interest. . . . Also worth mentioning,

in view alike of Sir Herbert Grierson's prelatic prepossessions, Scott's own Episcopalianism, and Mr. Muir's anti-Calvinistic writings (e.g., his 'debunking' life of Knox), is the religious issue. Such repudiations of Calvinism are thoroughly religious repudiations—i.e., culminating in a sort of milk-and-water mysticism, Calvinist in tone but not in logic. Mr. Muir's revolt against Calvinism, for example, is nothing but a reform of the religious ideology necessary to the hold of England over Scotland so as to make it meet the problems with which post-War development has represented the Ascendancy. His book is performing the function of *The Causes of the Lord's Wrath against Scotland* again. Mr. Muir's anti-Calvinism is as much a red herring as Hitler's anti-Semitism, besides being incompatible with his own religious standpoint.[107]

MacDiarmid's attack on *Scott and Scotland*, then, is based on his desperate need to assert not only the inviolability of the Scottish imagination from English corruption but, indeed, its innate superiority. To do this he must disprove Muir's Scottishness even if this means wholly contradicting all his previous assessment of the man and what he might do for Scottish criticism. Thus when he published his *Golden Treasury of Scottish Poetry* in 1940 Muir was not included as a poet. The uneven collection would have certainly benefited from his presence, but Muir was attacked in the preface:

None of these things in relation to Scots presumably matters to Mr. Muir, who is not a Scot but an Orcadian, with a very different psychology and historical and linguistic background, and who has nowhere vouchsafed any evidence of any particular knowledge of the Scots language or any familiarity with its literature adequate to warrant his criticisms. So far as his deprecation of "mere lyrics" is concerned, however, Mr. Muir is on the worst possible ground. His argument about the various forms in English poetry as against the two forms which have formed the unvarying staple of Scottish poetry is perilously like contending that a centipede is necessarily more vital and more complete than a quadruped or a mere biped, and his whole thesis indeed is like condemning wild strawberries because they have not the attributes of peaches.[108]

Such ludicrous political misreadings as these should not prevent us from seeing that *Scott and Scotland* was a concise and honest attempt to evaluate Scottish achievements in the light of comparable English ones and on the basis of this evaluation see how Scottish literature might develop. Muir did believe that in terms of tradition, immaturity of poetic forms and genres and moral vision, Scottish literature was inferior to English. Given his own desire to write a religious poetry, a poetry of transcendence, he was drawn to English poets like Herbert and Vaughan because he believed that the celebrated imaginative mode of the Caledonian Antisygyzy with its oscillating nature had, other than in MacDiarmid, retreated into mere vacillation allowing its proponents to exist in a sentimental void. Where MacDiarmid had seen Gregory Smith's book *Scottish Literature: Character and Influence* as defining the essential aspects of the Scottish imagination, Muir tended much more to T.S. Eliot's opinion that:

> It is true that Mr. Gregory Smith seeks for permanent characteristics of the Scottish mind which find expression in literature. But, with deference to his superior knowledge of his subject, the characteristics which he presents do not seem essential to literature, sufficient to mark any significant *literary* difference. Neither the love of precise detail nor the love of the fantastic which he finds in Scottish literature, is a literary trait; on the contrary, they are both more likely to be hostile to artistic perfection. Nor has the passion for antiquities, nor the persistence of local metres in verse, any extensive significance. To the extent to which writing becomes literature, these peculiarities are likely to be submerged.[109]

There is some truth to the fact that when Eliot wrote this in 1919 he was busy discarding his American provincialism, as he thought of it, in order to make himself an Englishman so that no doubt his too can be seen as covert sabotage against the Scottish cause. In any case his analysis of the relationship of Gaelic to Scottish literature and the fate of Lallans is, at this time, remarkably similar to that of Muir. Thus he wrote:

> Mr. Gregory Smith makes it copiously clear that Scots literature was the literature of the Lowlands, and that the Scot of the Lowlands was at all times much more closely in touch with his Southron enemy than with the Gaelic occasional ally. Whatever aesthetic agitation may have taken place in the Highland brain, the disturbance was not communicated to the

the Lowlander. We are quite at liberty to treat the Scots language as a dialect, as one of several English dialects which gradually and inevitably amalgamated into one language. Only Scotland, more isolated and differing from the others more than they differed from each other, retained its local pecularities much longer. The first part of the history of literature is a part of the history of English literature when English was several dialects; the second part is a part of the history of English literature when English was two dialects—English and Scots; the third part is something quite different—it is the history of provincial literature. And finally there is no longer any tenable important distinction to be drawn from the present day between the two literatures.[107]

While Muir enormously admired MacDiarmid's astonishing, but in his opinion singular, achievement in fusing elements of Lallans with the fecund energies of the modern European and American mind in a marvellously allusive and expressive synthetic art speech, he, like Eliot, believed that the long-standing debilitating paradox of Scottish writing had to be resolved in terms of English. To MacDiarmid all these assertions were anathema. Perhaps, too, the intensity of his response came from confusing his own consummate achievements with the whole range of possibility of Scottish writing to the degree that all Scottish writing must follow his example and prescriptions. Muir, somewhat cryptically, remarked that the skull shape of Borderers often tended to be Caesarian and MacDiarmid himself had a fondness for John Davidson's remark that:

> A poet is always a man of inordinate ambition and inordinate vanity. In his heart he says, "I want my poetry to be remembered when Homer and Dante and Shakespeare are forgotten."[111]

Given, then, that MacDiarmid's whole policy was the severance of all English connections and that *Scott and Scotland* moved in the reverse direction, it was inevitable that he should seek to rebut it. Inevitable, too, given the man, that the manner of these rebuttals should be erratic, spasmodic, bellicose and, in some instances, so extreme as to undermine the very point he was attempting to prove. As he grew older that heroic reckless quality of MacDiarmid's tended to degenerate, as did his prose style, into a very questionable kind of carelessness and this does not at all help our understanding of the case he attempted to make about Muir's alleged misreading of Scottish literature or the veracity of that case.

Since MacDiarmid believed that Scottish writing had nothing to do with English, indeed he could imagine no two less compatible cultures, he had, therefore, the immediate problem of defining an authentic Scottish literary tradition. This difficulty was not aided by the fact that, like Muir, he initially saw that the Scottish creative genius had been inured within a "Genevan prison-house" and, to an even greater degree than Muir, he was sceptical and dismissive of much of post-Unionist and Victorian Scottish writing. As he wrote:

> I asked him if he'd heard
> Of Burns or Sir Walter Scott,
> Of Carlyle or RLS
> He said he had not.
> "Some people think that these
> Are representative . . . I don't
> At least, you've little to forget,
> And should assimilate with ease,
>   From that false Scotland free,
> All that's worth knowing yet.[112]

While MacDiarmid's analysis of the Scottish literary situation is typically radical and bold it left him, in resurrecting a national tradition, with a difficulty almost akin with that faced by Christ with Lazarus. MacDiarmind was not one to play second fiddle to anybody, however, and his solution was that Scottish writing should, by an act of imaginative faith, leap backwards five centuries to its medieval roots. Ironically, his early impression of Muir was that he was one of the very few Scottish writers comparable with the Auld Makars.[113] Thus with odd, almost random, exceptions such as Fergusson, Smollett and Hogg through which the national spirit had intermittently flowed, MacDiarmid postulated that:

> It is necessary to go back behind to Dunbar and the Old Makars—great Catholic poets using the Vernacular, not for the pedestrian things to which it has latterly been confined, but for all "the brave translunary things of great art." The younger

Scottish poets are repossessing themselves of noble media and high traditions; and a splendid mystical and imaginative spirit is reuniting them over a period of five centuries with their mighty predecessors.[114]

In MacDiarmid's belief that, given inspired modern receptors, the creative energy of medieval Scotland was of sufficient voltage to discharge itself across the near literary vacuum of the intervening centuries, there is a certain splendour but also an arguable desperation. Part of that desperation can be seen in the predilection for Dunbar. Muir himself believed him a major but, in certain respects, limited poet and, in fact, preferred Henryson's placid depths to Dunbar's highly wrought surfaces but MacDiarmid tended to turn him into almost a cult figure for almost all the other members of his generation. Thus we find Neil Gunn writing:

> . . . harking back to Dunbar is professedly not a harking back for language so much as a harking back for greatness. Dunbar is great in breadth, in variety and ingenuity, in largeness of conception and utterance, after the fashion that Chaucer before and Shakespeare after him were great. It is this lost greatness that the renascent Scot would strive to see restored, recognising that its manifestation in a nation at any time is due not so much to the odd appearance of individual genius (generally forced to dissipate his best energies in rebellion), as to the existence within the nation itself of that aptitude for greatness out of which genius naturally flowers.[115]

Gunn here creates more problems than he resolves. He wants a national greatness manifested in common creativity and yet he can only, even in medieval times, locate it in one figure. Second, he assumes that Dunbar is a figure of Shakespearean proportions. It is perhaps this weakness of locating within history figures adequate not only to defining a definite Scottish imaginative mode but a major literary tradition, comparable to that of England, France or Germany, that increasingly drove MacDiarmid into pre-history and myth in order to establish authentic Scottish greatness. By the time he wrote the preface to *The Golden Treasury of Scottish Poetry*, MacDiarmid was not so much placing his faith in Dunbar and the medieval makars as in a tradition, mainly Gaelic, which was as yet not revealed to us but, it was implied, the appearance of which was imminent.

It is certainly no exaggeration to say that it is with Scottish literature as it is with an iceberg—only a small fraction of it is visible above the obliterating depths.[115]

Indeed, in MacDiarmid's further assertions about a submerged Scotland, we are made to feel that the untapped resources available to its imagination and about to be brought to the surface, make North Sea oil look like a drop in the nation's bucket. For this to be done MacDiarmid thought we must see Scottish history in its proper context. Thus he wrote:

> But 2000 years B.C. is a bagatelle; the Edda refers to exploits of about 3380-3350 B.C. and Dr. Albert's edition of *The Chronicles of Eri* (1936) is well entitled *Six Thousand Years of Gaelic Grandeur Unearthed*. Alas, the very great difficulties of making or obtaining verse translations in the beauties of the originals, have rendered it impossible for me to give in this anthology anything like a representative selection from the poets in question. . . . It is not too much to say that if literary considerations alone determine the choice, two-thirds of any such anthology will be "from the Gaelic", and every one of the poets named in the passage quoted above and about forty others, will earn their proper place at last in the bead-roll of the best poets our country has produced.[117]

While he was aware of the distinctive sensibility of Gaelic poetry in translation, Muir could not accept that this word hoard lay ready to be unearthed. Given his critical honesty it was even less possible for him to accept the absurd leaps MacDiarmid made from dubious knowledge of past Celtic civilizations to the belief that all that was needed was an act of national will which would not only reconstitute Celtic Scotland and throw off the English yoke but would also make Scotland a counterweight to Russian Communism.[118]

MacDiarmid's notion of a Celtic free society as opposed to Russia—this was prior to his endorsement in 1956 of the Russian occupation of Hungary—was based on his premise that the real mission of Scotland and Scottish literature was that of the advance of human freedom; we were for him a nation of democratic intellectuals with a vengeance. Thus he wrote:

> A friend recently asked me to define the Scottish genius, and I answered, 'Freedom—the free development of human consciousness', and in the course of the argument I cited the

misconceptions and difficulties that have arisen through successive attempts to force Scottish history, with its incomparably chequered character, into the mould of English constitutionalism; the radicalism of Scotland in politics versus the conservatism of England . . . the extent to which the religious genius of Scotland had sought freedom until it became stultified and subverted . . .[119]

Now while there have been heroic voices raised throughout Scottish history, it could scarce be otherwise in a nation so prone to giving and selling itself into bondage, it is a nonsense to suggest that as opposed to England, Scotland has a premium on the advocacy and attainment of human freedom and that her literature manifests this. As a matter of common sense MacDiarmid is, in this respect, much more like Blake and, to an even greater degree, D.H. Lawrence than any Scottish writer. Also MacDiarmid's belief in Scottish political radicalism as a force producing great literature is tenuous. His evidence for this is based on the work of relatively minor nineteenth-century poets who have nothing of the imaginative potency of Blake, Hazlitt or Shelley. Muir, in fact, believed that Scottish writing compared to English was sadly lacking in a tradition of liberty. Thus in a brilliant short essay on Rudyard Kipling (his mother was Scottish) he made the following interesting point concerning authors writing in English who come from without its tradition:

> In all this he was, like Carlyle and Conrad, who were also born outside England, against the main English literary tradition, which is purely human and based on liberty. He did not speak the same language as Marlowe and Milton and Blake and Wordsworth. His gospel, again like Carlyle's and Conrad's, was a gospel of work and hero-worship. Carlyle came from a country which was both poor and Calvinistic; Conrad from a long and indecisive struggle with the sea; and Kipling from the fatalistic and imperfectly settled East. It was natural, therefore, that they should have recognised with more than ordinary clearness the virtues of work, and that the idea of liberty should have roused their scepticism and even their hostility, as unjustified in the nature of things. Kipling had a profound understanding of the vital difference between good work and bad; he had hardly any appreciation whatever of the value of thought, and here he was

unlike Carlyle, whose conception of work was considerably wider. But it excluded just as strictly the idea of liberty.[120]

Thus, other than their evaluation of Christ, nothing could more completely divide Muir and MacDiarmid than the former's disbelief in the latter's thesis that the essence of the Scottish spirit was the pursuit of freedom, political and imaginative, which had been perpetually thwarted by England's Machiavellian hand in her affairs. Muir and MacDiarmid did not disagree about the critical points of Scottish history. In both men, three areas preoccupied them, Calvinism, the Union and Industrialization. In MacDiarmid's interpretation, however, not only the Union but Calvinism had been imposed on the Scots by English intrusion and the industrial revolution in Scotland had taken its particularly harsh course because of the movement and involvement of English capital. Muir, while disliking the Anglicisation of the Scottish personality as much as MacDiarmid and not denying some substance to such arguments, simply could not believe in a historical theory of such undiluted conspiracy. His intuitive vision of Scottish history was one of a nation with deep, self-destructive tendencies whose loss of freedom and economic decay were largely the results of a thrawn, perverse national will:

> This deterministic conclusion discouraged me when I came to it, and I went over in my mind what Scottish history I could remember, hoping to find some faint sign that Scotland's annals need not have been so calamitous as they were, and need not have led to the end of Scotland as a nation. I thought of the declaration of independence signed at Arbroath Abbey on April 6th, 1320: "As long as a hundred of us remain alive, we will never submit to the domination of the English: for we fight not for glory, nor riches, nor honour, but for liberty alone, which no good man giveth up save with life itself." I thought of Barbour's fine lines on freedom. But I reflected that Wallace had been betrayed, that David I had sold his country; I saw the first four Jameses thwarted on every side, Mary Stuart sold to the English, Charles I sold to the English, and Scotland itself sold to the English. I remembered Culloden and the Highland clans delivered helpless to Cumberland because of the intrigues and counter-intrigues of their chieftains and a few Lowland Scots; I

thought of the present feud between Glasgow and Edinburgh, the still continuing antipathy between the Highlands and the Lowlands; and it seemed to me that the final betrayal of Scotland which made it no longer a nation was merely the inevitable result, the logical last phase, of the intestine dissensions which had all through its history continued to rend it. I thought of the Covenanters at Bothwell Brig fighting one another and flying from their enemy; and that seemed to me a symbol of Scottish history and of the Scottish spirit, which even now is kinder to strangers than to those who were nursed in it. And there came into my mind a sight that I had seen as I stood on the banks of an Austrian mountain stream on a very hot summer day many years before. The stream was running very fast, and in the middle I made out two bright green snakes struggling in a death battle; I watched them for a few moments; then they were both swept, still fighting, over a cataract. The comparison was too swift and dramatic, I told myself, for the stubborn anger that burns through Scottish history; but nevertheless it would have been as impossible to put a stop to that as any of the disastrous turns of Scottish history. Perhaps with time this spirit of exaggerated individualism will no longer be able to work the harm to Scotland that it has worked in the past.[121]

In a sense, Muir's thinking about Scotland, in general, and its relations with England, in particular, is an attempt to make Scotland perceive the nature of its freedom as existing in an openness to life beyond the false imperatives and certitudes of dogmatic moralities and ideologies; creative literature is the great enemy of such forms of mental tyranny and genuine freedom exists in its mature self-responsibility. His attitude towards Scotland is very close to that of Ortega Y Gasset's analysis of the malfeasances of the Spanish spirit:

I mistrust the love of a man for his friend or his flag when I do not see him make an effort to understand his enemy or the flag of his enemy. I have observed, at least, that we Spaniards find it easier to be aroused by a moral dogma than to open our hearts to the demands of veracity. We are definitely more willing to hand over our free will to a rigid moral attitude than to keep our judgment always open, ready at any moment for the desirable reform and correction. One might say that we embrace the moral imperative like a weapon in order to simplify life for ourselves by destroying immense portions of the globe. With keen vision

95

Nietzsche has detected forms and products of resentment in certain moral attitudes. No product of resentment can evoke our sympathy. Rancour emanates from a sense of inferiority.[122]

Apparently not only often blind to, but at times productive of, such dark forces, there exists in MacDiarmid with his vision of English conspiracy, the consequent notion of the conspiratorial power of the English language for devitalising and extinguishing the Scottish tongue. As he wrote:

> I SHOULD use . . .'
> A language not to be betrayed;
> And what was hid should still be hid
> Excepting from those like me made
> Who answer when such whispers bid.[123]

Now, in part, MacDiarmid's case is undeniable. Loss of a language is one of the most severe forms of deprivation because it not only destroys the bonds between a people and its past but also it disrupts external communication and inner awareness. MacDiarmid believed that a whole range of not only psychological but physiological consciousness was lost as Braid Scots ebbed away. Muir certainly numbered this loss of language as one of the principal tragic Scottish losses—*Scottish Journey* is as much an elegy as it is a travel book—but he could not agree that the dialect could be resurrected nor, after initial misgivings, that English had never, or ever could be, a medium for a *Scottish* writer. As he wrote in one of his earliest essays on Scottish literature:

> The thing I am examining here, superficial in appearance, goes deep. No writer can write great English who is not born an English writer and in England; and born moreover in some class in which the tradition of English is pure, and it seems to me, therefore, in some other age than this. English as it was written by Bunyan or by Fielding cannot be written now except by some one who like them has passed his days in a tradition of living English speech. A whole life went into that prose; and all that Stevenson could give to his was a few decades of application. And because the current of English is even at this day so much younger, poorer and more artificial in Scotland than it is in England, it is improbable that Scotland will produce any writer of English of the first rank, or at least that she will do so until her

tradition of English is as common, as unforced and unschooled as if it were her native tongue[124]

Part of MacDiarmid's delight in Muir's early criticism was due to perceptions of this kind. Ironically, though he himself turned to English as the medium for his "poetry of ideas" not long after the publication of *Scott and Scotland*, he never surrendered his theoretical commitment to the primacy of the Scots language.[125] Also there was a considerable degree of truth in MacDiarmid's case that Scotsmen had abused rather than used English. As a major Modernist writing when "most of the important words were killed in the First World War", MacDiarmid shared that generation's belief that the shambles of that conflict had been almost created by the falsity of the preceding rhetoric. Like Hemingway, MacDiarmid wanted to redeem the lost connection between words and things and part of his endorsement of Lallans was because it had a stark, direct power of conveying life's essential and basic facts. Scottish Anglicised rhetoric had, as he saw it, continually falsified the true nature of Scottish life and, in a sense, the Great War was its ultimate and, MacDiarmid hoped, Pyrrhic victory. As MacDiarmid wrote concerning that extraordinary nineteenth century "moral philosopher" and rhetorician, "Christopher North".

The main purpose of all verbiage is simply to batter the hearer into a pulpy state of vague acquiescence in which a sense of mutual enlightenment can at least exist as an illusion. The most important words in the language—"living experience", "passion" , "beauty"—are the most effective for this purpose, and the clergy and the politicians in particular make great play with them. To such an extent has this gone that words have practically ceased to have any meaning; no wonder that Wyndham Lewis contends that a stiffening of satire or straight-speaking is needful in anything that wishes to survive the subtle misconstruings of the defensive reader or hearer. The fluent eye of the reader is apt to glide deceitfully over the page—or the adept ear of the hearer to act in an equivalent fashion—that the words have no time to make much more than an approximate impression at best. But most of the words are *clichés*,

97

verbomania in which the expression of thought in any real sense of the term has practically ceased to be an element at all.

Scotland, in particular, is dominated in every direction by an abracadabra impervious to all sense—overridden by meaningless phrases. This is not surprising, "Christopher North" was only the most extraordinary exponent of this sort of thing carried to the furthest degree, but it has long been not only general in Scotland but actually recognised and defended.[126]

Now this is true but it is equally true that, as Muir contended, the dialect employing different means, more those of oblique whimsy, had achieved a very similar result which was the obfuscation of Scottish reality for very dubious and often political ends. Arguably, then, much Scottish writing is not so much paralysed by an intractable linguistic problem but with a degree of spiritual malaise which takes place at a level prior to the choice of a verbal ·medium. In a short but extremely perceptive review of *Scott and Scotland*, Catherine Carswell indicated such a possibility:

A divorce between intellect and emotion is, as I think most thoughtful people will agree, an underlying cause of our literary shortcomings. But whether it can be attributed to circumstances of language in that degree which Mr. Muir would have us believe, is another question. Mr. Muir argues well and has picked his examples with care. Yet here and there we feel a sense of strain, as though there were doubts in his own secret mind, and as though he were aware of inconvenient truths which, if allowed full play, might interfere with the nice woof and warp of his fabric. And we ask ourselves whether that fabric is not devised less to demonstrate one defect in the Scottish body than to hide another. Language is a kittle subject, and lends itself to both sides of many an argument.

For example, Mr. Muir points to Dunbar and Henryson as examples of Scottish poets who, had they been followed up, would have founded a Scottish literary line instead of ending in the air. But to make his point here he is compelled to exaggerate the difference in language between these poets and their English contemporaries. Yet was this more than a question of spelling, and of some turns of thought and phrase? Was it more, for instance, than the difference between the mother tongue of a Dorset or a Northumbrian man and literary English? It is certainly not so wide a gap as that which was successfully negotiated by Provençal men who have written in Parisian French and in the dialects of Sicily or of Tuscany. With Gaelic it is, of course, another story. But were not Dunbar and Henryson, for all their Scottish birth and sentiment, in the true body of English literature, and hence English writers with Scottish souls? Is not the same true of Sir Thomas Urquhart? Have not Scottish ministers been able to preach in the mother tongue with all the force of their emotion and intellect combined? Yet there is scarcely a Scottish sermon worth reading today, which sad circumstance, to my mind, points to one thing only, namely that Scotsmen lack religious genius, for all their concern with theology.[127]

I do not know if "English writers with Scottish souls" is the complete answer to these troubled national creative paradoxes. Muir himself noted that one of the few good Scottish writers of English prose was Fletcher of Saltoun and, ironic though this is, it points to what is wrong with Scottish creative writing being not finally linguistic but pertaining more to national bad faith towards which there has been far too much literary complicity. Any form of language will be decadent if there does not exist a truthful spirit behind it. Also, in practical terms, Muir recognised that the great writer of his own generation, MacDiarmid, did not surrender his nationality by writing in English. As he wrote of one of MacDiarmid's earliest books of prose, *Annals of the Five Senses*:

> It is as if an alien were writing in English without attempting to be English in anything but his language. Now this has not been very often done. Stevenson did not do it, although in essentials he was as unlike an Englishman as possible; nor has Mr. Conrad done it, Mr. Conrad, who has almost succeeded in being more English than the English themselves. Mr. James Joyce has perhaps succeeded better than anyone else; and in a something exotic and almost excessively accomplished in his style, Mr. Grieve is not unlike Mr. Joyce; and I should say that, except Mr. Joyce, nobody at present is writing more resourceful English prose. Mr. Grieve is a Scot; that is, he is more intellectually subtle and on the whole less sane than the English who write English. Like Mr. Joyce he takes a delight in the subtle windings of the intellect for their own sake, and like Mr. Joyce again, that delight is in him partly sensuous. This, which must make the book appear foreign to English readers, is part of its

originality. It could only have been written by a Scotsman, and one of a type quite unguessed at by other peoples.[128]

Equally in the best of the new fiction of his age—part of Muir's critical genius was his invariably correct judgment of new writing—he saw that the Scottish novel was strengthened by its English connection:

> The question of language in contemporary Scottish literature is a very difficult one. Apart from "Hugh McDiarmid," the names most commonly connected with the Scottish Renaissance are those of Neil M. Gunn, Eric Linklater and Lewis Grassic Gibbon. Mr. Gunn's sensitive style is more obviously influenced by D.H. Lawrence than by Neil Munro; Mr. Linklater writes vigorous Elizabethan prose; Mr. Gibbon has struck out a style which does succeed in giving the rhythm of the Scottish vernacular. But all use English as their natural utterance; their literary inspiration is the great English writers, not Dunbar or Burns. On the other hand, they write about Scottish life for a Scottish audience, and not for an English one, like Stevenson. They write for this audience in English, it is true, but there they have little choice; for the Scottish people are a people who talk in Scots but think in English. These writers are, in any case, more intimately Scottish than Stevenson was, and that justifies one in calling the literary revival to which they belong a Scottish one. It is obviously only at its beginning yet; the promise for its future lies in the fact that for some time Scotland has been becoming more and more conscious of itself as a separate unity, and that this tendency seems bound to continue.[129]

It would be pleasant to conclude that, despite all apparent trends, such a spirit persisted.

NOTES

1. Muir wrote three novels *The Marionette* (1927), *The Three Brothers* (1931) and *Poor Tom* (1932). All are worthy of republication and the last is a masterpeice which Rebecca West, at least, appreciated for what it was. Her review is in *Modern Scot*, Vol.III, No.3 (Oct.,1932), pp.250-251.
2. See, for example, Christopher Harvie's remark in his *Scotland and Nationalism, Scottish Society and Politics 1707-1977* (London, 1977) that "Muir's stance was, however, marginal to the Scottish intellectual predicament." While Harvie's book seems to have been written more in haste than anger, it is a disquieting symptom of the manner in which not

only Muir but the whole creative generation to which he belonged is receding from Scottish consciousness. His own major contemporaries saw him as the least marginal of men.

3. See Article 18, "Burns and Holy Willie," below.
4. *Selected Letters* of Edwin Muir, ed. Butter (London, 1974) p. 114.
5. "W.B. Yeats", *The Estate of Poetry* (London, 1962), p. 45.
6. "Edwin Muir", *Contemporary Scottish Studies* (Edinburgh, 1976), pp.28-32. MacDiarmid's initial account of Muir as critic is as receptive of Muir's genius and promise as were Muir's account of his work.
7. *An Autiobiography* (London, 1968), p. 189.
8. *Belonging* – A Memoir (London, 1968), p. 219.
9. *Scottish Journey* (Edinburgh, 1979), p. 29.
10. "Scotland 1941", *Collected Poems 1921-1958* (London, 1967), p. 97.
11. *Collected Poems*, p. 228.
12. This is taken from a very interesting review of *The Story and the Fable*, "The Literary Life Respectable," by Q.D. Leavis, *Scrutiny, IX* (September, 1940), pp. 170-173.
13. *Selected Letters*, p. 64.
14. *Scottish Literature: Character and Influence* (London, 1919). p. 12.
15. *Scott and Scotland* (London, 1936), pp. 105-110.
16. Ibid., pp. 112-114.
17. *An Autobiography*, p. 220.
18. Ibid., pp. 51-53.
19. Ibid., p. 55.
20. "From a Diary", *New Alliance*, IV (Sept.-Oct., 1943), pp. 6-7.
21. *Belonging*, p. 45.
22. Ibid., pp. 137-138.
23. "On making Beasts of Ourselves," *The Uncanny Scot*, ed. Buthlay (London, 1968), pp. 148-153.
24. *An Autobiography*, p. 48.
25. *Poor Tom* (London, 1932).
26. "Foreword" to *The Estate of Poetry*, p. xi.
27. *An Autobiography*, p. 96.
28. "Tiresias," a review of *Transition, Nation,* CXXII (November 17, 1926), p. 509. Muir's critical and social thought contains many striking parallels with that of the Southern Agrarians; in both there is a sense of traditional order being ravaged.
29. *Selected Letters*, p. 35.
30. Muir's essay, "The Politics of King Lear," in *Essays on Literature and Society* (London, 1949) prefigures Kott's work in its analysis of Shakespeare's understanding of the nature of political terror.
31. *An Autobiography*, pp. 150-151.
32. *Belonging*,p. 114
33. *Scottish Journey*, p. 43.
34. *Circumjack Cencrastus* in *Complete Poems* Vol. I (London, 1978), p. 234.
35. *Letters*, pp. 70-71.
36. "The Scottish Universities and Some Other Considerations", *Modern Scot Vol. I., No. 4 (Jan., 1931), pp. 54-57.*

37. *Belonging*, p. 165.
38. "Why Scots Writers Emigrate," *Evening News*, Sept. 2., 1931, p. 4.
39. Ibid.
40. Ibid.
41. Letter in *Scotland in Quest of her Youth* (London, 1932), p. 167.
42. *Coleridge's Miscellaneous Criticism*, ed. Raysor (London, 1938).
43. "Why Scots Writers Emigrate."
44. *Circumjack Cencrastus*, p. 231.
45. "Why Scots Writers Emigrate."
46. "New Paths in Fiction – The Scottish Novel Since the War," *Glasgow Herald,* November 24, 1934.
47. *Circumjack Cencrastus*, pp. 253-254.
48. "Why Scots Writers Emigrate."
49. Ibid.
50. Ibid.
51. See Michael Grieve's account of this in *The Hugh MacDiarmid Anthology*, ed. Scott and Grieve (London, 1972), pp. xi-xvi.
52. *Letters*, p. 130.
53. "The Place of the Artist in Scotland," *Modern Scot*, Vol. II, No. 3 (Oct., 1931), pp. 192-193.
54. "The Contemporary Situation in Scotland," *Scrutiny*, V (Sept., 1936), p. 193.
55. *Belonging*, p. 226.
56. *Letters*, p. 190.
57. Ernest W. Marwick, "Lecture in the Crypt, Newbattle", *Saltire Review*, Vol. 3, No. 7 (Spring, 1956), p. 10.
58. *Collected Poems*, p. 234.
59. *Belonging*, p. 194.
60. "The Language of Scotland," a review of *Scott and Scotland, London Mercury*, XXXIV (October, 1936), pp. 556-57.
61. *Scots Magazine*, Vol. XXVI (October, 1936), pp. 72-78.
62. "Debatable Land," *Outlook*, I (Oct., 1936), pp. 87-90.
63. "Popularization," *Spectator*, No. 5503 (Dec. 15), p. 907.
64. Review of W.H. Hamilton's *Holyrood: A Garland of Modern Scots Poems, The Scots Observer*, (Feb., 16, 1929), p. 3.
65. *Albyn* (London, 1927), p. 17.
66. *Scottish Journey*, p. 68.
67. "This Scottish Tongue: The Renascence and the Vernacular," *Scots Magazine*, 18, No. 2 (May, 1933), pp. 107-110.
68. Ibid., p. 108.
69. Ibid.
70. Ibid., 109.
71. "Culture Now: Some Animadversions, Some Laughs," *Modern Occasions*, (Winter, 1971), pp. 162-178...
72. *Scott and Scotland*, pp. 176-177.
73. Ibid., p. 61.
74. "Edwin Muir," *Contemporary Scottish Studies*, p. 29.
75. *Scott and Scotland*, p. 35.

76. Ibid., pp. 40-41.
77. Ibid., p. 56.
78. Ibid., p. 56.
79. Ibid., pp. 60-61.
80. Ibid., p. 70-71.
81. *Robert Burns – The Critical Heritage*, ed. Low (London, 1974), p. 109.
82. See Article 1, "The Functionlessness of Scotland," below.
83. *Scott and Scotland*, p. 75.
84. Ibid., pp. 80-81.
85. Ibid., p. 40.
86. "The Cadelonian Antisyzygy and the Gaelic Idea," *Selected Essays of Hugh MacDiarmid*, ed. Glen (London, 1968), p. 58.
87. *John Knox: Portrait of a Calvinist* (London, 1929), pp. 307-309.
88. *Scottish Journey*, p. 46.
89. See Article 28, "Robert Louis Stevenson," below.
90. *Scott and Scotland*, p. 135.
91. Ibid., pp. 11-13.
92. "Complaint of the Dying Peasantry," *Collected Poems*, p. 262.
93. See, for example, Neil Gunn's discussion of Scott in his review of *Scott and Scotland* (footnote 61 above) and "Sir Walter Scott: A Centenary Commentary," *Modern Scot* Vol. III, No. 2 (Aug., 1932), pp. 111-123.
94. See Article 23, "Scott and Tradition," below.
95. Ibid.
96. "The Writer and his Public," *The Listener*, XXIV (Oct. 17), pp. 557-558.
97. "The Three Dreams of Scottish Nationalism," *Memoirs of a Modern Scotland*, ed. Miller (London, 1970), pp. 38-39.
98. See MacDiarmid's account of James MacPherson in *Scottish Eccentrics* (London, 1972).
99. This is from a review of Martin Green's *Dreams of Adventure, Deeds of Empire* (London, 1980), where considerable attention is paid to the Scottish contribution to the fiction of imperialism.
100. See Article 27 below.
101. *Literature and Oatmeal*, (London 1935).
102. "New Paths in Fiction; The Scottish Novel Since the War," *Glasgow Herald* (22 Nov. 1934), p. 5.
103. See Article 33, below.
104. See Article 12, "Literature in Scotland," below.
105. *Belonging*, p. 195.
106. *Lucky Poet* (London, 1972), p. 20.
107. Ibid., pp. 202-203.
108. *Golden Treasury of Scottish Poetry* (London, 1941), xxx.
109. "Was There a Scottish Literature?", *The Athenaeum*, August 1st, 1919, pp. 680-681.
110. Ibid., p. 681.
111. "John Davidson: Influences and Influence", *Selected Essays*, pp. 201-202.
112. *Circumjack Cencrastus*, p. 208.
113. Edwin Muir, "*Contemporary Scottish Studies*, p. 30.
114. *Albyn*, pp. 12-13.

115. "The Scottish Renascence," (pseud. Dane McNeil) *Scotts Magazine, 19*, No. 3 (June, 1933), pp. 201-204.
116. *Golden Treasury of Scottish Poetry*, p. xiv.
117. Ibid., pp. xii-xii.
118. See "The Caldonian Antisyzygy and the Gaelic Idea", *Selected Essays*, p.161.
119. Ibid., pp. 57-58.
120. "Rudyard Kiping," *The Listener*, XV (Feb. 5), p. 272.
121. *Scottish Journey*, pp. 226-227.
122. *Meditations on Quixote* (New York, 1963), p. 35.
123. "A Language No To Be Betrayed," *Complete Poems*, Vol. I, p. 665.
124. See Article 14, "A Note on the Scottish Ballads," below.
125. For an interesting discussion of this linguistic controversy see William Montgomerie, "Edwin Muir and Hugh MacDiarmid," *Gangrel*, Vol. 3, (1946), pp. 307.
126. *Scottish Eccentrics* (London, 1972), pp. 99-100.
127. "The Scottish Writer," *Spectator*, No. 5659 (Dec. 11, 1936), p. 1054.
128. See Article 32 below.
129. See Article 12 below.

1

The Functionlessness of Scotland*

Christopher Grieve sent me a letter a little while ago asking me to write something about the function of Scotland in the modern world. I replied saying that I could not imagine what Scotland's function could be, but that I would like to investigate the difficulty: perhaps it would be a way of coming to closer grips with the subject. This article is the result.

That nations have some historical function in the general development of civilisation—a function that changes with changing circumstances, it is true, but yet is operative in some way at every moment of their existence—is, I think, obviously true, however difficult it may be to determine what that function is. And it does not matter how small the nation may be: Austria, in spite of the lamentable size to which it has shrunk, has still a function; Latvia, though small and new, has a function. A nation that is effectively a nation, that has, in other words, some independent central organ directing and symbolising its life, has necessarily an objective importance, even if it is by mere virtue of its geographical situation. It affects and is affected by the other organic units surrounding it, and consequently influences, in a greater or lesser degree, the general course of civilisation. But there also exist hypothetical units, units which remain in a condition of unchanging suspended potentiality (which fail to achieve a crystallisation and create a central organ), and these remain in a sort of limbo,

*Free Man, (11 February 1931), p. 6.

half within the world of life and half outside it: a melancholy, unsatisfied,blindly aspiring state which romanticism is always ready to exploit, and for which the only cure is an active realism. Scotland is at present one of these hypothetical units.

And, being that, it has no functions. It has no calculable effect, as an entity, on the development of civilisation, though individual Scotsmen and Scotswomen, wrested from their context, may have in a very small way some such effect. If Scotland were really capable of merging with England, there would be no difficulty at all, and the hypothetical nation north of the Tweed would vanish, and the inhabitants of what was once Scotland be freed from the curse of a hypothetical existence and become active and genuine members of an organic civilisation. But even Scotsmen who are against the idea of nationalism will deny, with a heat they do not understand, that that is possible. Scotland has not become a real part of England, nor has it succeeded in remaining a separate and independent entity. That is its problem. All that effectively remains of it, therefore, is a name and an aspiration which, until very recently has never seriously wished to be fulfilled. The result is an emptiness and unreality quite peculiar to Scotland, and that only becomes intensified when such adjectives, as Scottish or Celtic have to be employed, for the words themselves evoke a disquieting sense of the merely contingent reality of the things they stand for. Into this semi-vacuum the population of Scotland are born, imaginary citizens of an imaginary country; and it is not surprising that so many should leave it. The only remedy for this state of things is either for the whole Scottish people to become English, or for Scotland to become a nation. The first has proved impossible.

A nation without a central organ to give it unity, a merely discarnate nation such as Scotland, is far more defenceless against the mechanical and purely materialistic forces of civilisation than any integral group could be. All that it can oppose to those forces is a floating tradition; and a tradition that has no concrete symbol to embody it soon fades, and presently there is nothing between the isolated individual and the operation of mechanical forces but a name or a memory. That has not yet happened to Scotland, but it has been happening for the last hundred years; and it probably helps to explain why so

106

many Scotsmen have excelled in engineering and business, and so few have done anything remarkable in the humane arts. Having a nation only in name, they inevitably become servants of pure undifferentiated "progress" at its most impersonal and its least humanly significant, servants of a thing that acknowledges no national boundaries, even one's own, that indeed scarcely acknowledges humanity, though created to serve it. So Scotland has earned the reputation of being a nation of engineers, servants of the machine. In other words, it has suffered more from the development of industrialism, from the effects of the industrial revolution, than any other part of the British Isles. It has suffered more, and both physically and spiritually, because against the rage of that revolution it could oppose nothing but the mere idea of a nation, an imagination that could do nothing to shield it.

It is this that makes a more human ideal necessary for Scotland now. An ideal for a people must to-day be a national ideal. All the evil of the world seems to be becoming more and more supernational and sub-national. Consequently any assertion of national independence now is far more essentially a challenge to that evil than to any other that may be accidentally connected with it. There are two main streams in the development of civilisation at present. One is in the direction of supernationalism; the other in that of nationalism. The first is essentially hostile to the old, complete human tradition; the second, in spite of the excesses and crimes of Chauvinism, is friendly to it. The ultimate aim of the first is uniformity, or, as it is correctly termed, standardisation; the second demands diversity as well. It is possible to fight for either ideal from the highest motives. But every one must make a choice, one way or the other.

2

Scotland's Problems*

If one accepts this book simply as a collection of essays one will find charming reading in it, and especially in Mr. Moray McLaren's "Scottish Delight", ingenious both in its analysis of Scottish character and in style, Mr. Compton Mackenzie's rectorial speech at Glasgow, a sincere piece of eloquence, and Mr. George Scott Moncrieff's "Balmorality", a skilfully conducted oblique attack on all that the word stands for. If, on the other hand, one regards the book as a scrutiny, its faults gape at once. One of the contributors has done his work excellently: Mr. Robert Hurd in his account of the present state of Scottish architecture. Two others, Mr. Thomas Henderson on the Scottish vernacular, and Mr. J. Inglis Ker on Scottish roads, have also dealt efficiently with their themes. but in taking up three subjects, the drama, music and painting, the editor seems to have somewhat overburdened himself; no clear picture of the real qualitative state of these arts in Scotland emerges from his essay; and one imagines that he has been more concerned to omit no names than to emphasize those who are really worth while. This, while justifiable enough in a survey, which must always have something statistical about it, is out of place in a scrutiny, which implies a close critical examination of data, as well as a point of view. The Rev. George F. Macleod in his paper on "The Church of Scotland in Quest of her Youth",

* [Review of *Scotland in Quest of Her Youth* ed. D. C. Thompson], *The Spectator*, No. 5447 (18 November 1932), pp. 709 and 711.

errs in the opposite direction; he has a point of view which, being romantic, prevents him from giving any objective statement of the present quandary of the Church of Scotland. But worst of all is the treatment of Scottish literature, where the most promising signs of national revival are to be seen. This subject is covered by a number of letters, all of them short, contributed at the editor's request by Scottish writers, his plea being that "any prolonged analysis of the position as regards writing would have been superfluous in the circumstances." The letters themselves, however, prove that such an analysis is by no means superfluous. I suggest that the editor should compile another scrutiny dealing with Scots literature, which needs above everything else some clarity about its position.

The two most interesting letters in the volume, those by Mrs. Catherine Carswell and Mr. Eric Linklater, prove this in the most striking way. For both Mrs. Carswell and Mr. Linklater hold that to be Scottish a Scottish writer need not deal with Scottish scenes. Mr. Linklater goes the length of saying: "I do not know who are Scottish writers and who are not." It is a point which deserves the most serious consideration, and has never received it. Mr Linklater goes on to ask: "Was Doughty not English because he wrote of Arabia?" a question which, however, loses a great deal of its point when one rembers that Doughty wrote just as much about Doughty as about Arabia in the most famous of his books. From the purely aesthetic point of view, which relegates the subject-matter to its properly subordinate place, the whole problem is no doubt absurd; but then aesthetics takes no account of nationality, and this question is a national and not a specifically literary one. It is a practical question, and though Mrs. Carswell and Mr. Linklater seem to have a good case, the fact remains that very few good novels have been written on foreign subjects, except by writers such as Conrad and Henry James, who virtually changed their nationality. Russian fiction is about Russia, French fiction about France, English fiction is about England, simply because in all of them the living tradition of a people comes to expression; there may be exceptions to this rule, but they are so few that they may be ignored; so that one can only conclude that Scottish fiction will be about Scotland. but the question is such a large one, and so important for Scotland at present, that it should be treated at length, along with several others—there are enough of them—in a companion volume to this.

These faults apart, the book is a pleasant enough conglomeration of reading matter. Mr. Moray McLaren's essay is the pleasantest, and the pleasantest thing in it is a prime piece of the Scottish vernacular, which the author attributes to an old Scottish farmer, but which one images was polished by himself. One feels grateful also for his quotations from the Ettrick Shepherd (by way of "Noctes Ambrosianae") particularly for "the auld male elephant, risin' up in his seraglio like a tower amang turrets." But it is invidious to praise Mr. McLaren for his quotations when he should be rather praised for a sensitive, penetrating, and, what is still more unusual, charitable study of his fellow-countrymen.

3

The Problem of Scotland*

A faculty of the Scottish mind which never seems to be dealt with in books about Scotland is its legend-creating power. This can be seen clearly if one compares English and Scottish history. King Alfred is the only great English legendary historical figure; while all the main characters in Scottish history, except its moralists and reformers, were quickly turned into mythical figures by the communal imagination, so that they came to resemble the heroes and heroines of an unwritten ballad. Wallace, Bruce, Mary Stuart, Montrose and Prince Charlie are more like inventions of fiction than historical names; it was the imagination of a people that effected this transmutation, and the implications of that imagination are not all flattering to Scotland. It was purely romantic, and it no longer exists actively: the Industrial Revolution cut across it and killed it. But it can still be seen in the disposition of Scotsmen to sentimentalise the past and shut their eyes to the present. Scotland's past is a romantic legend, its present a sordid reality. Between these two things there is no organic relation: the one is fiction, the other real life. The past does not enter into the present as it does in England; for Scotland's development ever since the Reformation has consisted in giving away its past piecemeal, until it squandered almost all its old

* [Review of *The Heart of Scotland* by George Blake and *Scotland and the Scots* by William Power], *The Spectator*, No. 5549 (2 November 1934), p.676.

heritage. While England was growing out of itself, Scotland renounced in turn its existence as an independent nation and as a separate community, and the ravages of the Industrial Revolution during the last century robbed it wholesale even of its racial characteristics. Glasgow is like a town where gold was discovered fifty or sixty years ago, not like the largest city of an old and civilised country. And Glasgow is an epitome of modern Scotland, possessing also its legend of a past when it was a pretty, trim little city as unlike its present self as possible.

These two books deal respectively with the real and the legendary Scotland. Mr. Blake confines himself to the present; Mr. Power ranges freely over the past and the future. He points to the glories of Scotland's Celtic tradition, and concludes with a vision of a regenerated nation with spacious towns and flourishing arts. Mr. Blake looks at Glasgow, the industrial region of Lanarkshire and the commercialised Highlands, and, honestly trying to answer the question whether the Scottish people will eventually lose their "cultural identity", comes to the following conclusion: "The forces often appear to have been too much for them. Largely huddled into drab industrial towns, they found it sufficient satisfaction to delight in the loveliness of the country round about them, blind to the economic ugliness that its empty and deliberately uncultivated condition represents. Notably slaves of jazz and the cinema, they will defend their unique Scottishness in terms of events and grandeurs long past and sadly soiled. For the most part they sit, curiously complacent, amid the ruins of their own civilisation, such as it is." That is the opinion of a man who has a sincere affection and admiration for Scotland, and it seems to me far more pertinent than anything that Mr. Power says, fascinating as his speculations are.

The present state of Scotland is mainly due to the Industrial Revolution. That revolution began by destroying the traditional life of the towns, and from the towns successive waves have been sent out into the countryside for the last fifty years, until now the acquired characteristics of Industrialism can be recognised as easily in a remote Highland village as in the spreading suburbs of Glasgow. Scotland became so radically industrialised because, having destroyed its past, it had no reserves to draw upon. "It is perfectly fair,' Mr. Blake remarks, "to say that the Reformation, as it shaped in Scot. wiped out tradition and produced Motherwell as a substit. for Culross." Scotland's industrial expansion was based on iro. and coal. The iron, Mr. Blake says, is almost worked out, and the coal coming to an end. Glasgow, a city of over a milion inhabitants, depends on these things. What is to become of it when they disappear? Or, rather, what is to become of the people who live in it? Actually a vast clearance is taking place in Scotland at present, compared with which the clearances in the Highlands last century were mere local incidents. It is a clearance not of actual human beings, like the Sutherland ones, but simply of the resources on which human beings depend for life. The workers of Airdrie and Motherwell are allowed to stay in their houses: the dole secures them that: but any reason for their staying there—and nobody in his senses would stay there by choice—is rapidly vanishing. The squalor of Industrialism remains, but industry itself is fading like a dream.

It is this industrial country in decline that Mr. Blake describes. He describes it faithfully, and this makes the book a valuable one, which everyone interested in Scotland or involved in its lot should read. He seems to have little faith in Scottish Nationalism; and it may be that the problem is too vast for nationalism to solve, except by introducing an economic revolution of some kind; for if an independent authority were to take over Scotland today it would take over a bankrupt concern. Nevertheless, the Scottish Nationalists seem to be the only people who are aware of this problem. Mr. Blake says many just things on Scotland's two chief surviving institutions, the Kirk and the school, showing that both, and the latter particularly, have degenerated greatly in the last fifty years. He paints a picture of Scottish home life which is, I think, highly flattering, and even praises high tea, which is surely going too far. But, apart from such idiosycrasies, his description of Scotland's state is so uncompromising and so badly needed that it deserves general gratitude.

In *Scotland and the Scots* Mr. Power sets out to trace the influence of the Scottish landscape on Scottish history, religion, poetry, music, and the plastic arts. It is an endlessly interesting and subtle question. Mr. Power throws off many suggestive observations during the course of his enquiry, and his reading is wide and miscellaneous. But his method is needlessly discursive; he rarely produces any proof in support of his opinions; and he finds evidences of the Scottish landscape and the Celtic culture everywhere, which is as bad as finding them nowhere. His conviction that all Scotland is Celtic makes him deny what history, literature and common observation alike demonstrate: that is, the profound difference between the people who live in the Highlands and the Lowlands. But the book is suggestive, as he claims, and anyone interested in the present state of Scottish literature will find a good deal in it that is worth reading. Both volumes are excellently illustrated, Mr. Blake's with fine photographs of Scottish scenery, town and country, and Mr. Power's with reproductions of well-known Scottish landscape paintings.

4

Scotland: That Distressed Area*

This is one of the best books that have been written about the Scottish question: indeed, probably the best. It gives briefly and clearly the results of a careful enquiry into the economic development of Scotland from 1907 until the beginning of the slump, with a short note on the state of things since. That development is described mainly by statistics; many of these statistics were not publicly available until Mr. Thomson got hold of them; and as he uses them they provide for the first time a means of definite comparison between the economic state of Scotland and of England as well as of six or seven European countries, such as Norway, Finland, Holland and Denmark, which have roughly the same population as Scotland.

There is no space in a review like this to give Mr. Thompson's actual figures, and the best way to show what he has proved about the state of Scotland will be to summarise his conclusions. Between 1913 and 1930, then, that is before the slump affected the question seriously:

(1) The population of Scotland declined, while the population of England and of nine European countries resembling Scotland in size increased.

(2) Unemployment was very much higher than in England or in those small countries. This in spite of a far heavier drain by emigration on the Scottish industrial population.

* [Review of *Scotland: That Distressed Area* by G.M. Thomson], *Criterion, XV* (January 1936), pp. 330-32.

(3) Scotland's national income fell, "so that the average Scotsman who started the century as rich as the average Englishman is now only two-thirds as rich".

(4) "The volume of *industrial production* in Scotland, which was still rising during the years 1907 to 1913, has since then fallen, so that in both 1929 (pre-slump) and 1930 it was not merely lower than in 1913 but actually lower than in 1907." During the same time production in England as well as in all western European countries except Germany increased, the increase in some cases being spectacular.

(5) Scotland's basic industries have fallen off, and she has failed to get hold of new secondary industries.

These facts speak for themselves, but a few figures may help to bring them home more vividly. From statistics compiled by the Insitut für Konjunkturforschung, Berlin, Mr. Thomson has extracted the following figures, showing the indices of production in several countries in the years 1913 and 1930. (I give only a few of the countries.) Going on these indices production in Norway rose from 57 in 1913 to 112 in 1930, in Finland from 44 to 83, in Denmark from 72 to 116, in France from 79 to 110. During the same time production fell in Scotland from 116 to 94. And Mr. Thompson says: *"Scotland is the only one of these European countries which shows an actual fall in production in the period between the start of the War and the start of the slump"*; for even Germany's production was slightly higher in 1928 than in 1913 (though it sank again in 1930) while Scotland's production had fallen even in 1928 by 16 points. The post-slump figures which Mr. Thomson gives are just as disturbing. During 1933 and 1934, 1075 new factories were opened in England and Wales and 510 shut—a net gain of 565. During the same time 34 new factories were opened in Scotland 65 shut—a net loss of 31. As for unemployment, Scotland had in 1931, "the year when the British Government extended official recognition to the world crisis, a mass of unemployment three-quarters of the total of workless in six countries whose aggregate population is six times as great as her own."

The point of this book is that it defines clearly for the first time the economic state of Scotland; and it is the state of a country slowly dying without having wakened to the fact. For, as Mr. Thomson says: "The character of the Scottish problem is

that of stealth, of a gradual attrition of physical and ⟨
resources, of a decline in strength which is only percept
comparatively long periods and which therefore displa
in outward signs not to the eye but to the memory." B
where it is openly displayed it is accepted as the natural state of
things. Mr. Thomson quotes a letter to the *Scotsman* by the Rev.
T. M. Murchison, a Church of Scotland minister: "Many
Highland parishes are becoming inhabited almost entirely by
the aged, school rolls dwindling, churches becoming derelict
because there are so few left to worship, minsters officiating at
ten funerals for every one marriage or baptism." If we were to
read such things in past history we should recognize them at
once as clear evidence of organic decay. But they are happening
at present; Mr. Murchison's letter was written in June this year.

Mr. Thomson merely states the facts about Scotland without
attempting any systematic explanation of them; and in this he is
right, for any explanation would have weakened the
overwhelming impression which his book produces. He is of the
opinion, however, that the economic decline of Scotland is
partly due to the centralisation of finance in London; and
indeed that decline may be merely one of the results of a general
process within Capitalism, the transition from the phase of
industrial capital to that of financial capital. But whatever may
be its cause, for Scotland it is a national domestic problem as
well as an economic one. In this book Mr. Thomson has tried to
rouse Scotland to a realisation of its state. But his book should
also be of interest to England, if she takes the Union seriously or
thinks of it at all. The attitude of the average educated
Englishman to the Scottish question is pained surprise at any
hint that Scotland might wish to dissolve the Union, combined
with a total lack of interest in Scotland as a part of the United
Kingdom. Mr. Thomson is convinced that Scotland would be
better off now without the partnership than with it, and indeed
the comparisons he has drawn between Scotland and such
small countries as Norway and Denmark justify him in his
belief. It is clear that Home Rule should in any case be freely
granted by England now, both for her own sake and for the sake
of Scotland; otherwise she may find that a still important part of
her kingdom will have sunk past hope and past recovery.

5

The Scottish Character*

People are often nonplussed on visiting a foreign or semi-foreign country by the fact that it does not correspond to the notion they had of it. We all have an image, for instance, of the Frenchman, the Englishman and the Scotsman. This image is really fanciful, for it comes from times when peoples lived in isolation from one another and knew very little about each other. We can travel about easily now, and countries are closer to each other than they have ever been before in the history of the world. These images of the Frenchman, the Englishman, the Scotsman, and so on, have accordingly faded; but they still survive, in a ghostly way. Many English people, for instance, still think of the Scotsman as a heraldic figure in a kilt, living at a (to them) unpronounceable place called Auchtermuchty. This figure spends his life going to church, drinking, arguing about theology, quoting Burns, playing golf, and singing comic songs in a pawky voice. He is a sort of cross between John Knox and Sir Harry Lauder. But he does not correspond to anything that a visitor will find in Scotland; for he does not exist; he is a fiction; and the best thing to do, before coming to Scotland, is to discard him.

In spite of this, there is a certain residue of truth in the picture. It is true that we neither go to church, nor drink, nor quote Burns, as much as we used to do; but we still argue, about theology and countless other things, which I think is all to the

* *The Listener, XIX* (23 June 1938), pp. 1323-325.

good; and a few of us play golf and sing comic songs, which is of less importance. But people in every country do these things nowadays; the English, for example, sing far more comic songs than we do, though in some way or other they manage to avoid the reputation for doing it. The real difference between the English and the Scottish is probably in the way they do these various things. In a church service a Scotsman expects more logic and less ritual than an Englishman. From drink he looks for a wilder hilarity. Again, he likes an argument to be carried on to its conclusion, without any concession to mere social convenience, and if need be with extravagant ferocity. He does not appreciate good-natured or polite agreement, which spoils the game. And so on.

I think the reason for most of these differences is the fact, which has often been admitted by impartial observers, that Scotland is a more democratic country than England. There is no more economic equality in Scotland, of course, than in England; but there is a greater sense of human equality. We have not got into the habit yet of putting down a man or an idea as upper middle-class, or some other class. I remember the shock of surprise this habit gave me the first time I went to England: I had read about it but never seen it in action before. We have not acquired, then, this habit of thinking in social classes, in spite of the fact that we live in them. The result is that if you ask any chance Scotsman a question, you will get neither a polite nor an impolite answer, but a reasonable human one, or at least one that is founded on an implicit respect for human reason. This applies to almost anyone you may meet. The reasonableness is not wrapped up in any way; and sometimes the answer is so exactly calculated to meet the question, that it may appear grudging. but it isn't intended to be; it is merely the rational response of one human being to another; and it has the virtue of letting you know exactly where you stand. Democratic people don't waste words, for they meet as man to man: that is the basis of intercourse. It is the formal recognition of class distinctions that makes a great number of words necessary, and that formal recognition has never been given in Scotland.

I don't think there is any more interest in the countless things that happen in the world in Scotland than in England but I think you will find a greater variety of opinion about them.

This, again, comes from a democratic habit of thought, for in a democracy every man feels he is entitled to use his own mind on everything, as far as it will carry him. So that even if you are an expert on something you must not expect a Scotsman to agree obediently with you; he keeps his right to give his opinion, even if it doesn't square with yours. He can be won over by argument, and will probably enjoy the winning over for the sake of the argument; but an appeal to authority, even if it is scientific authority, will very likely leave him unimpressed.

But this, like all similar generalisations, is only partly true. It hardly applies at all, for instance, to the Highlands. There anybody will agree with anything you say, if it is not actually blasphemous, for the sake of mere pleasantness, or to make you feel at home. This doesn't come from any weakness of character; it is simply that the Highland people have an unusually keen apprehension of your feelings and want to gratify them. So it is never safe, for instance, to ask anyone in the Highlands how far it is to the next town. If it is ten miles, you will probably be told that it is five. There is no dishonesty about this, for any other Highlander would accept the figure as it was meant and simply multiply it by two, and both parties would be satisfied. In the Lowlands you would be told, without any attempt to soften the fact, objectively, as it were, that it was a long way, and you would be given, after this warning, the exact mileage, down to the last half or quarter of a mile. The two responses come from different ways of looking at the world. A Highlander does not have the same absolute faith in the reality of miles as a Lowlander; he feels that some miles may be shorter than others; he thinks of the stretch you still have to cover, he enters into your anxiety and hopes that the road may not be so long as it seems. Or he may be a little ashamed that places are as far from each other as they are in the Highlands, and feel he has to justify these distances by modifying them. There isn't such a great difference between five miles and ten after all. And miles were probably invented by the Saxon invader.

But there is very little you can say about a country, especially if you belong to it; for as soon as you make any statement, you find scores of exceptions to it rising in your mind. A nation is really a collection of everybody, and there is no way of defining everybody. And on top of this the people in the different parts of

Scotland are different in various ways from one another, and have definite local characteristics. For instance, in my own county, Orkney, the people have the same sensitive manners as the Highlanders; yet they are very practical at the same time, and know the exact length of a mile. On the other hand, they find it difficult to say "No" to any question, and if they can they will get round it in some way. In the Lowlands a man will say "No" without hesitation and without addition, when 'No' is required. On the other hand, it is said that in the native language of the Highlanders, the Gaelic, there is no single word equivalent to "No" at all. "No" exists as a remote supposition, and can only be hinted at, with polite distaste, as a last resort. The Highlands pride themselves on being Celtic, and the Orkneys on being Norse, and yet they both have this curious dislike for the simple negative. A good part of the East Coast has a Norse atmosphere too, though not nearly so strong as in Orkney and Shetland; but there people can bring out a good round "No" without embarrassment. In the south and south-west of Scotland the word has become indigenous ever since the whole countryside said "No" to Prelacy and Erastianism in the seventeenth century. Many of the people there are still to all intents Covenanters. You will find among them Bible-reading shepherds and learned weavers.

I have been talking about the Scottish countryside till now, and it is the most Scottish part of Scotland. But there are the big towns, and big towns, no matter where they may be stationed, are much more like one another than the countryside around them. Glasgow, for instance, resembles Manchester, or London, or Berlin, or even Paris, far more radically than it resembles Auchtermuchty or Ecclefechan. Big towns follow a law and have a life of their own which seems to be independent to a great extent of the particular soil on which they are built. Outwardly they differ very largely; for some of them have style and some haven't. Edinburgh, for instance, has a definite style, and is one of the most beautiful cities in the United Kingdom. Glasgow has practically no style at all; it had the misfortune of being hastily huddled up in the middle of the industrial age of Victoria. It is not so much ugly, though some of the richer quarters contain masterpieces of ugliness, as careless and unbuttoned. Respectability is one of the vices which we share with the English; in fact, there is a case for maintaining that we took it over from the English and improved on it; for we cannot resist the temptation to work things out to the their logical conclusion. But Glasgow pays less tribute to respecatability than any other city in Scotland. The people there are, I think, the most easy-going, gregarious, warm-hearted and talkative people in all the country. They are very democractic, but their democracy isn't of the lean, suspicious kind; it bubbles over and carries everything before it. A man who tries to stand on ceremony in Glasgow is not snubbed; he is simply enveloped in a deluge of unceremoniousness where the point he has been trying to make gets completely lost. Glasgow is more crammed with vitality than any other Scottish town, or at least the vitality is less repressed and gets freer expression. Edinburgh has style, but Glasgow has this abounding, warm vitality.

I have not been able to say much about the people in Scotland, partly because there is so much to say. If I were coming up to Scotland for the first time, I would start with Glasgow. Having withstood that shock, I would go to Edinburgh. Then I would go to the Borders and the south-west, and stay for a while in the lovely little town of Kirkcudbright; and after that I would go straight up to the Highlands. In doing this I should find at least half-a-dozen different peoples, all of whom have the right to call themselves Scottish, and none of them is in the least like a cross between John Knox and Sir Harry Lauder. If I had any energy after that, I should go still farther north to Orkney and Shetland, where I should have a new surprise. When I try to imagine that novel journey, I see that if I were English I should be considerably nonplussed at several of the stages, and that the present talk would not be of much use to me. But nobody should object to being nonplussed; it is one of the chief pleasures of travel, and perhaps the only dependable one.

6

Bolshevism and Calvinism*

My purpose in this essay is to draw a comparison between Calvinism and Bolshevism (which seem to me to resemble each other in important respects), hoping that this may lead to a clearer understanding of both, and hence to a clearer awareness of what is happening in our own time. I shall try to remain as impartial as I can, for the fight for and against Communism is bound to go on; and to try to see clearly the logic that directs the combat and the fighters, though at first glance a purely passive act, is yet one which should be attempted for the sake of clarity, and one which, seeing the communists are still in an inconsiderable minority, may be of some use.

Calvinism has historically run its course; it has helped to change the face of society and as a factor in historical development has disappeared; it has thus for the student a double advantage over Bolshevism: we can see it completely in its rise, triumph, decline and fall, and we can estimate some of its consequences. I shall use Calvinism, therefore, as a light to examine the contemporary movement.

I shall begin with some of the resemblances between the two creeds. The following statements are true of Calvinism. First, it was a deterministic theory holding that certain changes were inevitable and that its own ultimate triumph was assured. Secondly, to concentrate its forces it possessed one central scripture reinforced by a mass of guiding exegesis, and

* *European Quarterly*, I (May 1934), pp. 3-11.

encouraged the unremitting study of that scripture, attributing to all secular literature, of whatever nature, a secondary importance. Thirdly, on the model of its scripture it set up a complete new system of life and created a new machinery which was designed to be at once theoretically sound and practically efficient. Fourthly, in its secular policy it was eminently realistic, employing the pretext of liberty, as all young movements do before they attain power, but using the same weapons as its enemies: that is, repression and discipline within, and craft and force without. Fifthly, while in its triumph still hostile to literature and other forms of traditional culture, it showed an extraordinary enthusiasm for education and an almost fanatical belief in its efficacy. Sixthly, it essentially sought and secured the victory of a class which was at the time under a stigma, for "the elect" were roughly the new commercial stratum which was already beginning to rise to the top. Seventhly, once it had triumphed it set up a dictatorship by committees and preferred the claims of the mass to those of the individual, exercising a strict control over people's private affairs. Eighthly, it revolted against the traditional conception of love and marriage, and while disgusted by the romantic attitudes of chivalry, made divorce easier, at once rationalising and loosening the marriage tie. And finally, it was in its policy international and revolutionary, from a convenient centre encouraging rebellion agains the old order in other countries.

Let us see how this picture fits Bolshevism. Bolshevism, too, is founded on a deterministic theory, envisages an inevitable triumph, is inspired by one book to which it attributes infallibility, relegates secular literature to a secondary position, has elaborated a complete new system and machinery of politics founded on its chief scripture, and is trying to perfect that machinery so as to achieve the utmost efficiency. It is eminently realistic in its policy, essentially seeks the victory of a single class, once under a stigma, and rules now in its triumph in Russia by a dictatorship of committees. It is in revolt against whatever romanticises the relations between the sexes, and to its adherents women are "comrades" just as to the early Calvinists women were "sisters". And finally it has an antipathy to traditional culture and a sanguine faith in education, and is both international and revolutionary.

124

These correspondences seem to me to be more than merely curious. But before going further I wish to make it clear that I am not attempting anything so foolish as an identification of Calvinism and Bolshevism, but only suggesting a parallelism. The creeds of Calvin and Marx do not coincide at any point. The Calvinist was essentially concerned with his relation to God; the Marxian is not concerned with God at all. The Calvinist wished to create a society completely governed by a religious discipline; the Bolshevist's ideal is a society purely secular. The two theories are so far apart that they seem to apply to separate worlds; everything in these two worlds is different: the objects themselves, the terms in which the mind conceives them; yet when one has admitted all this the haunting sense of a parallelism remains: it is as if the one world were a copy of the other, a copy in which all the objects are altered even to their names, but are yet recapitulated in the same logical order. To put it briefly, in content these two creeds are quite dissimilar, but in logical structure they are astonishingly alike.

And both have this further resemblance: that they are essentially logical. The water-tight system, the determinism assuring ultimate victory, the practical and realistic temper, the unity of aim rejecting everything which lies beyond its scope— literature, for instance—the direction of that aim towards the advancement of a chosen class, the rigid internal discipline: all these things follow self-evidently from one another. The water-tight system proceeds naturally from the possession of a central scripture, the determinism assuring certainty of success proceeds as naturally from the infallibility of that sytem, and so in turn with the practical temper and the unified aim and all the rest. Policy is international because the central scripture is a universal one, concerned in the first case with God's purposes with mankind and in the second with economic processes taken to be valid for all civilized societies. Policy is revolutionary because in both instances a class is seeking to wrest power from one politically superior. This in turn explains the enthusiasm for education and the hostility towards culture; for culture is a tradition whose ark is the class which is just about to be or has just been displaced, and education is a new culture, the kind of culture which the rising class finds most useful for its purpose. This new culture, however, has certain peculiar characteristics;

unlike the old, which was a growth, it is necessarily an improvization, a construction; and this being so its essential principles are system and logic, not experience. And this in turn helps to explain the Calvinist-Bolshevist attitude to marriage. For here tradition is particularly strong, and the attack must therefore be correspondingly incisive. Now every practical (as distinct from sentimental or romantic) attack on tradition takes the form of rationalizing certain things which before had been settled by custom and experience. To call women "sisters" or "comrades" is to strike deep at the traditional conception both of romantic love and marriage, and at the same time to affirm again the paramount claim of the new society; for a sister or a comrade is neither a wife nor a mistress, but a colleague in a common task which belongs to everyone without distinction of sex. In rationalizing marriage new revolutionary societies see that it is refashioned in accordance with the "one thing needful".

We can now have a clearer picture of Calvinism and Bolshevism. Deterministic, simple, practical, rational, anti-traditional, anti-romantic, functional: these qualities are qualities that cut clean through the complexity of life and custom and deliberately exclude everything which is useless or distracting or inimical to themselves. Simple and logical and exclusive; such are the ideas of Calvin and Marx; but perhaps their most essentially distinguishing attribute is exclusiveness. Revolutionary ideas may be divided into two classes: those which while seeming for a time to threaten tradition are yet absorbed into it; and those which create a tradition of their own, apart from the main tradition and at perpetual war with it; which are never completely absorbed, therefore, yet sometimes by their presence incite the main tradition to new efforts. Of this kind of revolutionary idea Calvinism is perhaps the greatest past example in modern history. Calvinism was for more than a century a civilization within a civilization; a narrower and more concentrated civilization within a looser and more complex civilization; tremendously efficient, therefore able, because of the very singleness of its aim, to effect great changes, to alter the destiny of the Netherlands and of Scotland, to make royalist England a republic and change its internal balance of power, and to colonize the New World; but powerless to change the main European tradition. For while Calvinism altered political and ecclesiastical forms it remained obstinately apart, its believers a peculiar people, eventually, by an inevitable transition, to become proud of being a peculiar people: it lived to itself and died of inanition. It died because it cut itself off from European civilization. It thought it was cutting off European civilization.

The type of man who produces and is in turn reproduced by such theories is well known to us in history from such figures as Wiliam the Silent, Cromwell and Knox. His virtues, with the exception of his central virtue of faith, from which all the others spring, are almost exclusively practical. He is admirably fitted to accomplish political, economic or religious changes in the objective body of society; he is often masterly in dealing with affairs and institutions, with objects in general. He accepts institutions simply as institutions and asks: How can they be made better, more rational, more in accordance with sound theory? He does not generally foresee the suffering which is caused by his changes, and when it appears he refuses to admit its justification. So after revolution comes repression tempered by education, for the same virtues which enabled him to direct the change now compel him to master its consequences. The Calvinist type, in general, has thus an unrivalled capacity for action, and a less than normal capacity for living. He creates conditions, therefore, that can only remain endurable by a sustained perseverance in action at the expense of living. The time comes when the other faculties of man, those that express themselves in contemplation, enquiry, invention, criticism, play and a hundred different ways, can no longer be denied; the exclusive convention falls to pieces, and its scattered elements are received once more into the main tradition.

But here an interesting question might arise. What if Calvinism had not lost finally in its main fight against the European tradition; what if, instead of contributing to modify that tradition in the long run, it had itself become the norm of European life, accepting only such scattered elements of the older order as it could use and digest? This speculation may seem idle, but it is very apposite to the present situation, for if Communism triumphs something like this is bound to happen. Communism is not only an exclusive creed, like Calvinism; it

127

becomes, once it has triumphed, an all-inclusive one. For while the secular aim of Calvinism was to emancipate a single class, that of Communism is to free the last class of all; and to do that is not merely to stand out against society, to set up a smaller civilization within a greater one, but to transform civilization radically in all its parts and leave nothing as it was before. If Communism triumphs there will be no returning to the old European tradition. The opposite will happen: the dispersed remnants of that tradition will be reassembled in the new order as the fragments of Greek and Roman civilization are reassembled in the fabric of modern sociery.

The decisive resemblance between Calvinism and Bolshevism, however, is in their working logic. And the decisive practical virtues of that logic are, first, its acceptance of determinism as a working hypothesis and, secondly, its exclusiveness. It is the logic of a class (in the first case the elect, in the second the proletariat) and so possesses an enormous functional efficiency; but it is also the logic of a class convinced that its eventual success is certain and unavoidable, and so capable of inspiring a faith far stronger than any that the declining order is likely to set against it. The tenet of predestination was to the Calvinists a theological dogma, but it was also the affirmation of a profound certainty that their power was growing and bound to grow and the power of their opponents declining and bound to decline, and that this was an invitable historical process beyond the control of their will (for election and damnation had nothing to do with individual merit). A determinism of this kind is founded in the last resort on a feeling that overwhelming objective forces beyond the control of the individual are on one's side; that the tide has turned and no human effort can stop it. Faith, which had upheld the old order, at this point deserts it for its enemy, and the old order is left to fight for a memory of former power, which has run through its fingers, it does not know how or when. That is what happened in the sixteenth century, and it may be that that is what is in danger of happening now. Communism has a faith and a driving logic as Calvinism had; in a world of confusion and doubt it knows what it wants and has an absolute faith that it will get it. And thus the fact that the logic of Calvinism and Communism are so alike is not merely a matter of curious interest; for it is the logic of a conquering class, a class conscious at all the forces of society, the declining forces no less than the growing ones, are working for it, and that nothing can retard or divert their final consummation. It is thus a concrete factor of considerable importance.

In this short analysis of Communist psychology I have tried to be as impartial as I can, but nobody can be quite impartial in the present state of society, and obviously I should have no right to criticise Communism at all unless I were convinced that there was a possibility of achieving a humanly satisfactory society without giving up the existing advantages of tradition and without having recourse to the machinery of Marxian determinism. That, I believe is possible, and could easily be done without acute dislocation, if the theory of Social Credit associated with the name of Major Douglas were put into practice. If it *is* put into practice, however, that can only be as a free response of the reason and the will to an economic necessity, not as a reaction dictated, just like the problem it has to solve, by that self-same necessity. The whole question at stake in the present psychological state of society is whether such decisions are possible at all, and is partly the growth of communist ways of thought that has brought this about. Communism sees only one choice for society, a choice relished by communists and disliked by their opponents, yet exercising almost as great an influence on the one as the other; for by persistently suggesting that there are only two possible attitudes, its own and the reverse, it circumscribes its opponents' way of thinking as strictly as its own. To believe that society can be both economically just and free, without being ruled by a dictatorship or subject to a political inquisition, requires a certain degree of freedom of mind, and freedom of mind on political questions is becoming more and more difficult to achieve. The whole Marxian argument is directed to proving that Communism is the necessary and inevitable next stage of historical evolution, and it amounts in reality to an overpowering suggestion. That fact, along with the obvious economic collapse of Capitalism, is what gives it such power, in spite of the relatively trifling number of active communists. It affects the ways of thought even of its opponents, and that is the technique of victory. Accordingly any real criticism of

Communism should concentrate on its technique, which is in danger of becoming the technique of everyone, including the man in the street. The number of people who believe that the reason and will can take an active part in the improvement of society is growing rapidly smaller; and despite the intellectual virtues of Communism, and its moral passion, it is vitally important that the tradition represented by such people, which is in the last resort the European tradition, should be maintained and if possible strengthened.

7

Knox in Scottish History *

As a writer on Knox, Lord Eustace Percy has the inestimable advantage of not being a Scotsman. Knox made a deeper impression on Scottish than any single figure has made on English history. We still live in his shadow, a shadow distorted by the changing lights of history, and the shadow, since it is near, is more real to us than the man himself. The shadow is fading, to the relief of some and the regret of others; but relief and regret, on such an intimate matter, imply that in Scotland we are of two minds, and that Knox is still a controversial figure.

Ideally it should be possible for us at this distance in time to view impartially the religious struggle of the sixteenth and seventeenth centuries, to see clearly the motives which made each of the opposing parties act as it did, to admit at least the necessity of the conflict. But we are, willingly or unwillingly, what modern Scottish history has made us, and modern Scottish history was mainly made by John Knox. Yet for the last two hundred years almost every Scotsman of first-rate mind, except Carlyle, has reacted against Knox's influence and the influence of his seventeenth-century successors. Burns reacted violently; David Hume, a man accustomed to moderate language, reacted even more violently. The reaction is still alive, and it is not astonishing, therefore, that an Englishman

* [Review of *John Knox* by Lord Eustace Percy] *London Mercury*, XXXVII (December 1937), pp. 212-14.

should now have produced what is probably the best book that has ever been written on Knox.

The great strength of this remarkable biography is its simultaneous grasp of the various elements, political, religious, national, international, dynastic, popular, which made up the concrete situation and the determined Knox's response to or rather action upon it. No other book illumines so clearly Knox's behaviour at every point by relating it to external political realities or inward religious hesitations. Where Lord Eustace Percy cannot explain Knox's actions by reason he leaves them in their obscurity. His grasp of the political forces of the time, their strength and their nature, is masterly, and his short survey of European history for the century before Knox touched it is impressive philosophically, as well as a dramatically effective prologue to the action that follows. He continuously shows Knox in relation to the whole European situation, as well as to the Scottish and English: in itself a remarkable feat of intellectual imagination. He is not so concerned with Knox as a man as other biographers have been; but he shows him on a greater stage, where his stature can be better measured. He has taken him away from Scotland for a little, to give him back again some inches taller. This operation, clearly a necessary one, has been performed with the utmost brilliance.

Lord Eustace Percy's interpretation of Knox as a religious genius, though worth the most serious consideration, is not so convincing. The portrait he draws is that "of a man with two strong sides to his character, but articulate upon only one of them, and that not the one which he himself valued most." On one side he was "a shrewd politician and lawyer", "a trenchant controversialist", "a matchless chaplain of an army with its back to the wall", "a preacher who could make the eternal war between God and Satan move before men's eyes", "a boisterous and (it must be confessed) a heartless caricaturist". On the other:

> He was not an evangelist in the usual meaning of the word. . . .
> No, strangely enough, his real spiritual bent was the mystic's. In the whole sweep of Old Testament and New, what first caught his ear was a voice which almost passes the range of human hearing: neither the word of God to man nor the words of man to God, but a fragment of "the huge soliloquy of God" Himself.

That is the seventeenth chapter of the Gospel of St. John, where, Knox said on his deathbed, he had "cast his first anchor". On this mystical side, Lord Eustace Percy holds, "He was almost wholly inarticulate, at least in public. . . . He lived by faith and preached the law; the Christ whom he knew as Saviour and Intercessor became on his pulpit lips the Judge of Nations." It is hard to judge how much this means if a man is known by his fruits. That Knox had a sincere personal faith cannot be denied, but what its nature was, what particular sustenance he drew from the seventeenth chapter of the Gospel of St. John, is almost impossible to say. That chapter is capable of countless interpretations, one of them is strongly Calvinist, and Scottish Calvinism has produced no mystic of note, unless Samuel Rutherford, a curious but much underrated writer, may be called one. If Knox was essentially a mystic, what misfortune made him so tongue-tied about it, and so voluble on all that concerned the public policy of the Church? We know nothing of Knox's religious experience, except that sometimes he was plunged in doubt and despair, as all believers have been: it is almost the only proof we have of his personal faith. His public faith is proved by his whole life after his conversion. Lord Eustace Percy thinks that Knox's tragedy consisted, roughly, in the triumph of the religious politician over the mystic. It may be so; it is at least a possible interpretation, and some interpretation is needed.

This book is of intense interest, not only to Scots readers; but perhaps its greatest value lies in its luminous exposure of the workings of history at a period which in so many ways resembled the one in which we are living.

8

Mary, Queen of Scots*

It is appropriate that the lives of most of the great figures in
Scottish history should be wrapped in obscurity: it supplies an
argumentative people with yet more food for argument. A
nation deserves the history it get; it also deserves the historians:
and Scottish historians are controversial. Where the events that
make up history are not bewildering enough for them, they
concoct an artificial obscurity to rectify the omission. The figure
of Mary Stuart is fatally involved in this manufactured
darkness. Her great misfortune as a historical figure was to be
the contemporary of George Buchanan, a professional
historian, and Maitland of Letherington, a potential one. So the
darkness that surrounds her is not the natural darkness of
ignorance; it is an adroitly woven and carefully safeguarded
darkness. And that being so it is practically impenetrable. We
do not know whether Mary was a cold-hearted murderess, or
the victim of murders still more cold-hearted. We do not know
whether she threw herself at Bothwell's head, or submitted to
him against her will. We know that she was brave, that she
behaved sometimes with admirable wisdom and self-control
and sometimes with extreme rashness, and that she had a
potent attraction for men without an equal capacity for keeping
them in subjection to her. It is possible that her irresistible
charm was her undoing: had she been dull and plain the

* [Review of *Mary, Queen of Scots* by Eric Linklater], *The Spectator*, No.
5474 (26 May 1933), p. 766.

Scottish lords might have remembered that she was a queen and forgotten that she was a woman. They could never forget that; they loved and hated her as only a woman can be loved and hated, and as very few queens have been; and there is in both their love and hate something of the exacerbation of the hopelessly ineligible suitor. It can be felt even in the words of that decent Don Juan of Calvinism, John Knox. She is doubly hidden from us—by the importunate distortions of Scottish jealously and the secure intricacies of Scottish intrigue.

Any biography of Mary must therefore be a thesis. Mr. Linklater's one is new, and he has stated it with great force and ingenuity. It is that Mary "was naturally chaste . . . and her political ambition was so strong and so deeply rooted as to occupy most of her thoughts. she believed in the rightness of her claim to the English throne, and she wanted to occupy that throne. . . . Therefore she refrained from taking lovers, because lovers might impair her political resolution and stain the reputation of one who was to be a great queen, and because lovers were not to her liking: since, despite a rich endowment of the external qualities of a sexual nature, her nature was not, in essence, strongly sexual." There is much to be said for this interpretation. Mr. Linklater adduces Mary's consent, in the one case cold and by all appearances politic, in the other case exasperated and angry, to the death of two men who had shown their admiration for her, Sir John Gordon and the French poet Chastelard. He might have supported it also by her most unfortunate choice of husbands, for both Darnley and Bothwell were men such as a woman of somewhat amateurish judgement in such matters might very conceivably have married. There is also the fact that she was far more sure in her choice of women friends than of men. All this goes to support Mr. Linkater's interpretation, which is a valuable contribution to the problem and deserves the most serious consideration. If it is the true one, then obviously Mary neither wrote the Casket Letters nor willingly married Bothwell, her husband's murderer, nor plotted with him her husband's death. If it is not the true one, it is still possible, though by no means certain, that she did these things. Darnley's peculiarly revolting murder, at once methodical and blundering, like the slaughter of a helpless animal by a clumsy hand, is just as incongruous with the passionate and impulsive Mary of most of her biographers as with Mr. Linklater's new version of her. Whether she was as passionate as Swinburne thought her, or as naturally chaste as Mr. Linklater thinks her, it is almost impossible to imagine her acting the part she is given in the Casket Letters; all that we know about her speaks overwhelmingly against it. The strongest argument against the theory that the letters are forgeries has nothing to do with her at all. It is that whoever composed them must have been a man of literary genius, with a powerful dramatic imagination, and we know of nobody in Scotland at that time who possessed those qualifications. That Letherington was suddenly visited by literary inspiration is extremely improbable. The matter will never be cleared up.

Mr. Linklater has cut straight to the heart of the problem; he has also given us a new and reasonable interpretation of Mary's character; and he has done all this in a hundred and fifty pages without sacrificing grace and wit of presentation. It is an admirable feat.

9

Fletcher of Saltoun *

This biography is very much a public biography, and Andrew
Fletcher's life seems to have been very much a public life. We
hear of him serving in Hungary as a soldier. We see him as a
young man defying Lauderdale in the Parliament House in
Edinburgh, joining with Monmouth in his brief rebellion and
incidentally shooting a man dead in a fit of temper (the one dark
blot on his career), writing pamphlets in excellent vigorous
English, standing out for the independence of Scotland at a time
when his contemporaries veered like weathercocks under the
winds of English flattery and bribery, introducing agricultural
improvements on his estate, advocating the reintroduction of
slavery as a cure for Scottish unemployment and the
introduction of conscription as a safeguard of liberty, coupled
with the death penalty for sexual offences. We see a man
animated from beginning to end by a passion for Scotland and a
passion for liberty, the first pure and consistent throughout, the
second limited greatly by the prejudices of his age as well as by
personal idiosyncrasies. But we have hardly a glimpse of
Fletcher as a human being unoccupied by any of these
activities. There is no evidence that he even possessed friends.
He never married, and it is hinted that this was because his
brother Henry forestalled him; but he seems to have accepted
the union between his brother and the woman he loved with far

* [Review of *Fletcher of Saltoun* by J. Mackenzie], *The Spectator*,
  No. 5579 (31 May 1935), p.949.

more philosophy than he accepted the Union between England and Scotland. The response which he roused in people seems to have been always either admiration or exasperation, never affection. A man who knew him describes him as "a low (short) thin man of brown complexion, full of fire, with a stern, sour look". His portrait shows that he had a quick choleric eye, a nose of portentous proportions and a somewhat ill-tempered mouth, combined surprisingly with a frank expression. The story of the debates which preceded the Union prove that his temper was indeed very fiery, and that he could not suffer contradiction, far less ridicule. A man endowed with such qualities would, one might have thought, have had an animated and restless private life. There is no sign that Fletcher had any.

There can be no doubt, either, however, that he was not only a completely honourable man, but a very remarkable one. His ideas were far in advance of his time, and he expressed them in a style of admirable clarity and force. He was one of the finest orators of his age, and had a passion which in any other man would surely have attracted a large following. Yet he attracted no following whatever. This is a mystery as deep as his apparent lack of private life, and may indeed have some connexion with it. His plan for a conscript militia certainly shows a somewhat inhuman nobility. His contemporaries harp greatly on his shortness of temper and his "pedantry". There is no sign of pedantry in his speeches, it is true, which rise sometimes to spontaneous eloquence without ever losing grasp of the argument. But an accusation so general must have had some cause, whether "pedantry" was the right name for it or not. One cannot help feeling that there was some truth in the words of "that excellent place-man" and trimmer, Sir John Clerk, who said that Fletcher "was a little untoward in his temper, and much inclined to eloquence. He made many speeches in Parliament which are all printed, but was not very dexterous in making extempory replies. He was, however, a very honest man, and meant well in everything he said and did, except in cases where his humour, passion, or prejudice were suffered to get the better of his reason." It is a painful sight to see a small man patronizing great one, and Fletcher's real epitaph was to be written by opponents less mean than Sir John Clerk. Nevertheless, the hiatus between Fletcher's great gifts and his ineffectuality as a public figure must be explained in some way, and a true explanation would probably find that it was due as much to his faults as to his virtues. Had he been a little different he might have secured a union between the two countries which was satisfactory to both, instead of one which Scotland felt for many years afterwards to be ignominious. Actually his inflexibility, as Mr. Mackenzie admits, helped to make Scotland's defeat in the negotiations more crushing. At the same time, he far surpassed the other Scottish statesmen of his day both in ability and in honesty. The best summary of his character is given by Macky, a contemporary: "He is a gentleman steady in his principles, of nice honour, with abundance of learning, brave as the sword he wears, and bold as a lion. He would lose his life readily to serve his country: and would not do a base thing to save it." A tribute such as that justifies all Mr. Mackenzie's admiration. This biography is a careful and solid piece of work such as one feels would have pleased its subject, without adventitious charm and without trimmings.

10

The Forty-Five*

Mr. Wilkinson's portrait of the Young Pretender has the great merit of being a credible human one, and that, curiously enough, instead of pricking the romantic legend, merely makes it more comprehensible. After reading the book one can see quite clearly that that legend was fed not only on the clan's devotion to a disinherited Prince who was trying to win back his throne against fantastic odds, but also on certain qualties in the chief actor. He was high-spirited, handsome, young, and a Royal Stuart, which equipped him perfectly to be a romantic hero; but he was also a man of considerable practical ability and great courage, generous to enemies who were dishonourable in defeat and pitiless in victory, considerate of the fortunes of those who fought for him, and cheerful in adversity. It is an attractive portrait; yet it raises a few questions, and one in particular that seems insoluble. For how could a man so clear-sighted and practical, according to Mr. Wilkinson, have set out on such an impossible adventure? Victory after victory fell to his Highlanders, it is true; but they all seem now a little absurd and unconvincing, somewhat like stage fights in spite of the bravery shown on the one side and the losses suffered by the other; and one cannot help feeling that it was the unreality of the whole triumphant march that overcame the Scottish commanders at Derby. Mr. Wilkinson blames them for forcing the Prince to

* [Review of *Bonnie Prince Charlie* by Clennel Wilkinson], *The Spectator*, No. 5445 (4 November 1932), p. 634.

turn back at that point, but he himself is unable to explain the inexplicable series of victories that led them there; and although the retreat was disastrous, to have marched on London through hostile country with Cumberland waiting to intercept them must surely have been worse. The fatal error was committed not at Derby but at the very beginning, when Prince Charles set out from France against the advice of his Scottish and English adherents and without bringing any aid from the French; and it is an error which it is impossible to explain in a man of considerable practical ability. The young prince seems to have been cursed with the quality which it used to be fashionable in business circles (before the slump) to call imagination, and is really a lack of true imagination, a failure to envisage the state of things as it is. He plunged; he forced the hands of the Highland chiefs, who were prepared to sacrifice themselves and their clans for him, though they were hopeless of the outcome. He made no impression on England. So it is not very surprising that the Scottish leaders should become hopeless at Derby when they saw that what their Prince coveted was not their allegiance but that of England, which was not prepared to raise a finger for him. The thought that they would have a better opportunity of escaping in their own country after the inevitable failure no doubt moved them too, as Mr. Wilkinson says; but that can be forgiven in men who saw execution in front of them as the reward of a course they had opposed from the beginning, and into which nothing but their loyalty had forced them. The result was a romantic legend long since degenerated into mawkish sentimentality, and the destruction of the ancient clan system and the desolation of the Highlands. Of the victors Mr. Wilkinson says: "They broke the power of the chiefs, they harried Episcopalian and Catholic priests alike, they destroyed religion and education." And all because an amiable, somewhat prosaic, headstrong young man would not be guided by heads wiser than his own.

Mr. Wilkinson tells his tale effectively, which must have required far more skill than it will be given credit for. It is a pity that his first chapter should be such unmitigated Wardour Street and strike such a gratingly false note; but after that the story is admirably managed. He is generous in his praise of the bravery and fidelity of the Highlanders, but hardly just to the

Scottish leaders, whose loyalty to a Stuart Prince forced them to bring terrible sufferings on their own countrymen. Their allegiance was a divided one; that was their tragedy, more moving in reality than that of their leader.

11

Facts and Flytings*

Scottish literature has seldom been written about except by Scotsmen, and as though it concerned only Scotland: a local interest. Herr Kurt Wittig is a German; he has studied his subject closely and with unusual concentration and, coming to it from outside, he is able to see freshly what has often been carelessly taken for granted. He approaches it systematically, as an object in itself of interest. He has made himself acquainted with Scottish Gaelic poetry, and I fancy that has not been attempted in any other book on the same subject. In this way he establishes a relationship between the two Scottish literatures and gives a fuller meaning to the Scottish tradition. It is generally thought that there is a vast difference between the poetry of the Highlands and the Lowlands. Herr Wittig brings out their similarities, which are striking, and exemplified not only in such things as the resemblances between the metrical forms of Highland and Lowland poetry, but in a realistic imagination, a particularised rendering of the factual, which is common to both. He adduces also a less important, but characteristic common trait, the custom of flyting which has persisted for hundreds of years.

Scottish poetry is very unlike English poetry, yet to define the qualities which distinguish them from each other is a difficult matter. Herr Wittig shows an intimate understanding of

* [Review of *The Scottish Tradition in Literature* by Kurt Wittig], *New Statesman*, LV (18 June 1958), p. 840.

Scottish poetry, but here he is less satisfactory; his distinctions are too sharp. He finds in Scottish poetry as compared with English "a stronger feeling for colour . . . imagery sharper and more detailed . . . greater metrical complexity . . . keener interest in nature, especially in its wilder aspects . . . the spirit of clannishness . . . flyting and extravaganza". And these qualities, he adds, are still more marked in Scottish Gaelic poetry, along with "a stronger folk element . . . a more 'democratic' spirit . . . 'more simplicity and straightforward diction' . . . and (in its understatements) greater restraint—if not grimness—in expressing tender feeling". These distinctions resemble too much a catalogue to be quite convincing, yet they do tell us something about Scottish poetry. Where they fall down is in implying that these qualities are to be found in Scottish poetry, and nowhere else. One has only to read to know that English poetry shows a strong feeling for colour, great metrical complexity, and a keen interest in nature, and that it displays a tact and restraint in expressing tender feeling greater than can be found in Scottish poetry. The differences between the two poetries lie deeper than a catalogue.

Yet Herr Wittig sees Scottish poetry very clearly, sees for the first time what has been seen so often that the impression has faded to a blur, and sees also now and then what has not been seen before. He traces already in Barbour the Scottish conviction that there is no getting round facts. He notes that Barbour occasionally "stresses that he has his knowledge from an eye-witness, gives the name of his informant, states expressly that he does not know a name or detail, reports two different verions, or presents something as a rumour the truth of which he cannot check". And then Wittig aptly quotes Dr. James Ritchie on the Scottish scientist:

> The genius of Scottish science bears a characteristic stamp—it is a faculty for minute detailed observation, for accuracy in small things.

There Herr Wittig throws light both on the Scotish tradition and the Scottish character, simply from observing a fourteenth-century Scottish poet.

He makes a more surprising, but very interesting, deduction from Barbour's religious attitude, relying again on close observation:

> He has a profound faith in God, yet nowhere does he refer to
> the Church as a mediator, mention its rituals, invoke its saints, or
> himself employ its symbolism, its dogmas. A century and a half
> before the Reformation, he converses with God face to face. . . .
> No wonder that the Scottish people were later to find the spirit of
> the Reformation so congenial.

This shows how deeply Herr Wittig has gone into Barbour's
mind, yet whether he is right in thinking that Scotland was
already reformed before it knew that the Reformation was to
come, is hard to say. However, he supports his case with ancient
Gaelic proverbs which embody somewhat the same conception:

> God, just and almighty, is the ruler of Destiny, but Christ is
> little mentioned, and no *specifically* Christian ideas are expressed.

It seems a position half-way to Predestination, but not yet in
sight of Calvin.

Herr Wittig impresses one as understanding the early
Scottish poets, particularly Barbour, Henryson and Dunbar,
more intimately than they have been understood before. On
Burns and Scott there is little new that he can say. On living
Scottish writers he is uncertain. He writes excellently on Hugh
MacDiarmid and Sydney Goodsir Smith, but Norman
MacCaig, who is a fine poet, has to share a single sentence with
eight other names. The treatment of Eric Linklater and Neil
Gunn is intelligent. But what makes the book remarkable is its
grasp of the potencies as well as of the performance of the
writers it deals with, particularly the earlier ones. It is probably
the best book that has yet been written on Scottish literature.

12

Literature in Scotland*

It is now about ten years since the Scottish Renaissance began to be talked about. There was no sign of a renaissance at the time except in the work of "Hugh McDiarmid", the writer who talked and wrote most indefatigably about it. He started several reviews, some weekly and some monthly, which never lasted for very long but produced work by young writers which otherwise might never have been produced. Most of that work was bad, but some of it was good: for instance, Mr. Neil M. Gunn's first stories, so far as I can remember, appeared in one of those short-lived magazines. After the last of them had stopped came *The Modern Scot*, a quarterly edited by Mr. James H. Whyte, which is the best literary review that has appeared in Scotland for many decades, and has now maintained for several years a critical level which is unique there. At the same time there has been a far more intensive literary production than the first twenty years of the century could show, as well as a considerable public interest in it. No doubt the growth of nationalist feeling in Scotland has helped greatly to canalize that interest. There is now, at any rate, an increasing public prepared to give a special welcome to Scottish work, and that is quite a new state of things, and provides for the first time for a century the possible conditions of a literary revival. but this is probably the most that can be said: there is a great deal of literary activity in Scotland; there is no Scottish literary

* *The Spectator*, No. 5526 (25 May 1934), p. 823.

movement to compare with the Irish movement whose chief figure was Mr. W.B. Yeats.

The main reason for this, I think, apart from the absence of genius in any great abundance, is that the Scottish renaissance is a renaissance without a centre, either social of intellectual. It has no convenient meeting point like Dublin where writers can discuss their aims, and no common literary purpose which would give directions to their production. the result is that Scottish writers receive no effectual criticism, and consequently no real help in their work. It is well known that the general level of book-reviewing in the English Press is very low; but in Scotland it is considerably lower. Again there are in England several reviews in which intelligent criticism can be had if one wants it; while in Scotland there is only one, and it a quarterly. In a country where criticism is indiscriminating or almost absent the work of its creative writers may be remarkable, but it is likely to be uneven. Scotland has three or four writers of original talent, but their work is far more uneven than it has any right to be, or than it would have been had they written for a country which possessed an acknowledged standard of serious criticism as well as the popular one represented by the Press. This lack of criticism is probably the chief danger to the present revival of literature in Scotland. With a little more enthusiastic complaisance it may end in a complete uncritical morass.

But though the present literary production in Scotland has no definite direction, there is one thing which clearly distinguishes it from that of Stevenson, Barrie, Crockett and Ian Maclaren at the end of last century. The Scottish characters in which these writers deal were intended primarily, like Sir Harry Lauder's humour, for foreign consumption. they were designed for the popular English taste; they were exports. This was not true to the same degree of Neil Munro's Highlanders, who came later, and it cannot be said at all, I think, of Mr. Neil M. Gunn's or Mr Lewis Grassic Gibbon's or "Fionn MacColla's" Scottish characters. These writers address themselves first of all to a Scottish audience, and not incidentally, as their predecessors did. Certainly Stevenson should not be blamed too much for his literary strategy, for such an audience did not exist in his time. And the fact that it does exist now is a clear proof of an immense increase in national self-consciousness.

In Scottish poetry there has been a change of a different kind. The most gifted poet writing in Scots at the beginning of the century was Charles Murray. He was a poet in the peasant tradition; he played skilful variations on immemorial simple folk themes which had been used hundreds of times, by Burns and his many predecessors and successors. The real originality of "Hugh McDiarmid" is that he employs Scots as any other poet might employ English or French: that is, to express anything which a modern writer may have to say. This had not been done in Scotland since she ceased to be a nation, since about two centuries, that is to say, before Burns. "Hugh McDiarmid" is an extremely erratic and uneven writer; but he is probably the most gifted poet who has written in Scots since Burns, and the innovation he has made (if it should turn out to be a true innovation, that is, if it is carried on and consolidated after him by other writers) is clearly of major importance. But here again Scottish criticism has failed. "Hugh McDiarmid's" use of Scots has been much praised and much blamed; but the question whether he has succeeded in reinstating Scots as a language capable of expressing the whole world of contemporary experience and thought just as satisfactorily as English or French has never been seriously considered. He has very successfully expressed his own individual talent, with all its excellences and defects; and as the result is original, that is sufficient to justify his means. But that Scots will ever be used again as an independent language capable of fulfilling all the purposes of poetry and prose is, I should think, very doubtful. It is not impossible, for Scots was once an autonomous language, and inherently there is no reason why it could not be an autonomous language again. But there is against that an overwhelming balance of probability. And if a language cannot be used for all the normal literary purposes of a language, no serious argument can be advanced for using it for poetry. "Hugh McDiarmid" is a poet of great originality, but if Scots does not become an independent language he will probably be known as a writer who fashioned a speech of his own, which has to be specially learned before he can be appreciated.

The question of language in contemporary Scottish literature is a very difficult one. Apart from "Hugh McDiarmid", the

148

names most commonly connected with the Scottish Renaissance are those of Neil M. Gunn, Eric Linklater and Lewis Grassic Gibbon. Mr. Gunn's sensitive style is more obviously influenced by D.H. Lawrence than by Neil Munro; Mr. Linklater writes vigorous Elizabethan prose; Mr. Gibbon has struck out a style which does succeed in giving the rhythm of the Scottish vernacular. But all use English as their natural utterance; their literary inspiration is the great English writers, not Dunbar or Burns. On the other hand, they write about Scottish life for a Scottish audience, and not for an English one, like Stevenson. They write for this audience in English, it is true, but there they have little choice; for the Scottish people are a people who talk in Scots but think in English. These writers are, in any case, more intimately Scottish than Stevenson was, and that justifies one in calling the literary revival to which they belong a Scottish one. It is obviously only at its beginning yet; the promise for its future lies in the fact that for some time Scotland has been becoming more and more conscious of itself as a separate unity, and that this tendency seems bound to continue.

13

Contemporary Scottish Poetry*

The difficulty about Scottish poetry is one of definition. Ever since the seventeenth century Scotland has produced two kinds of poetry—Scottish poetry, and poetry written in English by men of Scottish birth. Before James VI went to London at England's invitation this division did not exist. The Reformation, being part of an international movement, had helped it is true to dilute Scotland's national characteristics; Knox was the first Scotsman to write English prose. But Scotland's first English poet, Drummund of Hawthornden, came later, after the union of the crowns. Dunbar, Henryson and Gavin Douglas were Scottish in a sense that Burns and Scott could not be. They used the Scots language in the same way as the English poets were later to use theirs—that is, as a means potentially capable of sustaining all the forms of poetry, from the most simple up to the most complicated and ambitious. Gavin Douglas translated the Aeneid, and that he should have attempted a task shows how different was his attitude to the language from that of any Scottish poet after James VI. Verse translation into Scots since then has been confined mainly to versions of the Psalms and Heine's simpler lyrics.

The effectual reason for this great change, I think, was Scotland's loss of her separate nationality. Dunbar, Henryson and Douglas wrote as members of an independent society, with

* *The Bookman*, LXXVI (September 1934), pp. 282-83.

a civilisation of its own, and their poetry therefore touched the aspects of that civilisation at many widely separated points. Burns's poetry touched the life of a single class—the class which was farthest removed from the centre of national life, and therefore capable of continuing without alteration long after that centre ceased to exist. He was in the tradition of peasant poetry; Dunbar and Henryson were in the full poetic tradition of their time. Consequently, although Burns is a greater poet than either, his poetry compared to theirs is simple in feeling and restricted in scope. The change that took place in Scottish poetry after the union of the crowns was really a change from a full poetic tradition to a local one.

This brief historical excursus is necessary before one can understand the present position of Scottish poetry. Almost all Scots poetry since Burns has been local in setting, simple in feeling, and has dealt with a few restricted themes, mostly picked from the life of the country-side and the small towns. At its best this poetry has a great natural spontaneity; at its worst it is either literary, like Stevenson's verse, or helplessly sentimental. Charles Murray's "Hamewith" and Violet Jacobs's "Songs of Angus" contain some of the best folk-poetry written in the present century. Miss Marion Angus's talent is more dubious, and the titles of some of her collections of lyrics, such as "Sun and Candlelight" and "The Tinker's Road", give a fair idea of her facile and romantic imagination, which has not the home-spun strength of the peasant's. She has used folk-poetry as the basis of an art-form, and although the result is at times exquisite, it is also somewhat thin, like a country wine extracted from harmless and ordinary herbs. Another poet who has tried to give a romantic polish to folk emotion is Mr. Lewis Spence. "Plumes of Time" is written in what the author calls "Gentleman's Scots"—a language gathered both from mediaeval Scots and local dialect, with a slight admixture of the spoken speech of modern Edinburgh. The result is decoratively pleasing, though too fragile to bear the strain of intense poetic creation; being highly coloured, it produces the effect of excellently applied rouge. The face that this composition clothes is that of a Scottish peasant girl, and this juxtaposition gives Mr. Spence's poetry an unusual piquancy. It recalls simultaneously the kailyard and the green-room, and makes

151

one feel that an unimaginable marriagle is about to be consummated. But the union never takes place, or at best illegitimately. Mr. Spence's combination of staid sentiment and luscious diction is to be found in a good deal of modern Scottish poetry, and must spring from something in the national character. I imagine it can be traced to the breakdown of Calvinism, which is complete enough at present to enable poets to be free with words, but not with their emotions. "Plumes of Time" was really, I think, a protest against the exclusive dominance of the folk-song tradition; but being only a formal protest, in every sense, it was not effective. The author however has an excellent sense of form.

It is Hugh McDiarmid who has changed all this. He started with the reasonable assumption that if Scots was to be a language for poetry, it must be capable of expressing every shade of thought and emotion as clearly as English or French. Before this could be done the vocabulary had to be broadened and refurbished. So he plunged into Jamieson's Dictionary and emerged with what later became known as synthetic Scots. It was a rough-and-ready way of fashioning a language, and some of the confusion of its birth still adheres to the result. But though that is artificial, like Mr. Spence's diction, it has far more toughness and a far wider range, and McDiarmid has shown in a succession of volumes that it is capable of dealing with a great number of feelings and ideas which have been lost to Scottish poetry. His first two volumes, "Sangschaw" and "Penny Wheep", were mainly collections of short lyrics, exquisite in rhythm, individual in mood and not in the least in the Burns tradition. They were followed by a long, semi-philosophical poem called "A Drunk Man Looks at the Thistle", which is probably his finest work, and I think one of the most remarkable poems of the time. It is a farrago, but one expects a farrago from a drunk man; and the psychological transitions, from drunk to sober, from drunk to more drunk, are managed with real skill. His next poem, "To Circumjack Cencrastus", was even longer, but not quite so successful, being very careless in execution; it contained however some fine satire and a few lovely lyrics. This was followed by "Scots Unbound" which, except for one or two poems that are probably better than anything else he has written, lacks the vigour and daring of his earlier work. His latest volume, "Stony Limits", is partly experimental and partly propagandist, being divided between between adventures in new forms of English, which are not very successful, aand hymns proclaiming the triumph of Communism and Social Credit, which are vigorous but prosaic. As a transitional work this volume is interesting enough; but it has none of the intrinsic virtue of McDiarmid's early poetry, in which incongruous elements were united in the most daring and natural way. The incongruities are still here, but they are not united.

This is not the place to estimate Hugh McDiarmid's poetry, nor the time, for his latest work is obviously transitional. But it would hardly be denied, I think, that he is the most gifted poet in Scots since Burns. A more pressing question is whether the language in which he writes is actually, as it claims to be, a language able to sustain all the forms and degrees of poetry; for on the answer to that question depends one's hopes for the future of Scots poetry. McDiarmid himself has shown that he can use this language, and that in his hands it is capable of astonishing force and variety. It would be too much to say that he uses it with sureness; the language is too young. But I think he has shown that with good fortune, that is with assistance from other poets, present and future, it can be consolidated and win a place for itself. If something like that does not happen, then it is hard to see any future for Scots poetry; for the old folk-tradition cannot linger on for ever. since Scotland is not exclusively a country of cottars' houses and towns like Kirriemuir. Scots poetry was moribund; Hugh McDiarmid has wakened some hope fot it; and that, apart altogether from his intrinsic poetic gifts, makes him a uniquely important figure in contemporary Scottish literature. Two other poets, William Jeffrey and William Soutar, who have written mainly in English, have recently adopted Scots as their language, though whether this is a permanent policy it is hard to say. In any case their Scots is excellent, and not in the least influenced by Burns.

These two poets bring me to the second class of poetry—that written by poets of Scottish birth in English. This class obviously sems to belong to English poetry; for in poetry tradition means almost everything. The poetry of Mr. Jeffrey and Mr. Soutar could not have been written, I think, by a

Southern Englishman, but then neither could Wordsworth's. They are both poets of genuine inspiration but uneven execution, who would have achieved a greater reputation had they written less. I could add other names to theirs if I were writing about Anglo-Scots poetry; but the main question in Scottish poetry is at present the language question; and in any case a catalogue would be of no use to anybody.

14

A Note on the Scottish Ballads*

It is a thing worth noting that the one or two great poets whom Scotland as produced have been men in the ordinary sense uncultivated. Excepting Scott, those of whom we know anything have sprung from peasant or humble stock; and there was even before Burns, who set a fashion, a tradition of peasant poetry and a belief that an artificer of Scottish song might most congruously be a plowman or a weaver. In poets of this degree, so scarce in English literature, Scottish poetry has almost always been prolific; and against the solitary figure of Bloomfield it can set Fergusson, Ramsay, Tannahill, and a host of others, the worst of whom are sentimental and the best, if minor poets, most authentically poets. Outside these, among her imaginative prose writers, Scotland has shown a disposition for common and even mean conditions. Carlyle was the son of a mason, and George Douglas, the young student of Glasgow University who wrote one novel of passionate genius, "The House with the Green Shutters", and then died, was the illegitimate off-spring of a servant girl. Since English became the literary language of Scotland there has been no Scots imaginative writer who has attained greatness in the first or even the second rank through the medium of English. Scott achieved classical prose, prose with the classical qualities of solidity, force and measure, only when he wrote in the Scottish dialect; his Scottish dialogue is great prose, and his one essay in Scottish imaginative literature, "Wandering

* *Freeman*, VI (17 January 1923), pp. 441-44,

Willie's Tale", is a masterpiece of prose, of prose which one must go back to the seventeenth century to parallel. The style of Carlyle, on the other hand, was taken bodily from the Scots pulpit; he was a parish minister of genius, and his English was not great English, but great Scots English; the most hybrid of all styles, with some of the virtues of the English bible and many of the vices of the Scottish version of the Psalms of David; a style whose real model may be seen in Scott's anticipatory parody of it in "Old Mortality". He took the most difficult qualities of the English language and the worst of the Scots and through them attained a sort of absurd, patchwork greatness. But—this can be said for him—his style expressed, in spite of its overstrain, and even through it, something real, the struggle of a Scots peasant, born to other habits of speech and of thought, with the English language. Stevenson—and it was the sign of his inferiority, his lack of fundamental merit—never had this struggle, nor realized that it was necessary that he should have it. He was from he first a mere literary man, a man to whom language was a literary medium and nothing more, and with no realization of the unconditional mystery and strength of utterance. He sweated over words, but the more laboriously he studied them the more superficial he became, and to the end his conception of an English style remained that of a graceful and coloured surface for this thoughts and sensations. Below this were concealed, as pieces of unresolved matter, almost an irrelevancy, the plots of his novels, his knobbly or too smooth characters, and his thoughts which he had never the courage to face. What he achieved was more akin than anything else to what another foreigner, Mr. Joseph Conrad, has since achieved: a picturesque display of words, with something unspanned between the sense and the appearance. The other two Scots-English writers of the last half-century, John Davidson and James Thomson, the author of "The City of Dreadful Night", were greater men than Stevenson, less affected and more fundamental: but fundamental as they were, they lacked something which in English poetry is fundamental, and the oblivion into which they are fallen, undeserved as it seems when we consider their great talents, is yet, on some ground not easy to state, just. The thing I am examining here, superficial in appearance, goes deep. No writer can write great English who is not born an English writer and in

156

England; and born moreover in some class in which the tradition of English is pure, and it seems to me, therefore, in some other age than this. English as it was written by Bunyan or by Fielding can not be written now except by some one who like them has passed his days in a tradition of living English speech. A whole life went into that prose; and all that Stevenson could give to his was a few decades of application. And because the current of English is even at this day so much younger, poorer and more artificial in Scotland than it is in England, it is improbable that Scotland will produce any writer of English of the first rank, or at least that she will do so until her tradition of English is as common, as unforced and unschooled as if it were her native tongue.

Nor does this exhaust the possibilities, or impossibilities, of the Scottish manipulation of English. The superficially significant thing about Scottish writers is that they generally come from some humble rank of life; the superficially significant thing about English writers is that they come, as a rule, from some class cultivated, or with a tradition of culture. This difference is, taking a purely literary view, a matter of speech, but it is not entirely nor indeed chiefly so. What distinguishes the Scottish peasantry is not only its cradling in the dialect, but a whole view of life, a view of life intensely simple on certain great, human things, but naturalistic, perhaps in a certain sense materialistic. This simple vision of life, of life as a thing of sin and pleasure, passing, but passing with an intense vividness as of a flame, before something eternal, is the greatest thing which Scotland has given to the literature of the world. Everything which obscures the clearness of this vision, making it less simple than itself when it is most simple, is antagonistic to the Scottish genius; and here, and here only, in defence of their naturalism, of this terrific, sad and simple vision of life, the Scots are iconoclasts, and contemptuous of the thing called culture or humanism which in other lands has has such glorious fruits. Knox expressed the national temper when, disdainfully asserting that the image of the Madonna was only "a bit painted wuid", he threw it into the sea; and Carlyle repeated it on a grand scale in his Dumfriesshire judgments on all the figures which the culture of the West gave into his hands. Carlyle, in genius one of the greatest of all the writers born in Scotland, was in attainment one of the most patchy and immature, simply because he constantly passed judgments on men and cultures foreign to him; judgments which of Scotsmen and Scots culture would have been true, but which of them were valid perhaps only on some intensely human plane, and on every other absurd.

This sense of life and death, of pleasure and sin, of joy and loss, not thrown out lavishly into all the manifestations of life as Shakespeare threw them out, but intensified to one point, to the breaking point where a flame springs forth: that is the sense which has inspired the greatest Scottish poetry: the poetry of Burns, the poetry of the ballads. Burns, it is true, was more nearly than any other Scottish poet a humanist, and had more than any other a delight in the variety of life; but when he was greatest he came to simplicity, that simplicity of stark, fundamental human things which the ballads more perfectly than any other poetry express. He is not greatest in lines, magical as they are, such as

> Yestreen when to the trembling string
> The dance gaed through the lighted ha',

but in

> And sae I sat, and sae I sang,
>   And wistna o' my fate,

or in

> We twa hae paidl'd in the burn
>   Frae morning sun to dine,
> But seas between us braid hae roared
>   Sin' auld lang syne,

or in

> And I will luve thee still, my dear,
>   Though a' the seas gang dry.

The unquenchability of desire, the inexorability of separation, the lapse of time, and all these seen against something eternal and as if, expressed in a few lines, they were what human beings have felt from the beginning of time and must feel until time ends: these things, uttered with entire simplicity, are what at its best Scottish poetry can give us, and it can give them with the intensity and the inevitability of the greatest poetry. The ballads go immediately to that point beyond which it is impossible to go, and touch the very bounds of passion and of life; and they achieve great poetry by an unconditionality which rejects, where other literatures use, the image. In no poetry, probably, in the world is there less imagery than in the ballads. But this, once more, is not the sign of poetic debility, but of a terrific simplicity and intensity, an intensity which never loosens into reflection; and reflection is one of the moods in which images are given to the mind. There is nothing in the ballads but passion, terror, instinct, action: the states in which soul and body alike live most intensely; and this accounts for the impression of full and moving life which, stark and bare as they are, they leave with us. It is this utter absence of reflection which distinguishes them also from the English ballads, not only from those surrounding the name of Robin Hood, which are nothing but simple folk-art, but from really beautiful English ballads such as "The Unquiet Grave". There are several Scottish ballads containing, like it, a dialogue between two lovers, the one living and the other dead; but there is none which treats the subject in this way:

> The wind doth blow to-day, my love,
> And a few small drops of rain;
> I never had but one true love;
> In cold grave she is lain. . . .

> 'Tis down in yonder garden green,
> Love, where we used to walk,
> The finest flower that ere was seen
> Is withered to a stalk.

> The stalk is withered dry, my love,
> So will our hearts decay;
> So make yourself content, my love,
> Till God calls you away.

That is beautfiul, and as poetry as perfect in its way as anything in the Scottish ballads; but what a difference there is in spirit and in atmosphere. Here there is retrospection and resignation; but there only the present, the eternal present, and the immediate acceptance of it, exist, and we never escape from the unmixed joy, the absolute pain. There is philosophy in "The Unquiet Grave", the quality of a great reflective poetry; there is morality in it, the inescapable ethical sense of the English, and that feeling of ultimate surrender which goes always with a genuine morality. But see with what a total lack of moral compensation, or of moral bluntening, or of resignation, or of alleviation—with what a lyrical and unconditional passion the same theme is treated in a great Scottish ballad, in "Clerk Saunders":

> "Is there ony room at your head, Saunders?
>   Is there ony room at your feet?
> Or ony room at your side, Saunders,'
>   Where fain, fain wad I sleep?
>
> "There's nae room at my head, Marg'ret,
>   There's nae room at my feet'
> My bed it is fu' lowly now,
>   Amang the hungry worms I sleep."

Or, almost as simple and great:

> "O cocks are crowing on merry middle earth,
>   I wot the wild fowls are boding day;
> Give me my faith and troth again,
>   And let me fare me on my way."
>
> "Thy faith and troth thou sallna get,
>   And our true love sall never twin,
> Until ye tell what comes o' women,
>   I wot, who die in strong traivelling?"

I do not wish to make any comparison between these two poems, both great in their kind, or to praise one at the expense of the other. I wish merely, what is infinitely more important, to make clear what are the peculiar attributes of the Scottish ballads, and what it is that they have given to the poetry of the world. And it is pre-eminently this sense of immediate love, terror, drama; this ecstatic living in passion at the moment of its expression and not on reflection, and the experiencing of it therefore purely, as unmixed joy, as complete terror, in a concentration on the apex of the moment, in a shuddering realization of the moment, whatever it may be, whether it is

> I wish that horn were in my kist,
>   Yea, and the knight in my arms neist.

or

> And I am weary o' the skies
>   For my love that died for me.

or

> Yestreen I made my bed fu' braid,

160

The night I'll make it narrow.

or

> This ae nighte, this ae nighte,
> Everie nighte and alle,

> Fire and sleete and candle lighte,
> And Christe receive thy saule.

This world in which there is no reflection, no regard for the utility of action, nothing but pure passion seen through pure vision, is, if anything is, the world of art. To raise immediate passion to poetry in this way, without the alleviation of reflection, without the necromancy of memory, requires a vision of unconditional clearness, like that of a child; and it may be said of the Scottish ballad-writers that they attained poetry by pure, unalleviated insight, by unquestioning artistic heroism; and this quality it is that, in the last analysis, makes the very greatest poetry great, that makes "Lear" great, and "Antony and Cleopatra". In Shakespeare and in Dante it is united with other qualities through which its utterance becomes infinitely various and rich: in the greatest of the Scottish ballads there is this quality, and this alone. This, and not the occasional strangeness of their subject matter, is what gives them their magic, a magic of ultimate simplicity, of supernatural simplicity, as in

> O they rade on, and farther on,
> And they waded rivers abune the knee,
> And they saw neither sun nor moon
> But they heard the roaring of the sea.

from "Thomas the Rhymer". Or, from "Tam Lin".

> About the dead hour o' the night
> She heard the bridles ring.

There is here nothing but final clearness of vision which finds of itself, as by some natural, or rather, supernatural, process, an absolute reality of utterance which does not need the image. The thing is given in the ballads and not a simile either illuminating or cloaking it; and this absence of the image has in itself an artistic value, and produces an effect which can not be produced in any other way; it makes the real form and colour of things stand out with distinctness which is that, not of things seen by daylight, but those, more absolute, more incapable of being

161

questioned, which we see in dreams. When a colour is set before us in the ballads it has a reality which colour has not in poetry where imagery is used; it has not merely a poetic value, it has the ultimate value of pure colour. This is the reason why the ballad of "Jamie Douglas" gives us an impression of richness as of some intricate tapestry, though the means are as simple as

> When we cam' in by Glasgow toun
> We were a comely sicht to see;
> My Love was clad in the black velvét,
>   And I mysel' in cramasie,

or

> I had lock'd my heart in a case o' gowd
> And pinn'd it wi' a siller pin.

There the qualities of the velvet, the crimson, the gold and silver are seen as they are only seen in childhood, for the first time, and with something solid in the vision of them; something which we have perhaps for ever lost, and which the painters of our day, with their preoccupation with volume, are trying to rediscover; but which was given to the ballad-writers by the sheer unconditionality of their vision, and by that something materialistic in the imagination of the Scots which is one of their greatest qualities.

The art of these ballads may appear to us untutored, rough, falling occasionally into absurdities, and, regarding such things as diction and rhyme, showing a contempt for the perfection towards which all art necessarily strives. but the more we study them the more astonished we must become at their perfection on another side: that completeness of organic form which makes each an economically articulated thing. There is, it is true, a sort of logic of ballad-writing, a technique of repetition, of question and answer, not difficult to handle and handled in some of the ballads far too freely; but in the greatest, in "Clerk Saunders", "May Colvin", "The Lass of Lochroyan" and "Sir Patrick Spens", the technique is fused in the inevitability of the movement from beginning to end, so that one can see them in one glance as one sees a short lyric. The sensation which these give us is the sensation which can only be given by great conscious art. It is not a matter of the compulsory unity which folk-ballads, sung before a company, must have: for that one need only go to the

English ballads about Robin Hood, ballads definitely beneath the level of poetry, which can run on in the style of

> The King cast off his coat then,
> A green garment he did on,
> And every knight had so, i-wis,
> They clothéd them full soon,

for as long as one likes. the difference between that and

> The King sits in Dunfermline toun
> Drinking the blude-red wine

is the difference between a thing seen and shaped by a company of common men in a jovial mood, and a thing seen and shaped by a great spirit, lifted up on the wings of imagination. All these English ballads are timid, ordinary, and have the mediocre happy ending which crowds love. For example, three of Robin Hood's followers, we are told, go down to London, cast themselves on the King's mercy and nevertheless are condemned to death: they are reprieved at the last moment by the Queen. This would not happen in a great Scottish ballad. Johnnie Armstrong, in the ballad of that name, puts himself in the power of the Scots King, and he, too, is condemned to die, but there is no reprieve. The difference in treatment between the two episodes is the difference once more between great poetry, imagined by a heroic and sincere spirit, and second-rate folk-poetry, recounted by good-natured and insincere men. In the ballads of Robin Hood we are not told, as we are in the Scottish, what must happen, the circumstances being such and such; we are told what the ballad-makers wish to happen. The vulgarity of the happy ending, which has disfigured so much of the greatest English imaginative literature since, making it less great than it should have been, is already full-fledged here. I say vulgarity, for the fault of the happy ending is that it is vulgar; it is a descent from the level of aesthetic vision where tragedy is bearable to that of our ordinary wishes, where it is not; a complete betrayal of truth and beauty at the bidding of an impulse perfectly natural and perfectly common. This surrender negates form by its own spirit, just as the unflinching grasp of aesthetic vision holds and fulfils the form. The dependence of style upon this thing is in poetry absolute; and it is by virtue of their spirit, and because they are conceived and executed entirely on the level of aesthetic vision, that the Scottish ballads are opulent in examples of great form and great style, as, to quote an example of both:

> Why does your brand sae drop wi' blude,
>   Edward, Edward?
> Why does your brand sae drop wi' blude,
>   And why sae sad gang ye, O?
>
> O I hae kill'd my hawk sae gude,
>   Mither, mither;
> O I hae kill'd my hawk sae gude,
>   And I hae nae mair but he, O.

To write poetry such as that, not only an exquisite sense of form was needed, but a great and sincere spirit, an elevated and intrepid mind.

Looking back on that tremendous world mirrored in the Scottish ballads, one is tempted to exclaim, What a culture there must have been once in that narrow tract of land between Edinburgh and the Border, and what a tragedy it was that its grand conception of life and death, of time and eternity, realized in pure imagination, was turned by Knox and the Reformation into a theology and a set of intellectual principles! But Knox's work has been done; it has not been undone; and time alone will show whether it ever will be. Certainly only a people who saw life so intensely as a matter of sin and pleasure, of sin in pleasure and pleasure in sin, could have accepted with such passion a theology which saw life as a thing of transgression and damnation. There is somthing unswerving and, however we may dislike and deplore it, heroic, in the theology as well as the poetry of Scotland. A burning contemplation of things which take men beyond time made her equally the destined victim of Calvinism and the chosen land of the ballads. But of that national tragedy it is idle now to speak. To those, however, who deny that a poetry so immediate as that of Scotland, so entirely without reflection, can be great human poetry and of value in a world in which so much of the dignity of the life of men is involved in the fact that they are capable of reflection, one can only say that a mighty reflection, or rather something more than a reflection, is implied in the very spirit of the ballads, a reflection on supreme issues which is unerring and absolute and has come to an end; a reflection not tentative, not concerned with this or that episode in a poem, with this or that quality, moral or immoral, or with the practicality or impracticality of life but of life itself, finally and greatly; a reflection which is a living vision of life seen against eternity: the final reflection beyond which it is impossible for the human spirit to go. In the Scottish ballads life is not seen, as it is seen so often in English imaginative literature, as good and bad, moral or immoral, but on a greater and more intense level, as a vision of sin, tremendous, fleeting, always the same and always to be the same, set against some unchangeable thing. In this world, so clear is the full vision that pity is not a moral quality, but simply pity; passion not egoistic, but simply passion; and life and death have the greatness and simplicity of things comprehended in a tremendously spacious horizon. It is idle to attribute this simplicity, which is a capacity for seeing things as they are eternally, to the primitiveness of the existence which the ballads mirror. Life was at that time, as it has been always, complex, a mystery not easily to be pierced. If one wishes to see what mere simplicity without an over-powering vision of life seen *sub specie æternitatis* can do, one can go in any case to the folk-ballads surrounding Robin Hood. But the Scottish ballads have something which ordinary folk-poetry has not, that great quality, that magnanimity about life, inadequately called philosophic, which Arnold found in Homer.

Whether the Scottish genius will ever return to some modified form of the ballad as its preordained medium it is useless to consider to-day. Probably Scottish writers are fated hereafter to use English, and to use it, taking all things into account, not with supreme excellence. But it is difficult to avoid two conclusions: that the ballads enshrine the very essence of the Scottish spirit, and that they could have been written only in the Scottish tongue.

15

The Ballads*

Child's *Ballads* was first published between 1822 and 1896 in an edition limited to a printing of 1,000 sets, and has never been printed again until now. Perhaps out of piety to the author the reprint is a replica of the original; it has the drawback that the print is rather small for the overworked modern eye. But here is the work just as it first appeared, and it is still indispensable and still endlessly fascinating. Child's method is our guide to this day in dealing with the ballads. Further discoveries have been made since his great work appeared, new ballads and new versions of the known ones have come to light, but the excitement of discovery still breathes from his pages, and the sense of being the first in the field.

The majority of these ballads and most of the best are Scottish, and this may be due to the fact that the tradition of folk song lingered longer among the Scottish peasantry than the English, so that, half a century after Percy, Scott could still gather a new harvest of ballads for his *Minstrelsy of the Scottish Border*. Also, a great deal of Scottish poetry comes from the peasantry—one thinks of Burns and Hogg. So that while the ballads are almost lost in the rich variety of English poetry, in Scotland they are, perhaps, the main body of great verse, apart from the work of the Makars.

The world of the ballads is a world of pure passion and

* [Review of *English and Scottish Popular Ballads* edited by F.J. Child], *New Statesmen*, LII (9 February 1957), pp. 174-75.

absolute will and action, where love survives death and the lover cannot rest in the grave. It recognises three principalities which have power on the earth: Heaven, Hell, and Elfland. In the ballad of *Thomas the Rhymer* there is a geographical chart of the ballad landscape, showing "the path of righteousness', "the braid, braid road", and "the bonnie road that winds about the fernie brae". Elfland is a place of delight, but on a certain day one may be snatched from it to Hell. These beliefs were accepted for hundreds of years by the country people. They fell into occasional blunders: the widow's three dead sons come home, but though they come from Purgatory the sprays of birch on their hats grew on the banks of Paradise. Heaven and Purgatory and Hell the peasants accepted, as children of the Church; Elfland they must have kept as a secret world, until at last it dissolved into a fancy. Yet the persistence of Elfland is curious. Fairies were believed in by pious Christians less than a hundred years ago in the north of Scotland, and in some places are believed in still: in current Greek ballads lovers when they die still go where Eurydice went long before them.

The variety of ballad themes in every country is very striking. There is the riddling ballad where good luck or disaster, life or death, may depend on giving the right answer to an ambiguous question. It is found in many languages, and as Child points out, it goes back to Oedipus. There is again the ballad of the impossible demand:

> "Ye maun make me a Holland sark,
> Without ony stitching or needle wark.
> And yet maun wash it in yonder well,
> Where the dew never wat, nor the rain ever fell.
> And ye maun dry it upon a thorn
> That never budded sin Adam was born."

The strangeness of the questions transports us into a remote world; the answers can be found only by the Clever Lass. In India, Tibet, Persia, Turkey, old Russia and most of Europe, the Clever Lass seems to have been regarded as more quick-witted than the men, and the belief can still be found in some country places.

Harder to account for are the numerous ballads about the Elphin Knight who charms kings' daughters by the beauty of his singing, rides off with them, and then murders them. These ballads are mainly European and more widely diffused in the north than in the south. Sometimes the princess escapes by snatching the knight's sword and cutting off his head, or by pushing him into the sea when his back is turned; sometimes she is rescued by her brother; sometimes her brother arrives to avenge her after she is dead. This strange nightmare of the imagination must have been familiar for long to the peasantry of Europe. Yet the horror is relieved in some of the ballads by a wonderful touch of comedy. May Colven returns to her father's bower early in the morning after drowning her Elphin Knight, and is accosted by the parrot:

> Up then and spoke the pretty parrot:
> "May Colven, where have you been?
> What has become of the false Sir John,
> That woo'd you so late yestreen?"

> "O hold you tongue, my pretty parrot,
> Lay not the blame upon me;
> Your cup shall be of the flowered gold,
> Your cage of the root of the tree."

From his bed-chamber the king asks

> "What ails the pretty parrot,
> That prattles so long ere day?"

And the parrot answers

> "There came a cat to my cage door,
> It almost a worried me,
> And I was calling on May Colven
> To take the cat from me."

The parrot leads us back from the nightmare to the ordinary world; in the purely tragical ballads there is no place for these fancies.

The mark of the great ballads is their immediate grasp of passion and tragedy without reflection or moral comment. All is action and its tragic outcome, set down directly. The style of this poetry is as immediately recognisable as that of a great poet. It is not a popular style, but the style of a class, developed and perfected within ancient and strict boundaries: it is traditional. In the Scottish ballads, the style is very different

168

from that of Burns: it came from a folk imagination which had found an almost archetypal pattern where everything stood in its place as if it must remain there for ever. The pattern was so complete and so long established that it had no need to explain itself; it had passed beyond opinion. The imaginative pattern in turn dictated the patterned style, whose marks are brevity and direct statement:

> I wish that horn were in my kist,
> Yea, and the knight in my arms neist . . .

> But had I wist before I kissed
> That love had been sae ill to win,
> I had locked my heart in a case o' gowd
> And pinned it wi' a siller pin . . .

> "Tak hame your ousen, take hame your kye,
> For they hae bred our sorrow;
> I wiss that they had a' gane mad
> Whan they came first to Yarrow . . ."

The pattern of these poems is dialectical, and question and answer, even when they are equivocal, are accepted as soon as they are spoken. This is another way of saying that they are inevitable. Yet inevitable needs occasional relief, and the ballads find it now and then in one of those sudden inspired expansions of the theme which deliver us from the action. In *Sir Patrick Spens* we see nothing but the wintry setting out, "the auld moon wi' the new moon in her arm", the storm gathering, the ship sinking; and then—

> O lang, lang may the ladyes sit
> Wi' their fans into their hand,
> Before they see Sir Patrick Spens
> Come sailing to the strand.

> And lang, lang may the maidens sit
> Wi' their goud kaims in their hair,
> A'waiting for their ain dear loves,
> For them they'll see nae mair.

We are back in the greater world again, as we are when the parrot speaks. The art which could do such things was untutored, but never without pattern and style. Many of the lines are clumsy, almost ludicrous; it is always surprising to find what fine lines

169

there are in the poor ballads and what poor lines in the good.

We can trace the figures and stories used by poets in the ages of written work. We do not know, except conjecturally in a few cases, where the ballad themes came from. Who were the originals of the Clever Lass, the Elphin Knight, the Demon Lover, the Cruel Brother, the Cruel Mother, the Jealous Sister? Were there any origins for these figures, or are they to be taken as types that recur always in human life, living allegories? There are few historical figures, such as Jamie Douglas and the Earl of Moray. The ballad of *Sir Patrick Spens* is considered by some to commemorate a historical disaster, though Child doubts it. Yet even if in 1281 or 1290—the alternative dates—a ship was wrecked between Norway and Scotland, drowning the Scots lords, the ballad soon forgot it. The old women who still sang it a hundred years ago did not know anything about Alexander III of Scotland or the Maid of Norway. History, if it was really history, had receded to such a distance that nothing was left but the poetry. The transit of the ballad through so many generations gave it the distance which a conscious poet must achieve for himself. One can discern now and then in transmission the voice of some obscure individual genius speaking, but even that may be an illusion. There are versions of *May Colven* in which the parrot, which strikes one as an original invention, does not appear. But it seems pretty certain that the pattern—and the pattern is the main thing—was preserved by the peasant community itself.

The ballads—and the folk-songs—are distinguished from the rest of poetry in that the poet cannot be distinguished from the audience. The succeeding generations who preserved them knew nothing about poetry except that it came into their lives from the past as an inheritance. They received it and handed it on. In the transmission it changed, through carelessness or innovation. Child gives ten versions of *Sir Patrick Spens* and eight fragments from other versions. They are very unequal in quality. Poetry must have seemed to these peasants an integral part of their life, a thing without which life could not be natural and whole—not a rare and special delight which could be enjoyed only by a few. It embodied a tragic vision of life, and the figures in the tragedy were not peasants, but great representative figures, kings and knights and ladies, as they are in Shakespeare. The folk-songs provided the comedy and pathos, and were about the singers themselves. Universal education and the Open Society have driven this poetry away so far that it is almost impossible now to conceive of poetry as a natural activity; and it has become to us a miracle that poetry like the ballads should ever have existed.

16

Robert Henryson*

Henryson's poetry has two main virtues; one the property of his age, the other more specifically his own. The first is as important as the second. He lived near the end of a great age of settlement, religious, intellectual and social; an agreement had been reached regarding the nature and meaning of human life, and the imagination could attain harmony and tranquillity. It was one of those ages when everything, in spite of the practical disorder of life, seems to have its place; the ranks and occupations of men; the hierarchy of animals; good and evil; the earth, heaven and hell; and the life of man and of the beasts turns naturally into a story because it is part of a greater story about which there is general consent. Henryson, like Chaucer, exists in that long calm of storytelling which ended with the Renaissance, when the agreement about the great story was broken. There is still an echo of the tranquillity in Spenser. But in *The Faerie Queene* he deals with the delightful creatures of his fancy, and Chaucer and Henryson deal with men and women, wolves and sheep, cats and mice.

The virtue of the story while it lasted was that it made everything natural, even tragedy; so that while pity had a place, there was no place for those outcries against life which fill the tragic drama of the next age. The framework and the nature of the story excluded them. And the pity itself is different from that of the Elizabethans, as deep, but tranquillised by the knowledge

* From *Essays on Literature and Society* (London, 1949), pp. 7-19.

that tragedy has its place in the story. The poet accepts life, as the Elizabethans tried to do, but is also resigned to it; the acceptance implying the resignation, and the resignation the acceptance. This attitude makes the age between Chaucer and Henryson the great age of the story. The Elizabethan drama arose when the long peace of storytelling was broken.

The sense that all life, whether of the animals or of men, is a story and part of a greater story, is then one of the surviving virtues of Henryson's poetry, strong enough still, in spite of all that has happened since, to produce a composing effect on us and remind us of a standard of proportion which has been lost. It is the virtue of an age, not ours, and it required to embody it a particular form of art, not ours, and in the practice of that art Henryson was almost perfect.

> Upon ane tyme (as Esope culd Report)
> Ane lytill Mous come till ane Revir syde;
> Scho micht not waid, hir schankis were sa schort,
> Scho culd not swym, scho had na hors to ryde:
> Of verray force behovit hir to byde,
> And to and fra besyde that Revir deip
> Scho ran, cryand with mony pietuous peip.

We recognise the narrative art of an age, which passed with that age. In Henryson what delights us is the perfection with which it is controlled, its speed, which is neither hurried nor lumbering, and the momentary touches of humour and fancy which, while never retarding the story, give it interest and vivacity: "Scho culd not swym, scho had na hors to ryde."

Henryson's personal contribution to that consummate art was a fanciful eye for detail and a profound sense of situation, most usually comic, but in one or two cases tragic. *The Moral Fabillis of Esope the Phrygian* is his great humorous, and *The Testament of Cresseid* his great tragic work. During the last century *The Fables* have been overshadowed by *The Testament*, and their beauties neglected. But to appreciate the sweetness and harmony, the endlessly lively and inventive quality of Henryson's poetry, it is necessary to know them both; otherwise he runs the danger of being considered a poet of moderate capacity who, by a piece of good luck, wrote one great poem.

Most of the fables, though not all, are humorous. Henryson's humour is not quite like anything else in Scottish literature,

173

more subtle and pervasive than the humour of Dunbar or Burns or Scott, more urbane, more indirect, less specialised, and saturated with irony. It is an assumption more than anything else; it remains implicit in the selection of detail and the choice of expression, and rarely comes to the point of statement. The fables transport us into a mood in which we see everything as Henryson sees it, with the same tender ironical humour, but without being able to explain very clearly how the mood has been induced. His sense of the ridiculous is so delicate and exact that the faintest emphasis is sufficient to indicate it, and more than the faintest would distort it. His more obvious strokes of humour, therefore, do not represent him best; as, for instance, when the fox kills a young lamb at Lent, dips it in the stream, and fishes it out, crying: "'Ga doun schir Kid, cum up schir salmond agane.'" The quality which transmutes these fables and our mood as we read them is less obvious and more delicate, and consists in a fine decorative sense of the absurd. We find it in the account of the Burgess Mouse, on her way to visit her sister in the country:

> Bairfute, allone, with pykestaf in hir hand,
> As pure pylgryme scho passit out of town,
> To seik hir sister baith oure daill and down.

We find it in the lament of Pertok the hen for Chanteclere carried of by the fox:

> "Allace," quod Pertok, makand sair murning,
> With teiris grit attour hir cheikis fell;
> "Yone wes our drowrie, and our dayis darling,
> Our nichtingall, and als our Orloge bell,
> Our walkryfe watche, us for to warn and tell
> Quhen that Aurora with hir curcheis gray
> Put up hir heid betwix the nicht and day.
>
> "Quha sall our lemman be? quha sall us leid?
> Quhen we ar sad, quha sall unto us sing?
> With his sweit Bill he wald brek us the breid.
> In all this warld wes thair ane kynder thing?
> In paramouris he wald do us plesing,
> At his power, as nature did him geif.
> Now eftir him, allace, how sall we leif?"

In this passage Henryson's sense of the ridiculous is touched with pity, as it often is, and the pity with fantasy. The pity is

174

real, but as we feel it we smile at it, yet without thinking the less of it. The touches in these verses are exquisite:

> Our nichtingall, and als our Orloge bell, . . .
> With his sweit Bill he wald brek us the breid. . . .
> In all this warld wes thair ane kynder thing? . . .

These felicitous inventions run through *The Fables* and give the dry stories their delightful life. They stray even into the Moralitas with which each fable ends. These little sermons have been blamed for their dullness, but one suspects that in many of them Henryson retains his irony. It is difficult to believe that a man with such a fine sense of the ridiculous could have written without knowing what he was doing, "The hennis are warkis that ffra ferme faith proceidis", at the end of a fable where hens and various beasts play their part. And the more serious of the Moralitas have a sincerity that is far from dullness.

The allegory is a form which the modern taste finds stilted and unreal, because the great story as Chaucer and Henryson knew it is dead. But while that story lasted the allegory was a perfectly natural convention—the most convenient device for telling it. *The Fables* belong to that modest kind of allegory which finds in the lives of the animals a pattern of human life. It has obvious merits; it simplifies life; it so reduces the dimensions of the human situation that we can easily grasp them; it divests the characters of all adventitious pomp and glory, as well as of all that passes in our time under the name of ideology; it lays bare with a force beyond the reach of literary naturalism the solid egoistic motives of action. This is doubtless what once made it such a popular and democratic form of art.

But in Henryson it assumes virtues of a rarer kind. Human snobbishness becomes touching and forgivable to him when he finds it in the Burgess Mouse. The crimes of the Fox and the Wolf become imaginatively comprehensible, and to that extent excusable, since all the animals act in accordance with their nature. The result is that the animal allegory, when it is not employed satirically, runs the danger of making us indiscriminately indulgent to all the faults and crimes of mankind; and the more lively the imagination of the poet, the more completely he enters into the nature of his allegorical

175

characters, the Lion, the Wolf, the Fox, the Cat, the greater this
danger becomes. So the fable has to be followed by the
Moralitas, that human proportion may be preserved.

There are one or two fables in which Henryson achieves a
profound effect of tragedy and pity, and moves us quite
differently. An instance is *The Preiching of the Swallow*. It is
distinguished from the other fables by the solemnity of the
opening:

> The hie prudence, and warking mervelous,
> The profound wit of God omnipotent,
> Is sa perfyte, and sa Ingenious,
> Excellend ffar all mannis Jugement;
> For quhy to him all thing is ay present,
> Rycht as it is, or ony tyme sall be,
> Befoir the sicht off his Divinitie.

The argument proceeds in this vein to the conclusion "That
God in all his werkis wittie is." The seasons are advanced in
illustration of this, and Henryson describes how he walked out
on a spring day to watch the labourers in the fields; and
thereupon he suddenly comes upon the tragic theme of the
poem. A flock of birds alights on a hedge near by; they are
having a loud dispute with a Swallow, who has been warning
them of their danger.

> "Schir Swallow" (quod the Lark agane) and leuch,
> "Wuhat haif ye sene that causis yow to dreid?"
> "Se ye yone Churll" (quod scho) "beyond yone pleuch,
> Fast sawand hemp, and gude linget seid?
> Yone lint will grow in lytill tyme in deid,
> And thairoff will yone Churll his Nettis mak,
> Under the quhilk he thinkis us to tak.
>
> "Thairfoir I rede we pas quhen he is gone,
> At evin, and with our naillis scharp and small
> Out off the eirth scraip we yone seid anone,
> And eit it up, ffor, giff it growis, we sall
> Haif caus to weip heirefter ane and all."

In June Henryson walks out agin "Unto the hedge under the
Hawthorne grene" and the birds come and resume their
dispute. The Swallow cries:

> "O, blind birdis! and full of negligence,
> Unmyndful of your awin prosperitie,

Lift up your sicht, and tak gude advertence;
Luke to the Lint that growis on yone le;
Yone is the thing I bad forsuith that we,
Quhill it wes seid, suld rute furth off the eird;
Now is it Lint, now is it hie on breird.

"Go yit, quhill it is tender and small,
And pull it up; let it na mair Incres;
My flesche growis, my bodie quaikis all,
Thinkand on it I may not sleep in peis. . . .

"The awner off yone lint ane fouler is,
Richt cautelous and full off subteltie;
His pray full sendill tymis will he mis,
Bot giff we birdis all the warrer be;
Full mony off our kin he hes gart de,
And thocht it bot ane sport to spill thair blude;
God keip me ffra him, and the halie Rude."

The lint ripens and is gathered and spun into thread, and the net is woven for the fowler's use. Winter comes; the fowler clears a place in the snow and strews chaff on it to attract the birds, and while they scrape and scratch he throws the net over them.

Allace! it was grit hart sair for to se
That bludie Bowcheour beit thay birdis doun,
And ffor till heir, quhen thay wist weill to de,
Thair cairfull sang and lamentatioun:
Sum with ane staf he straik to eirth on swoun:
Off sum the heid he straik, off sum he brak the crag,
Sum half on lyve he stoppit in his bag.

The poem produces a strong feeling of approaching danger and of a blindness that no warning can pierce. It is filled with pity and a sort of second-sight which makes one think of Cassandra:

"This grit perell I tauld thame mair than thryis;
Now ar thay deid, and wo is me thairfoir!"

There is an echo of the last line in *The Testament of Cresseid*.

The continuous interest and liveliness of the detail makes *The Fables* one of the most delightful books in Scottish literature. Detail is a matter of invention, an imaginative conclusion from the facts given; it creates the body of the story, which otherwise would be a mere bare framework. Situation is an imaginative conclusion of a greater scale, and gathers up a larger number and variety of elements. Henryson's genius is shown in his invention in both kinds, and *The Testament of Cresseid* is his great achievement in situation. It seems to have been his own invention purely; Mr. Harvey Wood in his consummate edition of Henryson implies it, and Sir Herbert Grierson is of the same opinion. "It was no light thing", he says, "to come after Boccaccio and to succeed in making a real addition to a great dramatic story, something that without needless challenging of comparison does, in its impressive way, complete that tragic tale."

In his essay Sir Herbert speculates on the reason why Henryson should have been moved to add to a tale already accepted, and in the course of doing so he says the best things that have yet been said about the poem. "Chaucer had, in his courtly and detached manner, avoided any moral judgment upon Cresseid . . . . The only moral which he will enforce at the end of the whole tale is the religious one—that all earthly things are vanity. . . . but Henryson is not content with what, after all, is an evasion— he, a Scot and a Schoolmaister, with a Scot's and a schoolmaster's belief in retribution. The result might have been disastrous—a dry or piously unreal didactic poem. But it is not, and that for two reasons. In the first place, Henryson retains Chaucer's sympathy with Cresseid. . . . In the second place, his morality is sound and sincere, not the preacher's conventional acceptance of standards which he has not made his own. For the retribution which overtakes Cresseid in the poem is the retribution of her own heart. . . . It is not the leprosy we think of as her penalty but the last encounter with Troilus and its reaction on her soul." And Sir Herbert goes on to say that when the poem ends it has produced "a real *catharsis* leaving us at peace with Cresseid as Chaucer's poem scarcely does".

There is only one thing in this criticism with which one is tempted to disagree. I mean the assumption that Scots and schoolmasters have a belief in retribution stronger than that of Italians and Englishmen and playwrights, that Henryson was the retributive kind of Scotsman and schoolmaster, and that the spirit of the poem is in any sense a spirit of retribution. It is filled with pity. Indeed what Sir Herbert brings out so convincingly is that the poem is a more humanly satisfying end to the story than either of the earlier versions had provided, and exhibits a profound humanity which will not rest content with anything less, as the crown of the story, than a genuine reconciliation of

178

the heart. In seeking this reconciliation through retribution Henryson was no more peculiarly Scottish than in refraining from doing so Chaucer was peculiarly English, or Boccaccio peculiarly Italian. This is not a matter of nationality. It would be superfluous to labour the point if there were not a sort of conspiracy to make Henryson a bleak and harsh writer, if Miss Agnes Mure Mackenzie had not called *The Testament* stern, and other critics had not cited it as a proof that the Scots have always been dour and harsh in their human judgements. As well call Dante harsh for his treatment of Francesca, or Shakespeare dour for having Desdemona and Cordelia murdered.

The keynote of the poem is sympathy, as Sir Herbert Grierson points out, not judgment, though its theme is judgment. But the judgment is transformed when it is accepted by Cresseid in a moment of realisation; and that, indeed, is what brings about the reconciliation of which Sir Herbert speaks. Henryson's humanity is clear from the beginning of the poem; perhaps indeed humanity is a better word to describe his temper than sympathy: a humanity so simple that it needs only the most ordinary words to give it utterance, the more ordinary the better. He sees misfortune, not guilt, in Cresseid's conduct after she was turned away by Diomede:

> Than desolait scho walkit up and doun,
> And sum men sayis into the Court commoun.

He pities her "mischance" when she was forced to

> go amang the Greikis air and lait
> Sa gigotlike, takand thy foull plesance!
> I have pietie thou suld fall sic mischance.

He interposes his charity between her and her accusers:

> Yit nevertheless quhat ever men deme or say
> In scornefull langage of thy brukklines,
> I sall excuse, als far furth as I may,
> They womanheid, they wisdome and fairnes;
> The quhilk Fortoun hes put to sie distres
> As hir plesit, and nathing throw the gilt
> Of the, throw wickit langage to be split.

He attributes Cresseid's misfortunes and faults to chance, and

179

absolves her of all guilt; and this is the assumption running through the poem. He does not bring her to judgment, as some critics have implied; he shows the judgment of fate and of her own heart overtaking her. His humanity in dealing with her is perfectly simple, but its simplicity contains this surprise.

It is this simple and yet surprising humanity that brings about the finest effects of style in the poem; I mean those lines which seem at once the result of exquisite poetic judgment and of a humanity so obvious that it has become sure of itself and seizes at once the ultimate situation, formulating it in the fewest possible words, words which seem just adequate and no more, and in that appear to achieve a more secure finality: all that might have been said being made superfluous by the few simple words that are said. When Cresseid is stricken with leprosy and goes to her father for comfort, Henryson leaves one line to tell of their grief: "Thus was thair cair aneuch betwix thame twane." In Cresseid's Complaint one line suffices to draw the contrast between her present and her former condition: "Quhair is thy Chalmer wantounlie besene?" The incident of Troilus' meeting with her at a corner as he returns to Troy from fighting the Greeks is itself a compressed summary of the tragic situation, and is contained in three lines:

> Than upon him scho kest up baith hir Ene,
> And with ane blenk it come into his thocht,
> That he sumtime hir face befoir had sene.

When she is told by her companions who it was that stopped beside her and threw a purse of gold in her lap, she compresses her fault into the cry: "O fals Cresseid and trew Knicht Troilus!" Troilus, after hearing of her misfortunes and her death, seems again to be saying all that can be said when he exclaims:

> "I can no moir.
> Scho was untrew, and wo is me thairfoir."

The epitaph which he inscribes on her tomb is in the same high concise style:

> Lo, fair Ladyis, Crisseid, of Troyis toun,
> Sumtyme countit the flour of Womanheid,
> Under this stane lait Lipper lyis deid.

No other Scottish poet has risen to this high and measured style,

180

and Henryson himself does not attain it often, though he does as often as the subject requires it. Yet it is a style which one would have expected to suit the Scottish genius, with its seriousness and its love of compressed utterance. And that it does suit that genius is proved by Scottish folk-poetry, and particularly by the Ballads, with their complete seriousness and their extreme compression. But this gift, which belongs to the Scottish people, ceased after Henryson to belong to Scottish poets. Seriousness, though not compression, went for a long time into theology, a theology which was never more than mediocre. To the poet was left only a sort of secondary, official seriousness, that of "Man was made to mourn" and "But pleasures are like poppies spread." The Scottish poets followed the tradition of Dunbar, who expressed the exuberance, wildness and eccentricity of the Middle Ages, not that of Henryson, who inherited the medieval completeness and harmony, and the power to see life whole, without taking refuge in the facetious and the grotesque. Yet Henryson embodies more strikingly than any poet who has lived since the fundamental seriousness, humanity and strength of the Scottish imagination.

181

17

Robert Burns*

"Few men had so much of the poet about them," said the father of Alan Cunningham, "and few poets so much of the man: the man was probably less pure than he ought to have been, but the poet was pure and bright to the end." It is the only humane judgment passed on Burns by a contemporary: all the others have a touch of cant in them, something morally or socially superior. The most dully respectable circle in literary history sat and watched Burns in his sober hours, driving him regularly to the extreme where goodfellowship was not very strongly flavoured with decency. The goodness of his father early drew to the house people with an affectation of deliberate virtue. It attracted the pious Murdoch, the model dominie, who loved to recollect in after years the admonitions he had given to genius. Later Burns, now a young man, was permitted for a time to breathe the musty controversial air of liberal theology as it was propounded in his county, and he found it so good that he was moved to poetry. This was, however, his only experience of emancipated society. His fame and his journey to Edinburgh again enveloped him in the stupendous Scots respectability of that time; the elegant and priggish minister Blair, the virtuous and respectable Dugald Stewart, "the historian Robertson", sat beside him wondering visibly whether their young genius would become a really respected poet and a prosperous and godly farmer. Their society must occasionally have appeared to

* *Freeman,* VII (9 May 1923), pp. 202-4.

him like the reading of an interminable, dull tract. But indeed his educated friends, except for one or two women, had only virtue to recommend them, while his boon companions were equally without sense and sensibility. In spite of a lifelong desire for friends, he found only moralists and tipplers; and although he could move these by the astonishing spectacle of his thoughts and passions, so that when he spoke from his heart they wept, he received nothing back from them to give him happiness, nor, except in states of drunken effusion, any direct human comprehension. As his life grew poorer he turned to these states more and more rather than to the intelligent men of virtue who had less than nothing to give him, and who gave grudgingly.

It was after his visit to Edinburgh that his nature, strongly built and normal, disintegrated. He had hoped, in meeting the first shock of his astonishing triumph in the capital, that an escape was at last possible from the life of hardly maintained poverty which as a boy he had foreseen and feared. He left Edinburgh recognising that there was no reprieve, that hardship must sit at his elbow to the end of his days. Fame had lifted him up on the point of an immense pinnacle; now the structure had melted away and, astonished, he found himself once more in his native county, an Ayrshire peasant. Some fairy had set him for a little in the centre of a rich and foreign society; then calmly and finally, she had taken it from under his feet. There is hardly another incident in literary history to parallel this brief rise and setting of social favour, and hardly one showing more the remorselessness of fortune in the world. The shock told deeply on Burns, working more for evil than the taste for dissipation which he was said to have acquired from the Edinburgh aristocracy. His character gradually fell to pieces. The more narrowly decent want constrained him, the more he took to the drink; yet to the last a little good fortune was sufficient to set him back for a time in a self-respecting life. Sometimes the recognition of his degradation aroused in him a violent, almost suicidal remorse. While drinking one afternoon with a friend he was advised a little officiously to be "temperate in all things". At that he started up, drawing his sword, but immediately afterwards threw it away and dashed himself in a fit of shame on the floor. Such an extreme betrayal of himself showed the extent of his pride and the degree in which he had offended it, and in offending it had come to despise himself.

He desired above all things to love and to be loved, yet it is doubtful whether once in his life he had a deep and sincere passion. His imagination demanded something more than the dairy-maids and mason's daughters of his parish could give him; but when he dreamed of the Edinburgh women whom he was later to know, his realistic mind quickly cut the reverie short. But it was not only the imperfections of mason's daughters that kept him from loving; there was an obstacle also within himself, a thirst for love which probably no single love affair could have quenched, a too great desire to love which by its vehemence defeated itself. Before long he got into the habit of "battering himself into a warm affection," to use his own words. Yet libertine though he was in fact, he was anything but a libertine in nature. He could imitate the light seducer, but he could not lightly seduce. All his amours for the first and happier part of his life were attempts to experience, or to delude himself that he experienced, the kind of love for which he sought in vain all his life. In the last years of his life, his amours revenged themselves for their unsuccess, as such things normally do, by becoming mechanical.

He had experienced hardship, sufficient disappointment and indignity: the astonishing thing was that he remained the sanest of all poets, saner than Shakespeare or than Goethe. He had no Werther, and it was not within his power to feel or to conceive the deep disgust with life which Shakespeare uttered through Macbeth. Often he was dismayed with his own life, and had thoughts of putting an end to it; but something earthy was so strong and unquestioned in him that he was incapable of doubting the value of life itself. His hopelessness was never that of a hopeless man, but of one who, like his fellows, in the midst of discouragement, lives hoping. His sorrows were those of a naturally happy disposition; but they were probably on that account more poignant, for they sprang out with the unpremeditation of agonized surprise. He expressed again and again in his poetry the feeling of eternal separation and of irrevocable fate; but although he threw all his heart into the cry, there was something remaining, something solid and complete which brought him back again to himself. He had not that power, or that weakness, which enabled other poets to submerge themselves in an emotion, and become the passion which they felt; he was always in his poetry a man feeling love, grief or anger, and the man came as clearly through the words as the emotion. From this deep-rooted sanity, which was a sort of completeness, he could never be moved. It put a stamp on the smallest of his poems, and is still the thing by which we recognize him. It was what made him include in a love poem, and with perfect propriety, a verse such as this:

> I hae been blythe wi' comrades dear;
>   I hae been merry drinking;
> I hae been joyfu' gath'rin gear;
>   I hae been happy thinking:
> But a' the pleasures e'er I saw,
>   Tho' three times doubled fairly,
> That happy night was worth them a'
>   Amang the rigs o' barley.

He would bring the whole perspective of life into a verse, and thus give a wider and more human reality to the sentiment of a song than other poets could attain by letting themselves go to the final lengths of passion. His sense of completeness prevented him from writing of love in the void; his lovers were altogether in the world, and their love was, like everything else in the world, not immune from the reflections of comedy.

His vision of the world was unusually complete. Generally praised as a lyric poet, he was more truly a kind of dramatist. He expressed very seldom in his songs the emotions of Robert Burns, and when he expressed them, he often did it badly. "To Mary in Heaven" and "Man was made to Mourn", poems obviously composed under the stress of deep personal emotion, were among the worst he wrote, and had none of the absolute sureness of dramatic lyrics like "Tam Glen" or "Whistle and I'll come tae ye, my lad". In his songs he put himself in a certain attitude, or rather, a certain number of attitudes, and the voices which spoke through them were those of the entire Scots peasantry of his time. All his songs written for women were especially exquisite; in throwing the emotion of a woman into a song he did not once fail. But even in his songs for men the voice was not often Burns'; it was generally that of the ideal young Scots peasant who is one of his chief creations. He himself became this Scots peasant, generalizing himself in his race and in his class, and changing with the mood into "the rakish rook, Rob Mossgiel", the canny lover stealing away beyond the Lugar to his Nanie, the sober married man who "will take cuckold frae nane", the stiff-necked democrat pointing to "yon birkie ca'd a lord". So complete, so universal was he here that it may be said of him that he created the modern Scots peasant. He did not make the Scots peasantry any better morally, perhaps, but he gave them something which is more valuable than morality, an aesthetic consciousness of their joys and griefs, their nature and destiny, and left them with some added touch of humanity and of poise.

His songs showed this strong and true dramatic power; but its main achievement was "The Jolly Beggars." In spite of its bestiality (a word, as good as any other, which Arnold was to find for it a hundred years later) that poem was of all his works the most full of "the glory and the joy" which he found as he walked "Behind his plough upon the mountain side". He filled it with a sense of Bacchanalian ecstasy in which lust became a form of rapture, and every kind of freedom was possible; but all was seen with a sort of divine carelessness, with a charity which had become impartial. He indulged the flesh more riotously in "The Jolly Beggars" than any poet has done since; but also, "penetrating the unsightly and disgusting surfaces of things", he "unveiled with exquisite skill the finer ties of imagination and feeling"—one of the functions of poetry, as Wordsworth said. "It is the privilege of poetic genius," he said, writing about "Tam o' Shanter", "to catch, under certain restrictions of which perhaps at the time of its being executed it is but dimly conscious, a spirit of pleasure wherever it can be found—in the walks of nature, and in the business of men." Burns caught this "spirit of pleasure", and in a poem in which there was not a weak line, not an uncertain intonation, rendered it with a vigour and pliancy which must have astonished himself. He painted corruption in colours so festive and at the same time so objective, that his picture had not only a poetic, but a philosophic value.

In sense of life, in humour, in dramatic force and truth, in organic vigour of style, he was great; but his most divine power was probably that of putting into words more simple and unalterable than any others in Scots or English literature, emotions and thoughts felt by every one. In verses such as

> Thou'll break my heart, thou bonnie bird
> That sings beside they mate;
> For sae I sat, and sae I sang,
>   And wistna o' my fate,

or

> Had we never lov'd sae kindly,
> Had we never lov'd sae blindly,
> Never met—or never parted,
> We had ne'er been broken-hearted,

he found a simplicity more simple than that of Shelley's love lyrics or even than that of Wordsworth's verses on Lucy. Perhaps this simplicity was of a sort which men so cultivated as Shelley and Wordsworth could not have attained. Perhaps only in a great dialect language like the Scots could it have been expressed. It acquired its inevitability by virtue of that propriety of expression which was Burns' most perfect endowment, enabling him to describe what he chose in the best and fewest words; a tinker or a provincial beauty; a scene of devotion or a carousal.

He was much blamed for his faults while he lived, and he has been blamed more since; and the censure which during his life was mischievous, driving him to new excesses, has been since, one suspects, uttered more out of the critics' determination to produce the patents of their respectability than out of any deep detestation of Burns' vices, bad, no doubt, as these were. Coleridge called him "a degraded man of genius"; but it is doubtful whether Burns' vice was as demoralizing as Coleridge's respectability. Throughout the complete tragedy of his moral downfall, felt poignantly by himself, he maintained his integrity; and although he died at the age of thirty-seven of recurrent excesses and accumulated disappointment, his life was more dignified than Coleridge's: he did not compromise and deceive himself. More than any other poet of the last two centuries he has helped to humanize his own countrymen and the English-speaking peoples generally, and to instill into them not only a more sensitive manner of feeling, but also a more philosophic habit of thought. No one was better fitted than he for the task; no one was farther removed from all perversity of feeling, all singularity of thought. He was a norm of humanity, a model, in everything but his life, for all men. As a consequence there is no writer on whom the blame of succeeding generations lies more lightly; Burns will always be loved, except by a few timid Presbyterians like Stevenson, with a special, warm indulgence. This attitude is one of the lessons which his poems have taught mankind.

18

Burns and Holy Willie*

Mr. Ramsay MacDonald recently unveiled some new statuary in the Burns Mausoleum at Dumfries and made it the occasion for a speech. This event was not of any intrinsic importance, but it has considerable symbolic interest. The setting itself was involuntarily symbolic. The unveiling of the statuary took place in a churchyard; between one and two hundred people were gathered within the gates; outside were several thousands, some unemployed among them. When Mr. MacDonald started by addressing his audience as "friends", there were some jeers from the crowd outside, and shouts of "What about the means test?" But these interruptions soon subsided, and Mr. MacDonald succeeded in making a very long and very involved speech, after having released the Scottish Standard which draped the figure of Burns at the plough.

The symbolism implicit in this scene is quite casual and involuntary. The churchyard could hold only a certain number of people; the "platform party" (in Scotland one is always hitting against platform parties) was naturally chosen from the more well-to-do admirers of the poet: landlords, baronets, and officers in the British Army. Objectively one can see that, Scotland being what it is, a ceremony in honour of its greatest poet should take just this form and no other. But at the same time one is driven to ask what can have happened to Burns since his death to make him now the implicit property of the middle

* *Left Review*, II (November 1936), pp. 762-64.

and upper classes, when he was the property of the poor man at the beginning. This change may be briefly described by saying that Holy Willie, after being the poet's butt, has now become the keeper of his memory.

In "Holy Willie's Prayer" Burns uses words about his friend Gavin Hamilton which might have described himself:

> He drinks, an' swears, an' plays at cartes,
> Yet has sae mony takin' arts
>> Wi' great and sma',
> Frae God's ain priest and people's hearts
>> He steals awa'.
>
> An' when we chastened him therefor,
> Thou kens how he bred sic a splore,
> An' set the warld in a roar
>> O' laughing at us:—
> Curse Thou his basket an' his store,
>> Kail an' potatoes.

Burns set the world in a roar of laughing at the people who now unveil statuary in his honour. Why is it that they are so kind to his kail and potatoes?

One reason for this is that the figure of Burns has become quite vague, and that the vaguer he becomes the more universally he pleases his countrymen. His words no longer mean anything. When he makes Holy Willie say:

> O Thou, that in the heavens does dwell,
> What, as it pleases best Thysel',
> Sends ane to heaven and ten to hell,
>> A' for thy glory,
> And no for onie guid or ill
>> They've done afore Thee!

nobody stops to reflect that these words may have some relevance still, if not theologically, at least as a description of actual life; for the strength of Calvinism was that it did not ignore the facts of actual life, where one is saved and ten lost not for any good or ill they have done. The vagueness of Burns as a national symbol can be gathered best, however, from Mr. MacDonald's own words:

> Bare-footed, broken-hearted, baffled, thwarted, crucified by weaknesses, made all the more so [*more so what?*] on account of the unusual amount of the divine inspiration which he had, this

190

strange, complicated personality, torn hither and thither, who never sinned but who was his greatest and most ungenerous condemner of the sin, a man who knew good and evil, a man who never deceived himself, a man who asked all other men to be honest—God knows, if any man who ever breathed the breath of mortal life could lead the great pilgrimage of men who knew their shortcomings, but who had determined to be honest, Burns, by his life, by his confessions, by his tortures, by what he said and what he asked other people to benefit from [*what can that be?*], is entitled to be the leader of that honest pilgrimage of men.

This is perhaps the vaguest Burns we have yet had to swallow; but he was swallowed amid applause, according to the newspaper reports. This is because there is nothing left in him which could offend any taste, expensive or poor, except a taste in the slightest degree critical.

But to make Burns go down without a single thought of care something still more was needed, and Mr. MacDonald supplied that too:

They are quite right, those who say that Burns taught more effectively revolution than anybody who has tried on the same game in the world. But Burns's revolution was not a revolution of circumstances, which is futile; Burns's revolution was a revolution in soul, a revolution in being, a revolution in manliness, a revolution in humanity. And that, my friends, may be like the mills of God; it may "grind exceeding slow," but it is grinding, it is grinding, it is changing, it is changing fundamentally. It creates a new type of man, who can not only demand the rights of citizenship, but is prepared and is determined to exercise the duties and the responsibilities of citizenship at the same time.

The distinction in the last sentence should not be lost sight of; this new type of man shows no determination in *demanding* the right of citizenship, he merely *can* do so; all his determination comes into play when he contemplates his duties and responsibilities. To what party can this new type belong? And what part had Burns in its creation, when he started this revolution?

I think I have said enough to show that Burns has been unostentatiously but securely swallowed and digested by Holy Willie during the century and a bit since his death. Burns was not the revolutionist whom Mr. MacDonald makes him out to be, but he was an honest writer. And though he was a revolutionist, he showed his sympathy with the French Revolution in a quite practical way, without stopping to consider whether it was a mere revolution in circumstance or a revolution in soul. We cannot imagine the Burns whose statue Mr. MacDonald unveiled sending arms even to the constitutional government of Spain against the expressed wishes of the established order, as the living Burns did to the leaders of the French revolution against a similar prohibition. Something has happened to him since his death, and it is what happens to all writers after their death, no matter what they have written. It may not be true that all writers reflect the economic ideology of the society in which they live—I do not think it is—but it does seem to be true that their writings are finally and in the long run made to reflect that ideology, by a process of elimination and transformation, until the most influential classes in society can finally put their seal on the result. This necessity for social elimination and transformation probably accounts for Mr. MacDonald's sharply condemnatory but vague references to Burns's recent biographers (he could only have meant Mrs. Catherine Carswell's plain-spoken and entirely sympathetic *Life*). For an honest biography helps to destroy the imposed image and to undo the careful work of social transformation.

19

Burns and Popular Poetry*

For a Scotsman to see Burns simply as a poet is almost impossible. Burns is so deeply imbedded in Scottish life that he cannot be detached from it, from what is best in it and what is worst in it, and regarded as we regard Dunbar or James Hogg or Walter Scott. He is more a personage to us than a poet, more a figurehead than a personage, and more a myth than a figurehead. To those who have heard of Dunbar he is a figure, of course, comparable to Dunbar; but he is also a figure comparable to Prince Charlie, about whom every one has heard. He is a myth evolved by the popular imagination, a communal poetic creation, a Protean figure; we can all shape him to our own likeness, for a myth is endlessly adaptable; so that to the respectable this secondary Burns is a decent man; to the Rabelaisian, bawdy; to the sentimentalist, sentimental; to the Socialist, a revolutionary; to the Nationalist a patriot; to the religious, pious; to the self-made man, self-made; to the drinker, a drinker. He has the power of making any Scotsman, whether generous or canny, sentimental or prosaic, religious or profane, more whole-heartedly himself than he could have been without assistance; and in that way perhaps more human. He greases our wheels; we could not roll on our way so comfortably but for him; and it is impossible to judge impartially a convenient appliance to which we have grown accustomed.

The myth is unlike the man; but the man was its basis, and no

* From *Essays on Literature and Society* (London, 1949), pp. 57-63.

other could have served. We cannot imagine Wordsworth or Shelley or Tennyson or Shakespeare turning into a popular myth; and Burns did so because his qualities made it possible, and because he deserved it. No other writer has said so fully and expressly what every man of his race wanted him to say; no other writer, consequently, has been taken so completely into the life of a people. The myth may in some ways be absurd, but it is as solid as the agreement which rises in Scotsmen's minds whenever Burns utters one of his great platitudes:

"O wad some Pow'r the giftie gie us
To see oursels as ithers see us!"

"the hert aye's the part aye
    That makes us right or wrang."

"The best laid schemes o' mice and men
    Gang aft a-gley."

When the Burnsites are assembled on the Night, they feel Burns invisibly present among them as one of themselves, a great man who by some felicitous stroke has been transformed into an ordinary man, and is the greater because of it—a man indeed more really, more universaly ordinary than any mere ordinary man could ever hope to be. This feeling is a tribute to Burns' humanity; it is a claim to kinship; it is also a grateful recognition that here is a poet for everybody, a poet who has such an insight into ordinary thoughts and feelings that he can catch them and give them poetic shape, as those who merely think or feel them cannot. This was Burns' supreme art. It seems to be simple. People are inclined to believe that it is easier to express ordinary thoughts and feelings in verse than complex and unusual ones. The problem is an artificial one, for in the end a poet does what he has a supreme gift for doing. Burns' gift lay there; it made him a myth; it predestined him to become the Rabbie of Burns Nights. When we consider Burns we must therefore include the Burns Nights with him, and the Burns cult in all its forms; if we sneer at them, we sneer at Burns. They are his reward, or his punishment (whichever the fastidious reader may prefer to call it) for having had the temerity to express the ordinary feelings of his people, and for having become a part of their life. What the Burns Nights ignore is the perfection of

Burns' art, which makes him one of the great poets. But there is so much more involved than this, his real greatness, is scarcely taken into account.

Ordinary thoughts and feelings are not necessarily shallow, any more than subtle and unusual ones are necessarily profound. It may be said that Burns was never shallow and never profound. He did not have "Those thoughts that wander through eternity" which consoled Milton's Belial in Hell; and he could not be shallow as Tennyson sometimes was. He was sentimental, but sentimental with a certain solidity and grossness; there is genuine feeling behind his mawkishness, not merely a sick refinement of sensibility striving to generate the illusion of feeling. He could rise to the full height of the ordinary, where simplicity and greatness meet:

"Thou'll break my heart, thou bonie bird,
That sings beside they mate;
For sae I sat, and sae I sang,
And wist na o' my fate."

His rhetoric, his humour, his satire, his platitude have all the same solidity, the same devastating common sense. There is a great difference between *A Man's a Man for a' that* and

"Kind hearts are more than coronets,
And simple faith than Norman blood."

The one speaks positively to us; the other says nothing. Burns became as amorphous as a myth because he was as solid as a ploughman. He became legendary because he was so startlingly ordinary. He was the ordinary man for whom Scotland had been looking as it might have looked for a king; and it discovered him with greater surprise and delight than if it had found a king, for kings are more common. His poetry embodied the obvious in its universal form, the obvious in its essence and its truth, the discovery of which is one of the perennial surprises of mankind. If Burns' poetry had not been obvious, he could never have become the national poet of Scotland.

But the national poet of Scotland is too conventional a term for him; the poet of the Scottish people is better, for all claim him. And by the people I do not mean merely the ploughman and the factory worker and the grocer's assistant, but the lawyer, the business man, the minister, the bailie—all that large

195

class of Scotsmen who are not very interested in literature, not very cultivated, and know little poetry outside the poetry of Burns. It is these who have fashioned the popular image of Burns; and this is what really happens when a poet is taken into the life of a people. He moulds their thoughts and feelings, but they mould his too, sometimes long after he is dead. they make current a vulgarised image of him, and a vulgarised reading of his poetry; they take him into their life, but they also enter into his; and what emerges as the popular picture is a cross between the two. What is good in this bargain is self-evident—that the words and thoughts and feelings of a great poet become the common property of his people. The disadvantages I have tried to describe; they are natural and inevitable; compared to the single great advantage they do not matter very much, unless to those who cannot endure a normal dose of vulgarity. But they exist, and those who are advocating a more popular note in poetry at present should take them into account. For Burns is an object-lesson in what poetic popularity really means—the prime object-lesson in the poetry of the world, perhaps the unique instance.

It is good, then, that there should be "poetry for the people", as its advocates call it. But there is another side of the question, and I found it illustrated while turning over an old number of the *Criterion* the other day, and coming on an editorial note by Mr. T.S. Eliot. A letter by the Poet Laureate and his friends had appeared in *The Times* under the heading, "Art in the Inn". Mr. Masefield proposed making use of the country public-house for "verse-speaking, drama and readings of prose, and thus encouraging a wider appreciation of our language and literature in its highest forms". Mr. Eliot was disconcerted by this proposal, as a number of us would be; for he "had always thought of the public-house as one of the few places to which one could escape from verse-speaking, drama and readings of prose. If the public-house is to fall into the hands of the English Association and the British Drama League, where, one must ask bluntly, is a man to go for a drink?"

With this most people would agree; propaganda of this kind rests on a false basis; but Burns, at any rate, does not need it; when he is quoted or recited in pubs, the act is quite natural and spontaneous. But the more serious part of Mr. Eliot's comment comes later."I suspect that two distinct intentions, both laudable, have been confused. One is, that there should be a public for poetry. But what is important is not that this public should be large, but that it should be sensitive, critical and educated—conditions only possible for a small public. The other intention is, that people should be made happier, and be given the best life of which they are capable. I doubt whether poetry can be made to serve this purpose for the populace; if it ever does, it will never come as a result of centralised planning."

Now, when Mr. Eliot doubts "whether poetry can be made to serve this purpose" (of giving people the best life of which they are capable), he is evidently thinking of poetry as everyone who takes it seriously thinks of it; the poetry, to guess at his own tastes, of Dante, Shakespeare, Webster, Donne, Dryden, Baudelaire, the French Symbolists; but the list can be indefinitely extended, and for the genuine lover of poetry it will include Burns, shorn of his popularity, a name of the same kind as those other great names. If there is to be a public for these poets, and for what is good in the poetry of our own time, obviously Mr. Eliot is right in saying that it must be "sensitive, critical and educated"; for without such a public poetry could not be preserved, and its traditions would be lost. Mr. Eliot asserts that this public is bound to be small, and no doubt that is so; but there is a fringe surrounding it which is not small, a working liaison between the discriminating few and the undiscriminating mass. Nothing can be done by propaganda or organisation to extend that fringe; but by merely existing it produces an effect among the mass which is different from the effect produced by popular poetry; for it is qualitative. What the advocates of poetry for the public should aim at is the dissemination of a feeling for quality, not the production of poetry which will be read in greater and greater quantity. This cannot be done by propaganda for popular poetry; but a beginning might be made by reform of our schools, where poetry is so often "taught" in a way to make the pupil dislike it and misunderstand it.

Burns exists in both worlds—the world of quality and the world of quantity. The world of quantity has grown so powerful and established such a firm hold on him that it is difficult to extricate him from its grip. He has certainly fulfilled one of the

197

functions which Mr. Eliot doubted whether poetry could fulfil—"that people should be happier"; he has done much more than that; and what he has done is good beyond doubt, with this limitation which does not apply to other poets—that he has not brought poetry to people, but simply Burns. It may be that Burns is enough for many people who read him; but Shakespeare, or Milton, or Keats is not; to read one of them is to wish to read the others, and to discover poetry. Yet though Burns invisibly appears on Burns Nights, obedient to the summons, one feels that he too would have agreed with Mr. Eliot's opinion that the public for poetry should be "sensitive, critical and educated"; for he knew something by experience which his admirers do not know—the desire for perfection and the endless pains of the artist.

20

Robert Burns, Master of Scottish Poetry *

The movement which made Burns the acknowledged master of Scottish poetry was unlike any other in the history of Scottish literature. Time had prepared everything for it; two centuries of religious terrors had faded under the touch of reason and enlightenment, and the mysterious problems of election and damnation, riddles rather than problems to the new reason, had turned into amusing doggerel:

> O Thou, wha in the Heavens dost dwell,
> Wha, as it pleases best thysel'.
> Sends ane to heaven and ten to hell,
>   A' for thy glory,
> And no for any guid or ill
>   They've done afore thee!

Calvinism, once feared as a power or hated as a superstition, became absurd under the attack of common reason. The growing powers of the Enlightenment encouraged the change in the universities, the churches, in popular debate, and among the people. The ideas of liberty and equality did their part; Scotland became a place where a man was a man for a' that; the new humanistic attitude to religion led people to believe that "The hert's aye the pairt aye that maks us richt or wrang." The story of the Fall itself became a simple story of human misfortune to two young people whose intentions had been so good, "Lang syne, in Eden's bonnie yard".

* *Glasgow Herald* (24 January 1959), p. 6.

> Then you, ye auld sneck-drawing dog!
> Ye cam to Paradise incog.
> And played on man a cursed brogue
>   (Black be your fa!),
> An' gied the infant warld a shog,
>   Maist ruined a'.

Yet the new humanistic theology could not make Satan entirely to blame either.

> But fare ye weel, Auld Nickie Ben!
> O wad ye take a thought an' men!
> Ye aiblens might—I dinna ken—
>   Still hae a stake:
> I'm wae to think upo' yon den.
>   Ev'n for your sake!

Popular Scottish religious thought and the art of a great poet had brought Scottish poetry to this stage, and the poetry was a new poetry with a strong premeditated dash of the Enlightenment, something of Voltaire's contes and Bernard Shaw's plays. This poetry replaced for over a hundred years the traditional Scottish kind. But it held no key to the old Scottish poetry, and there was no way back.

Yet there were two Scottish poets, ten years younger than Burns, who wrote in a different mood and a different style during Burns's later years. They do not belong to the new poetry. And they give us a sense of what was lost by the new poetry when it was established. What was lost was the sense of the strange, a quality in which the old poetry, both simple and sophisticated, had been so rich. The settlements of the Enlightenment had been so conclusive that they left no room for wonder, except of the semi-official kind, which the solver of old riddles assumes in self-defence, when he finds that there is nothing in life which is simply strange. Hogg was not troubled by such second thoughts. He found it easy to describe that day late in the evening when Bonnie Kilmeny came home. Like his ancestors, Scott was attracted by what was remote and strange in the imagination, not by what was touching or pathetic (the mouse, the daisy), but rather

> The herring love the merrie munlight,
> And the macherel love the wind.

And he brought back Proud Maisie to ask her question for her.

> Proud Maisie is in the woods
>> Walking sae early.
> Sweet Robin sits in the bush
>> Singing sae rarely.
> "Tell me, thou bonny bird,
>> When shall I marry me?"
> "When six braw gentlemen
>> Kirkward shall carry ye."

It was a question that grew harder to ask as the new poetry got into its stride. The simply strange went out of Scottish poetry and was replaced for a while by pretended terrors; the old legends of witch-gatherings in the Scottish countryside had to stop at the amusing point, and the drunken farmer and his grey mare Meg stop at the Brig o' Doon so as to provide a wonderful, farcical, harmless spectacle.

As for what Burns added to Scottish poetry, nothing comparable has been done by one poet in one generation, or has endured for so long. His poetry does not disclose any terrible truth about human life, such as we find in the old poetry; it holds us simply by its strong familiarity, its knowledge of everyday Scottish country and small town life, intimately seen, and the life of the people blossomed as it had not blossomed before, and as it was not to blossom again. Burns saw it so clearly that he could see it in proportion, not merely at those moments which strike the deepest notes of poetry, though these he could strike with perfect simplicity and assurance:

> Thoul't break my heart, thou bonny bird,
>> That sits beside thy mate,
> For sae I sat, and sae I sang
>> And wistna o' my fate.

That is great poetry. But what strikes us more in Burns are those occasional verses from a great love-song such as "The Rigs o' Barley" which gave a sense of the general heightening of the feelings of one who is in love, and who seeks for emblems of love in the borderlines of occupation and distraction:—

> I hae been blythe wi' comrades dear;
>> I hae been merry drinking;
> I hae been joyfu' gatherin' gear;
>> I hae been happy thinking.

As if that happy night that "was worth them a'" had by some happy chance been combined with them.

21

*There Was A Lad**

The great posthumous misfortune that befell Burns was to have
a teetotaller for his first biographer. On the authority of a man
who knew nothing about drinking he acquired the reputation of
having drunk himself to death. It was quite undeserved, as we
know now; yet the popular legend supported by Burns's own
drinking songs composed when he was sober, still lives on. The
harm done by biographers is almost impossible to repair.

Mr. Hilton Brown's book, which sets out to do a great deal of
necessary repairing, is so good that it is a pity it should be
occasionally disfigured by an assumption of cynical realism
which does injury both to Burns and, one feels, himself.
Essentially his attitude to Burns is sympathetic and
appreciative; but his detestation of the sentimental legend of
Burns is so inveterate that it drives him to make such
extravagant statements as that "For Burns women existed for
one end and for one end only", forgetting for the moment that
Burns wrote "Mary Morison" and "My luve is like a red, red
rose", and that the feelings of the poet must have been the
feelings of the man.

Antagonism to the Burns legend may distort our image of
him as badly as acceptance of it, and when Mr. Brown picks out
prudence as one of Burns's characteristic qualities, one feels
that he is simply having a tilt at the legend. Burns had no

* [Review of *There Was A Lad* by Hilton Brown], *The Observer*, No.
8251 (24 July 1949), p. 7.

judgment in farming, plunged into one love affair after another, never thinking where they would lead him, got involved in what, according to Scots law, seems to have been bigamy, all with an entire disregard of the consequences. Every man is prudent in some way. But one does not insist on the caution of Don Juan, or on the practical good sense of Micawber.

Mr. Brown does not attempt a biography; but he does lay the foundations for what may some time be a genuine one. He clears away misconceptions; he deals honestly with the difficulty of seeing Burns clearly; he pierces some of the mists; and he looks with his own eyes. Perhaps the most interesting section of the book deals with Burns's dramatic image of himself and the pains he took to impose it upon his acquaintances. One feels it is from this self-dramatisation that the Burns legend originally arose. When a man is a natural actor he becomes more easy to understand in one way and more difficult in another. We see he is an actor, but we are left to guess what is behind the acting.

Burns was the most natural actor in the world; he had many parts and was convincing in most of them. He was the romantic lover when he wrote "Mary Morison", the practised seducer when he wrote to his raffish friends, the repentant sinner when he exclaimed that continued sensuality petrified the feeling. Mr. Brown seems inclined to think that the practised seducer was more real than the romantic lover. Both must have been real; yet the actor who wrote "My luve is like a red, red rose" carries more conviction than the one who advised his acquaintances on the arts of seduction. There is less vanity in him.

Mr. Brown invites controversy, because he says so many things that are new. His chapter on Burns's image of himself is full of illumination; that chapter on the technique of the poems is as good in a different way. He has seen Burns from an independent point of view, and his book will be indispensable to anyone who writes again about Burns.

22

A Romantic Poet *

It is sometimes the fate of writers who are understood by everybody in one age to be incomprehensible to another one. "Childe Harold" appealed immediately to the heart of its generation; it no longer appeals very strongly to our hearts, so that we have to understand it with our minds. And as there is very little in it for the mind, we are forced to try to understand why it was understood. Except for one or two lyrics, none of them quite perfect, a smally body of satire (none of it so good as Dryden, or even as Rochester), and parts of "Don Juan", almost all of Byron's poetry is dated in a sense in which the poetry of his greatest contemporaries—Wordsworth, Coleridge, and Keats—is not.

He outdistanced them at once in reputation for reasons which were comprehensible enough: he was a resounding poet, even if he was not a good one; and, possessing far more social sense than his rivals, he was able to catch more quickly and surely something which was in the air, and express before anybody else just what a great number of people wanted to have expressed for them. Nature had also made him look like a poet, and he assisted it to the best of his ability by a strenuous régime of excess and soda-water. On the top of all this he was an excellent publicity agent; he saw to it that both his poetry and his life had news value; he managed to requisition Europe as his

* [Review of *Byron: The Years of Fame* by Peter Quennell], *The Scotsman* (31 October 1935), p. 15.

background, and there, under a spotlight manipulated by himself, bade his native land goodnight and requested the dark blue ocean to roll on. It was a marvellous performance—the performance of a juvenile lead who had succeeded in deposing the more responsible members of the cast, and reducing them to their proper and inferior stations.

The ideal way to treat such a figure is the one employed by Charles Maurras in his brilliant book on Musset and George Sand. There Maurras demonstrated how the creed of romanticism actually worked out, a demonstration at once abstract and concrete, drawn both from general principles and observation. Mr. Quennell has not adopted this method; while on the whole averse to the particular kind of romanticism that was expressed by Byron and Musset and George Sand, he has no general criticism to pass upon it; and he treats Byron simply as an interesting human figure, whose life presents certain problems.

In his statement of these problems he is entirely admirable. It would be hard to put one's finger on any point where he is unfair either to Byrton or the many women who victimised or were victimised by him; and the whole management of the biographical material is beyond praise. Byron's vain, film-star side is shown without mercy: the curl-papers, the biscuits and soda-water, the slimming; but the reality of the Childe Harold side is also acknowledged: the pre-destinarianism, the feeling of ancestral guilt, the "fallen spirit" gambit, the fascination with what Conrad later called "the destructive element", a fascination which may have been one of the causes for his fatal attraction to his half-sister. What his relations with Augusta Leigh were has, of course, never been proved, and, indeed, cannot be, as Mr. Quennell very reasonably says; but he agrees that the worst interpretation is the most likely one. There is no doubt, at any rate, that the emotion which Byron felt most deeply and excitingly was the emotion of guilt; possibly it was necessary to him, as Mr. Quennell suggests; all his relations with women, at any rate, were involved with it; and of his relations with women none could have evoked it with more intensity that his affair with Augusta.

Mr. Quennell traces Byron's life from his return from the Continent in 1811 with the first two cantos of "Childe Harold", to his departure, in disgrace, five years later. During that time many women, including Lady Caroline Lamb, Lady Oxford, Augusta Leigh, and Annabella Milbanke, occurred in his life; he made an appearance in the House of Lords with applause; awoke to find himself famous; boxed; had innumerable affairs with female admirers; slimmed; got into debt; ill-treated his wife until she demanded and secured a separation; appeared assiduously in society as an *âme damnée*, and, finally, had to flee the country before the storm of innuendo which had gathered round his association with his half-sister.

Mr. Quennell seems to suggest that during this time all that Byron really wanted was peace and quiet, and holds that he did not really pursue women, but was rather pursued by them. Pursuit has an equivocal side, however; the rabbit does not pursue the snare; and it can be said of Byron that he succeeded in placing himself in a position where pursuit at least presented no very striking difficulties. When he was not pursued he showed a certain displeasure; and Lady Caroline Lamb's first ostentatious avoidance of him was followed by painful consequences. Also, he had a strong desire for power, as well as for public recognition, and there can be little doubt that he found a partial satisfaction for that desire in what was called at the time his "conquests", an enlightening term.

If one were to go upon Byron's portrait of himself in his poems and upon the history of his love affairs, one would be forced to think of him as a highly disagreeable character. He had certainly a very disagreeable side, as is shown in the brutal snobbery of his references to Keats, and also in his treatment of the women who loved him, when they became burdensome. But he was not nearly so bad as he made himself out; and Mr. Quennell's explanation of his apparent heartlessness strikes one as convincing.

> Had Byron (he says) been a less good-natured lover—had his gratitutde for affection been less immediate—it is probable that he would have caused infinitely less suffering. As it was, he found it difficult to say "No"—at least, at the beginning of a relationship, till desperation persuaded him to snap his chains. The brutality he sometimes displayed, when he struck for freedom, was directly proportioned by the indulgent facility with which he lost it.

He preferred to paint this weak good-nature as something vc like villainy, and considered it better to be thought wicked than feeble-willed. The fatal complications in which he involved himself during the five years of his public success in London might as readily have been brought about by weakness as by double-dyed infamy; and indeed, seen through Byron's predestinarian spectacles, the one became indistinguishable from the other. Mr. Quennell's book makes it easier to perceive this; his Byron is at least a human if not quite a likeable figure: a man even to be admired, though not in the ways he wished. The story of these five years is told with extraordinary skill, perhaps sometimes too amusingly, but also with genuine understanding. It is a very curious story, and well worth reading.

Scott and Tradition*

When one tries to relate Scott to tradition and see how he affected it and was affected by it, one discovers that there are two problems to deal with, two traditions to take into account. For Scott is both an English and a Scottish writer; he is related as closely on the one side to the line of English novelists whose greatest representative is Fielding as he is on the other to the anonymous ballads of his own country which he collected so lovingly and watered down so conscientiously. He derived from both those traditions, and in turn he influenced both.

There is an additional complication: the fact that he was caught up in the contemporary romantic movement. As a young man he had translated Bürger, and he chanced to live in a country which, for some reason or another, was regarded as peculiarly romantic. It was natural that he should yield enthusiastically to such a combination of advantages; yet he was not actually romantic in any deep sense, as Coleridge and Shelley and Hölderlin were; he was a shrewd improviser who made the best use he could of the situation, a situation which sentimentally had moreover quite a sincere appeal for him. His passion for ruins, heraldry, ancient customs and picturesque legends was perfectly sincere, and all these things were much in demand at the time.

On the other hand he had never any inkling of "The lost traveller's dream under the hill", to quote Blake's great

* *The Modern Scot,* III (August 1932), pp. 118-20.

romantic line. Lost travellers he did have a partiality for, but he liked to turn them into lost heirs, and once their estates were restored to them, they were not likely to go on dreaming under hills. His sense of mystery was very like that of the ordinary writer of mystery stories. Once it had served its end in complicating the plot of a novel it disappeared; it was a literary sham. Scott's working imagination was not really romantic at all, but sensible and practical, the imagination of a man of action.

In a short note like this one can therefore ignore the romantic elements in his work. To get some idea of how he affected the English novel and the Scottish poetic imagination, the best handy method is to compare him with his predecessors and successors in those respective traditions.

The eighteenth-century English novel was a criticism of society, manners and life. It set out to amuse, but it had a serious intention; its criticism, however wittily expressed, was sincere, and being sincere it made for more civilized manners and a more sensitive understanding of human life. Scott marks a definite degeneration of that tradition: after him certain qualities are lost to the novel which are not recovered for a long time. The novel becomes the idlest of all forms of literary art, and by a natural consequence the most popular. Instead of providing an intelligent criticism of life, it is content to enunciate moral platitudes, and it does this all the more confidently because such platitudes are certain to be agreeable to the reader. It skims over every aspect of experience that could be obnoxious to the most tender or prudish feelings, and in fact renounces both freedom and responsibility. Scott, it seems to me, was largely instrumental in bringing the novel to that pass; with his enormous prestige he helped to establish the mediocre and the trivial.

How much of the moral responsibility for this rests on him, and how much on his age, which was awakening to gentility, it is probably impossible to determine. The fact remains that all that Scott wrote is disfigured by the main vice of gentility: its inveterate indifference to truth, its inability to recognize that truth is valuable in itself. No doubt there have been countless genteel writers in the history of English literature. But Scott was the first writer of really great powers to bow his knee unquestioningly to gentility and abrogate his responsibility. As a result the tradition of English prose fiction was devitalized for more than half a century.

When we turn to his influence on Scottish literature we find the same story. There were not many genteel Scottish writers before Scott; there have not been many ungenteel ones since. His gentility can be seen in his *Border Minstrelsy* which he loved and yet could not but Bowdlerize. But the difference he introduced into Scottish poetry can be seen most clearly by comparing his own poems in the ballad form with the old ballads themselves. It is pretty nearly the difference between

> I lighted down my sword to draw,
>> I hackéd him in pieces sma',

and

> "Charge, Chester, charge! On, Stanley, on!
> Where the last words of Marmion,

the difference between a writer fully conscious that he is dealing with dreadful things and one who must make even carnage pleasing and picturesque.

Scott was a man of great native genius and of enormous inventive powers. But has any other writer of equal rank ever misused his gifts and indefatigably lowered the standards of literature with quite such a clean conscience?

24

Sir Walter Scott *

Scott is one of the most perplexing figures in literature. Not that there is any difficulty in his writings: they are generally quite straightforward, and at their best, in isolated passages, in the delineation of certain characters, achieve that "classic reconciliation" which Mr. Buchan claims for them. But only in isolated passages, in certain characters so solid that they walk out of the context; and it is here that Scott is so baffling. A writer who could create characters as real as Dandie Dinmont, Dugald Dalgetty, Andrew Fairservice, Bailie Nicol Jarvie, Edie Ochiltree, Cuddie Headrigg and his mother—the list must run into scores—should also have been able to create a world for them to live in; but what Scott provided is what his novels are made of—flesh and blood as solid as Fielding's, pasteboard as flimsy as Bulwer Lytton's. It is impossible for such substances to coalesce, and they never do in the Waverley Novels; the genuine characters live not in the world Scott gives them, but in another which cannot be found in his books at all; and so, in spite of their solidity, they have a sort of meaninglessness, they are related to nothing. Why did he never create their proper world for them? One feels that it must have been potentially in his mind in some form. Perhaps a final reserve of power was lacking in him, or remained unexerted. And that probably accounts for the feeling which Scott gives us: that not only was he incontestably a great writer, but also something highly

* *The Spectator*, No. 5439 (24 September 1932), pp. 364-65.

questionable and slightly absurd: a very great writer very greatly watered down.

There must be some partial explanation for such a mystery, and Mr. Donald Carswell, whose *Sir Walter* is the most independent as well as the wittiest of the various books about Scott that have appeared in the last few years, touches indirectly upon it in a recent article in *The Modern Scot*. Scott, he says, "presents the case, probably unique, of a man of high genius who was not faithful to his artistic vision—not actually unfaithful, but faithful only 'in his fashion.' He was an artist of the rarest creative gifts, but for some reason was always ashamed of the fact. . . . He wrote to his friends that he had no use for posthumous fame: what he wanted was contemporary success." "What he wanted was contemporary success"; he wanted Abbotsford as well; he wanted also to pay off the load of debt in which Abbotsford among other things had involved him: and the satisfaction of those wants kept him busy all his writing life; it perpetually drove him on, leaving him at most only a stolen moment now and then for his genius—to which he was faithful "in his fashion" between anxious thoughts of Abbotsford and Constable. One must remember in judging the Waverley Novels that they were written under the compulsion of urgent necessity, a necessity imposed by the wants of a man who demanded contemporary success. The conflict between the best-seller and the imaginative artist may then partly account for the discrepancies in Scott's novels. But not wholly, for one often feels that, apart altogether from Abbotsford and Constable, he did not care. Mr. E.M. Forster notes that "he has neither artistic detachment nor passion," and it cannot be gainsaid. He remains, in spite of all the explanations that have been found for him, a peculiarly inexplicable figure: a great writer without the significance that should belong to greatness.

The amalgam of flesh and blood and pasteboard which was his vision of the world he presented in a style notorious for its carelessness. Yet carelessness is not its worst fault—a careless style may sometimes be vigorous and expressive; its worst fault is bookishness. It is bookish in much the same way as Stevenson's, though with infinitely less skill. It is both artificial and slip-shod, and so presents an almost impenetrable barrier between the thing described and the reader. In his more rapid scenes Scott is like a man in an immense hurry who is encumbered with a very heavy overcoat, which, from sheer pressure of haste, he cannot stop to slip off.

There are moments, however, when literary convention as well as public approval allowed him to slip off his overcoat; and it is then that he shows the rare creative gifts of which Mr. Carswell speaks. In his use of Scots dialect he is a great and sensitive artist. The language his characters speak is not ordinary spoken Scots, but spoken Scots deliberately heightened, consciously used as a means of literary expression, as Synge long afterwards used the speech of the Irish peasantry. Take his harangue by Edie Ochiltree; he is showing Lovel his secret cave:

> "Few folks ken o' this place; to the best o' my knowledge, there's just twa living by mysell, and that's Jingling Jock and the Lang Linker. I have had mony a thought, that when I faund mysell auld and forfairn, and no able to enjoy God's blessed air ony langer, I wad drag mysell here wi' a pickle aitmeal—and see, there's a bit bonny dripping well that popples that self-smae gate simmer and winter—and I was e'en streek mysell out here, and abide my removal, like an auld dog that drags its useless ugsome carcass into some bush or bracken, no' to gie living things a scunner wi' the sight o't when it's dead—Ay, and then, when the dogs barked at the lone farmstead, the gude-wife wad cry, 'Whist, stirra, that'll be auld Edie,' and the bits o' weans wad up, puir thins, and toddle to the door, to pu' in the auld Blue-Gown that mends a' their bonny-dies—but there wad be nae mair word o' Edie, I trow."

The Scottish peasantry do not speak in such flowing periods. This style is Scott's own invention, and it shows an extraordinarily sensitive feeling for words and rhythm. In pure eloquence—an eloquence that recalls the Elizabethan drama—his Scots dialogue is unsurpassed by that of any other Scottish or English novelist. When they are using their own language his characters speak out for themselves like no other characters in prose fiction; they have an endless supply of vigorous, rhythmical and eloquent speech. This speech, moreover, has immense flexibility and range, and can express with equal force the pawky philosophy of Bailie Nicol Jarvie, the sickly querulousness of Andrew Fairservice, and the grief of the old fisherman Mucklebackit over his son Steenie's death at sea—in its unexaggerated pathos perhaps the finest passage in all the Waverley Novels.

It is characteristic of Scott that he should have relegated those eloquent figures, the only true children of his genius, to an obsequiously subordinate place in his books. His lifeless heroes and heroines hold the stage; it is their fates, we are asked to believe, that are important; and those humbler figures are mere servants or runners of errands. It is as if Scott shrank from dealing immediately with life as he knew it around him, and could seize it without fear only when it was separated from him by a broad barrier, in this case the barrier of class. The same terror of immediate reality can be seen in his portraits of women; he could never paint a passable portrait of any woman until she was past the dangerous age; his novels are full of vigorous beldames and sexless dolls. there is a weakness here that cannot be explained by his desire for contemporary success: an inner weakness, perhaps an inner terror; a need to put a good safe distance between himself and any deeper inquiry into human life. But if he was a great failure he was also a great man; and his achievement, fragmentary and in some ways absurd, still remains intact a century after his death.

25

Sir Walter Scott (1771–1832)*

Looking at Scott's life as a whole, one cannot but be struck by a deep cleft in it. This was shown early and may have been implicit in his parentage. His father was a lawyer, strict, conforming, respectable. His mother was impulsive and affectionate, a lover of poetry with a head stuffed with lawless tales. Scott inherited her love of poetry and her memory for stories; but in practical life he followed the example of his father. This antithesis clung to him permanently, making him pay in his novels a lip-service to lawlessness, while at the same time expressing a respectable man's reprobation of it. The division had another aspect as well. His mother's stories were about the past, and mainly about the past of the wild Border from which she came. His father was a faithful adherent of the Hanoverian House, who lived in the present and had no use for romantic legends. Scott set himself to live in the present; but he found himself pulled back into the past again and again, harmlessly in imagination and fatally in practice. Abbotsford is only understandable as the realization of an early dream which he had perhaps forgotten in the busy turmoil of his life, but which still determined his actions. The money which he made by his legal business and literary work gave him the means to realize this dream; yet of the last he wrote in words which would have pleased his father: "No man shall find me rowing against the

* "Sir Walter Scott (1771-1832)" in *From Anne to Victoria,* ed. Bonamy Dobrée (London, 1937), pp. 528-45.

stream." In his writing he never rowed against the stream; but in building a replica of an ancient Border community at Abbotsford he rowed against it systematically. The situation was roughly similar to a dozen or so in the Waverly Novels, where the young hero gets himself involved in a romantic adventure by some explained or unexplained necessity, without denying that the opposite side is right. In the novels the hero always returns at the end unscathed. Scott himself was never able to return; the necessity that drove him to create the extravagance of Abbotsford was a deeper one, and it finally destroyed him.

This conflict and its consequences he concealed from himself in his novels in the wish-fulfilment of the happy ending and in anonymity. It was his respectable paternal side that made him refuse to put his name to the Waverley Novels. He gave a number of reasons for this, but the only convincing one was: "In truth, I am not sure it would be considered quite decorous of me, as a Clerk of Session, to write novels." It was his father's side too that made him conceal his extravagantly fanciful business dealings with James Ballantyne, and perhaps his mother's side that drove him into them. Yet these two parts of his nature, the lawless and the conforming, the imaginative and the practical, never appeared in direct conflict; it would be more true to say that they played a complicated game of hide-and-seek with each other. In the novels this game is seen in an accommodating arrangement of experience whereby the blameless hero is able to indulge all the joys of lawlessness without coming to harm. In Scott's life the form it took was much more ingenious; it let him be a romancer and an anonymous gentleman of means at the same time, for his stories provided him with a very good income; but that income in turn paid for his most fatal romantic exploit, that is Abbotsford; so that it might be said that one side of him grew by a sort of blackmail on the other. The respectable side had finally to pay for all the excess of the fanciful; for in life such opposites have to meet sometime. But in the novels they never meet, and the result is that Scott's picture of life is always partly true and partly untrue in a very defined way; we can separate the one from the other as we cannot separate them in any other fiction of the first rank. There are dozens of characters in his novels

216

whom one feels he does not even wish to make real; almost all his women except the old ones, almost all his young men except those of the lower classes. His imagination was hampered by practical considerations. His love for Scotland was equally hampered by his adherence to the established order of the Union. This rendered his novels and his patriotism romantic in the bad sense, and made him get out of his two worlds, the past and the present, the cheapest they could give him; that is romantic illusion and worldly advantage.

To generalize on a man so great in outline and so complex in nature as Scott must seem useless; but a short sketch such as this cannot avoid it. Perhaps his main quality was a splendid largeness and generosity. He was incapable of jealousy. He was continually helping other people, and even after his ruin he could not rid himself of the habit. His novels show that he was incapable of hatred. He was what is called a quick judge of character, but he never judged people in the ordinary sense, except in two known instances; for he was harsh to one of his brothers and unfair to Constable. His Abbotsford experiment cannot be set down to snobbish love of display; it was a fatal realization of a dream which he had dreamt in childhood. His powers were probably crippled by his parental heritage, by his romantic attachment to the past and his prosaic respect for the establishment. If he had thrown himself into the real life of his time and looked forward to the future instead of clinging to the past, one feels that both his life and his writings would have been greater. "What a life mine has been!" he wrote towards the end, "half educated, almost wholly neglected or left to myself, stuffing my head with most nonsensical trash." This was his epitaph on his life, written in a moment of dejection. The "most nonsensical trash" must have been the mementoes of Scotland's past with which he filled his imagination and his rooms. The question is whether he had any choice; for there did not exist round him in Scotland a life as whole as the life represented by his mementoes and relics. Scotland in his time was neither a nation nor a province; it was a part of England and yet not a part of England; and this No Man's Land gave the final impress to his imaginations and his life.

His novels show the same largeness and generosity. He is probably the greatest creator of character and situation in

English literature except Shakespeare. His work, it is true, is consistently spoilt by the disparity in it between the man of imagination and the man who wanted to have the approval of the Edinburgh upper classes. Yet he was not merely a great writer spoilt, but a very great writer spoilt. Certain scenes in his novels are on the highest plane of poetic imagination: the scene in *Redgauntlet* where the Jacobites realize that all is lost because of an act of magnanimity by the English Government; the scene where Jeanie Deans pleads her case in London; and countless scenes in the pathetic style which have never been surpassed. His Scottish dialogue is an instrument for expressing all the varities of human feeling, and his mastery over it was absolute. His Journal will be read as long as his novels, as one of the most moving autobiographical documents in the English language. His long poems are second-rate; but he wrote several lyrics which, like parts of his novels, belong to the highest world of imagination. These expressed a sense of the vanity of action which ran completely counter to the glorification of action in his stories, and in them the tumultuous world of romance seems to die beyond resurrection. These lyrics belong to a private but very profound stratum in Scott's nature; his novels, with their splendid variety and richness, rather to his public character. The public and the private character never came together. If they had, one feels he would have been one of the greatest writers in English literature. As it is, he is very great on the level of obvious greatness, and perhaps the most remarkable man that his country ever produced.

26

The Scorpion*

This new biography draws unpublished material about Lockhart in the National Library of Scotland and letters in the possession of Sir John Murray and Mrs. Walter Maxwell Scott of Abbotsford. Miss Lochhead is to be congratulated on her industry and her sympathy for her subject, but she fails to make Lockhart attractive and irresistible—her own words. Indeed I feel that if she had shown less kindness to him she would have understood him better. For Lockhart remains a dark figure; one might as well try to be kind to Heathcliff or Iago. Not that he was on the same scale; what was bad in him came from weakness and a sense of his own sterility. His one great book is his life of Scott; Miss Lochhead rightly dismisses his novels as failures; even the best of them. *Adam Blair,* is very melodramatic. He will be remembered by his book on Scott and his attack on Keats.

He is difficult to understand because he gave out so little to take hold of except in his domestic life, where he felt safe and happy, and in his friendship with two very disagreeable men. John Wilson and Croker, both of coarser character than himself. Under their protection, and perhaps encouraged by their example, he discharged his venom at other writers in comparative safety, and anonymously.

Once when he was left uncovered, "he spent agonising

* [Review of *John Gibson Lockhart* by Marion Lochhead], *The Observer*, No. 8512 (25 July 1954), p.9.

weeks", Miss Lochhead says, "wondering whether the secret of his authorship would be discovered." In an abject letter to Croker, he admits having written an "Open Letter to Lord Byron", but cannot now for his life understand how he had come to be accused or even suspected of it, concluding: "I am a most unfortunate fellow." He had told Byron that it was more important to be a gentleman than a clever poet, and insinuated that Byron had used his quarrel with his wife "to affect utter broken-heartedness and yet be snatching the happy occasion to make another good bargain with Mr. John Murray." Not a word to show that he was sorry for the pain he had caused Byron; nothing but indignant grief at having been found out.

This incident not even Miss Lochhead can make attractive. She returns now and then to Lockhart's "pride". A man with any pride could not have written that letter to Croker, nor have made the brutal attack on Keats. From all the signs, Lockhart was devoured by envy and jealousy, and was too timid to give way to them except under cover. It was Scott, and his marriage to Scott's daughter, that in time helped to civilise him.

He could admire men of an older generation such as Coleridge and Wordsworth—he could hardly see them as rivals—but he was not a perceptive critic: fragments of "The Prelude" came his way and he found them disappointing. On the other hand, he did have the courage to refuse for *The Quarterly* an essay by his old friend Wilson on Wordsworth, written in the old snarling style. He asks Wilson:—

> Could one make "The Q.R." talk of W. W. as the fat, ugly cur, for instance?

And he returns the essay "most sorrowfull".

Towards the end, when family sorrows were gathering round him, he rose above his jealousies and envies, and wrote to a friend after the death of his son Walter:—

> Well, I suppose there is another world—if not, sure this is a blunder.

And a little later to his daughter Charlotte:—

> My dear and now only child, bear up, and learn to endure evil which is the staple of this mortal life.

He had added more than his quota to the evil of the world, and had once light-heartedly called himself "The Scorpion"; yet these words, called out by ordinary grief, still move us. Nevertheless, in spite of the life of Scott, in spite of Scott's indulgence and Miss Lochhead's kindness, it is hard to like him.

27

Best Sellers of Yesterday: VI William Black*

There is a slight awkward difficulty in writing of "the best-sellers" of yesterday; the term is a modern one, and the distinction it draws was not so universally recognised, and did not so generally apply then as now; for yesterday literature had not yet been logically commercialised. Novelists, whether good or bad, appealed not to a specialised puplic, but—as Mrs. Leavis has shown so clearly—to the public in general, which embraced indiscriminately the two reading classes that now exist side by side in separation, the high-brows and the low-brows. One of the effects of this was that the best-seller had to take some account of the more intelligent members of the community, had to pay a certain respect to literary standards. This was all to the good; but on the other hand, gestures of respect are easily taken at more than their face value by an entity as amorphous as the public; good will is accepted for performance; and a well-intentioned but mediocre writer may easily pass as a first-rate one.

This is what seems to have happened to William Black, and he is quite incomprehensible to-day unless we assume the existence of a single, mixed public. A born writer of best-sellers, he would impose too great an intellectual strain on the contemporary low-brow reader; his books are too well written; they contain too many allusions to Greek mythology and German poetry; they refer too frequently to such comparatively

* *The Listener*, VIII (7 September 1932), pp. 344-45.

unknown writers as Thomas Warton, as if everybody must be familiar with him; they set off at the smallest excuse on long and methodical descriptions of sunsets—a sunset for every emotional crisis—descriptions whose popularity can be explained only by the continued prestige of Ruskin and the still powerful influence of Wordsworth. Moreover, they contain sprightly dialogues on matters of general interest, dialogues that make the reader feel he is in very superior society and read now like a cross between Mr. Aldous Huxley and Mr. A.S.M. Hutchinson. The whole attitude is that of an author resolved to write a work of literature, resolved not to let literature down. That probably is why, after his great success, Black is so completely forgotten; why his name, unlike that of Rhoda Broughton, who was his contemporary, wakens no echo whatever in the mind: his work has too much literary pretension to pass muster among best-sellers now, and not sufficient literary merit to be interesting on other grounds

Black's literary aspirations were vain, then; and in spite of all he could do he continued to turn out nothing but books that sold. A best-seller is generally a story in which the author both has his cake and eats it; but it can also be one in which he goes on swallowing two cakes that violently disagree with each other without suffering any discomfort, indeed with complete enjoyment. Black's books belong to the latter class. the two things that he swallowed and flourished on were, first, Victorian respectability which, granting all its merits, was an oppressively narrow affair; and secondly, a wayward freedom which was in some undefined way exempt from the trammels of that respectability and never infringed or violated it. The strictest convention had to be vindicated, the most irresponsible liberty allowed. Perhaps the simplest way of achieving such a thing was the best. So Black introduced into most of his books some foreigner, generally of the female sex, in whom waywardness is both more graceful and more excusable. He introduced French girls and Italian girls and Greek girls, above all, Highland girls. He planted them in the middle of respectable English life; he described, with that somewhat fictitious sympathy which we give to people who are not so fortunate or unfortunate as to live within the conventions which encase ourselves, their delightful blunders, their justifiable, indeed righteous aberrations. He described these not only with sympathy but with delight, the pathetic delight of a schoolboy

223

dreaming of truancy while he is listening to the droning voice of his master and knows that there is no escape. His sympathy holds out even when his heroine pushes freedom past all permissible bounds, when she decides, for example, like the French heroine of *A Daughter of Heth*, to run away with a married lord. But the delights of truancy cease there; he firmly prevents the transgression; he sends a threatening sunset, and when that fails follows it up with a terrific tempest in which the recalcitrant heroine is struck down, and her lover's yacht, waiting impatiently outside Saltcoats, founders with the loss of all hands but one—not the lover. Yet the victim retains our sympathy, as an indigenous Victorian heroine would not have done; she has an excuse, the excuse of a freedom which, while delightful, is inevitably punished if it is pushed too far.

But in most cases freedom does not lead to such tragic results as in *A Daughter of Heth* and *Macleod of Dare*, another tragic best-seller (two books which unmistakably prove that a best-seller need not have a happy ending, if only virtue remains triumphant). It plays charmingly on the surface, in the whole scenes of novels of which *A Princess of Thule*, with its extremely correct and yet ostensibly unconventional Highland heroine, is the best example; it is indeed better than freedom, for it is in reality only another and novel kind of respectability, not ours, making for the same kind of righteousness. But here one is confronted with a real difficulty. If freedom is not freedom at all, but only a different kind of respectability, the whole point vanishes; the truancy is not really truancy, the escape not really escape. At this point Black is extremely vague; indeed it is questionable whether he saw the problem at all. Like many people in his time he was conscious of the irksome narrowness of Victorian life, resolved to support it, yet perpetually on the look out for any little liberty, real or vicarious. He was besides a man of very limited imagination; he genuinely believed that foreigners were fundamentally and completely foreign—foreign, if one may put it in that way, even to themselves, foreign and romantic by nature, just as they appeared to him. He saw that a Highland or a French girl was exempt from the restraints of Victorian respectability; he did not draw the further conclusion that they were subject to a respectability perhaps as strict; though at the same time it must have been a vague divination of this that made him regard their escapades as harmless. So law and liberty were reconciled.

The wayward, or rather the apparently wayward, heroine was, then, Black's chief vehicle of a freedom that could be deliciously indulged without the slightest responsibility—an adroit, almost high-brow solution of an essentially low-brow problem. His second was just as high-brow. For we are as entirely irresponsible for the doings of Nature as for those of the French or the people who speak Gaelic in the North-West of Scotland. Besides, the freedom of Nature was accorded a peculiar reverential regard in Black's time, and people were likely to be far more deeply convinced that a mountain, for instance, was created by God than that the French or the modern Greeks were. So the licentious excess sometimes characteristic of sunsets was looked upon not merely as excusable, like the more playful indiscretions of young ladies of foreign nationality, but as edifying and even moral. A sunset could be as flaunting, as riotous, as lawless as it pleased; for a sunset had neither responsibility nor, what was still more important, sex. Even storms, often more deleterious in their results than even the most serious infringement of respectability, were more than countenanced; and Black had no hesitation in backing the unchained license of the storm against the circumscribed human license of his heroine.

The possibilities of release which this invocation of Nature opened out were tremendous. The longing for infinite freedom could be satisfied by the recurrent spectacle of unfettered sunsets, the desire for destruction glutted without remorse by the violence and the effects of earth-shaking tempests. No wonder that Black was popular during the most oppressive period of Victorianism. Our attitude to Nature has changed since Black's time. It is the persistent recurrence of his sunsets that helps to make him unreadable now; yet it must have been largely for his sunsets that he was read so widely then. No natural phenomenon seems to be so charged with general and easily tapped emotion as a sunset; but the particular Ruskinian response that Black made to it is gone. Yet as the passion which he flung into his long succession of sunset-pieces came from his heart, some of his descriptions are impressive in their way. Take this one from *The Strange Adventures of A Phæton*, whose plot is the most broken-backed of the many broken-backed plots that Black gave to the public, being an account of a rambling journey from the South of England to Scotland, a barefaced excuse for repeated descriptions of Nature: "Darkness fell over land and sea. The great plain of water seemed to fade away into the gloom of the horizon; but here, close at hand, the pools on the shore occasionally caught the last reflections of the sky and flashed out a gleam of yellow fire. The wild intensity of the colours was almost painful to the eyes—the dark blue-green of the shore-plants and the sea-grass; the gathering purple of the sea; the black rocks on the sand; and then that sudden bewildering flash of gold from some solitary pool. The mountains in the South had now disappeared; and were doubtless—away in that region of darkness—wreathing themselves in the cold night mists that were slowly rising from the woods and the valleys and the streams".

There is real beauty, a real sense of wonder, in that description; it is not so drenched in yearning, so penetrated with what Ruskin called the "pathetic fallacy", as scores of others that could be quoted from these novels; yet as it is a repetition of a performance already given a countless number of times it is also a mechanical indulgence, and so one is not surprised that the next sentence should state flatly: "Such was our one and only glimpse of Wales". Black is perpetually giving himself away in this fashion. The accumulated emotion has been discharged, a need has been satisfied, and will be satisfied again, by another sunset, whenever it arises; but after every relief the author and his characters remain exactly the same, as staunchly, as strictly, as impenetrably Victorian as before. A catharsis more businesslike, more adapted to the needs of a great commercial nation, could not be imagined.

Yet the man who provided it had obviously to be above the average intellectual level of the more naïve purveyor of best-sellers. He had to be romantic in the cheapest sense, but he had also to have a genuine devotion to literature, for the natural descriptions on which so much of the effect of his books depended were steeped in literary influences. His senses had to be trained in a quite artificial and even subtle manner, but without affecting his fundamentally trite way of looking at life; he, in short, to be both a man of culture and an intelligence as commonplace as Rhoda Broughton. It seems an inexplicable combination. Yet it was a combination fairly common in the tasteless Victorian age, and very common in the land of Black's birth. For he was born in Scotland, a country where even among the ignorant reading is regarded as a virtue, but where it very seldom has much effect on the reader's sensibility or original disposition, retaining too often a sort of theoretical quality. Moreover, he had studied art as a young man and had the painter's eye, the academic painter's eye perhaps, for natural things, including sunsets. His devotion to literature was also genuine up to a point, which is defined appropriately enough perhaps by the fact that he was literary editor of *The Examiner* and later editor of *The London Review*; that he relinquished the latter post to become assistant editor of *The Daily News*; that he threw up that post in turn after the decisive success of *A Daughter of Heth* to devote himself to novel writing; and that in 1887, after achieving a dozen or so of best-sellers, he was chosen to write the volume on Goldsmith in the English Men of Letters series. The flavour of his books, faintly literary and sentimentally romantic, permeates with extraordinary persistence their very titles: *A Princess of Thule, Madcap Violet, Macleod of Dare, The Beautiful Wretch, Judith Shakespeare, Sabina Zembra, Briseis.* The beautiful wretch ("wretch", as archly applied to wayward young women, was a term of which he grew somewhat nauseatingly fond in his latter days—occurs again and again in *Briseis*, one of the last and worst of his novels) might serve as a formula for the majority of his heroines.

I have said nothing of Black's plots, for his appeal to the public could not possibly have depended upon them, so perfunctory and casual, so almost non-existent in most cases, are they: and this may perhaps explain why *A Daughter of Heth* and *Macleod of Dare* could end in disaster without affecting their sales. He achieved popularity by dangling before his readers' noses an illusive hope of freedom, and by gratifying that hope with a debased Wordsworthianism. He did this in all good faith, for he himself was clearly deluded by that hope, and believed firmly in the nobility of Nature. He would be an incongruous figure among contemporary true-blue best-sellers; yet he is at one with them in an essential respect, that he vulgarised everything he touched. If that is done with enough thoroughness, even the "story" for which reviewers are always crying can evidently be dispensed with.

28

Robert Louis Stevenson *

In the general eclipse of Victorian reputations no one possibly has suffered more than Stevenson. For while the fillip of ironical or hostile criticism has galvanized his colleagues into a new life—a life which is probably unwelcome to them—Stevenson has simply fallen out of the procession. He is still read by the vulgar, but he has joined that band of writers on whom, by tacit consent, the serious critics have nothing to say. So extraordinary, indeed, is the neglect into which he has fallen that when one surveys his literary period, the period of Meredith, Hardy, Swinburne, Bridges, Pater, Henry James, Mr. Geore Moore, Mr. Kipling and Mr. Shaw, it is only by an effort of memory that one contrives to include him. Partly, no doubt, this has been brought about by the overwhelming triumph of two movements: the sociological propandist movement represented by Mr. Shaw and Mr. Wells, and the realistic movement inaugurated in England by Gissing and Mr. George Moore, carried on by Mr. Galsworthy, and still busily practised by few hundred novelists. This latter movement was so powerful some years ago that when Mr. Frank Swinnerton wrote his intelligent and destructive book on Stevenson it seemed final. For some time, however, the realisitc convention has itself been disintegrating under criticism, and so it is more easy to see Stevenson now with unpartisan eyes.

Stevenson died in 1894 in his forty-fourth year. That is to say,

* *The Modern Scot,* II (October 1931), pp. 196-204.

he was still, for a novelist, a young man. Moreover he was younger than his years, for he had spent his childhood and youth in a country where everything combined to prevent an imaginative writer from coming to maturity. After three centuries of a culture almost exclusively theological, imaginative literature in Scotland in Stevenson's time was tolerated, where it was tolerated at all, only as an idle toy. That a novel should influence the character or humanize the emotions was an un-Scottish idea; and if Stevenson's relatives and advisers had contemplated such a secular operation it would have seemed to them illegitimate and insidious; for by its working morality, which should come uncontaminated from its pure source in religion or philosophy, entered the character by clandestine ways, indeed stole past conscience by lulling it to sleep, and took the soul by carnal wiles.

So one of the earliest ideas which must have been implanted in Stevenson's mind by universal suggestion was that story-telling was an idle occupation, and could be tolerated only as long as it remained so. He had before him, moreover, the example of his great countryman Scott, and he was probably too young, and too securely enclosed in national literary prejudice, to see that Scott's immense powers too were made idle by the general expectation of his countrymen that they should be idle. His fate indeed was typical of the fate of all Scottish imaginative writers since the Reformation who have not been, like Carlyle, directly and loudly concerned with ethics. In a country whose culture is almost exclusively religious, conscience finally becomes a matter concerned with only two spheres, the theological and the crudely material. There is no soil on which an artistic or imaginative conscience can grow, and no function for the novelist therefore except that of a public entertainer. If he refuses to accept the *rôle* he can, it is true, hit back at his audience as George Douglas did so savagely in *The House with the Green Shutters*. But that, though an exhilirating, is an unprofitable exercise, and for criticism at once serious and urbane, the civilizing delineation of Fielding or Thackeray, there was hardly any scope in Scotland in Stevenson's day. So one may account in great measure for the tragedies of Scott, Stevenson and Sir James Barrie, all of them writers of genius, and all of them stultified. What distinguishes

Stevenson from the other novelists of his race, however, is that he was not eagerly ready to be stultified; he suffered under his annulment and struggled against it; he strove to become the writer he was by endowment; he persistently aspired to be something more than a purveyor of light relaxation for serious church-goers; and there is little doubt that had he lived he would have been the first Scottish novelist in the full humanistic tradition.

There was another constricting national influence which Stevenson, like his most notable predecessor, had to struggle against, and overcame only in the last book he wrote. For Scotland was not only a religious, it was also a puritanical country, and not only puritanical, but ruled by a puritanism which had withered into a dry gentility. There was little gentility about puritanism in the sixteenth and seventeenth centuries; on the contrary it was an extremely frank creed, calling wickedness by its bluntest objective names; and no words recur oftener in Knox's writings and conversation than "whoredom", "adultery", "fornication", and the like. Yet if an overwhelming pressure of reprobation is directed against any class of transgressions for a great length of time, finally it will become sinful ever to mention them; and by Scott's age a convention the direct reverse of Knox's, and yet a belated consequence of it, had come into operation. That convention, the convention of silence, is still the mark of the more puritanical classes in Scotland as elsewhere, and Knox's vocabulary would now seem as indecent to them as D.H. Lawrence's. The effect of this convention on Scott was to make him turn all his heroines into dolls, and deprive them effectually of sex by the simple expedient of depriving them of life; so that when he wanted to portray a living woman he had to wait until she had passed the compromising years. In his long and impressive gallery of robust and passionate old women, there is not one but had done something or other in her youth; yet whatever could it have been? The question can no longer be answered; but two things are clear, that it was done in the fabulous past, and that it is a thing that cannot be allowed in the Waverley Novels. This is how the convention of silence affected Scott. It affected Stevenson in a different way; it made him keep woman out of his novels altogether for a time. He admitted her at last in the guise of Catriona, but there his failure was so lamentable that he might have been pardoned for never having anything to do with women again. He refused to give in, however, and finally he prevailed against the convention; for in his last book he drew full-length portraits of two women, one old and the other young, which are the most natural and exquisite in Scottish fiction.

He shared another fault with Scott, and he has been nauseously praised for his boyish irresponsibility. This too may largely be put down to his early environment. A society which makes a writer a mere entertainer tacitly deprives him of any civic status, puts him among the superior mountebanks, and, if he is a man of independence, drives him into a showy Bohemianism. The defiantly picturesque pose which Stevenson assumed was in part at least the cloak under which he hoped to conceal his humiliating function, that of having to please everybody. Having a conscience, moreoever, he began by taking his task very seriously; he set out even more deliberately than Scott to please everybody; he insisted almost importunately in pleasing, and convinced himself that this was one of the main duties of a writer. Yet at the same time he had an exquisite distaste, an uncannily sharp eye, for the time-server, the ingratiating windbag, and the type recurs again and again in his stories; he cannot get away from it. Beginning with Ben Gunn in *Treasure Island*, a tender if contemptuous portrait, the type is drawn with an ever colder and more destructive humour in the later stories, until in his last book the subtly repulsive figure of Frank Innes sums up the whole tribe. Is it fanciful to see in those portraits a distorted reflection of Stevenson the teller of time-serving tales in the mind of Stevenson the serious artist and the Calvinist? The Calvinist certainly had something to do with it. Volubility itself is an offence in puritan countries, but volubility exerted to please is an incomprehensible offence; it is both abject and unnecessary. Stevenson was, moreover, an admirer of the hardier virtues; it was one of his complaints that "our civilization is a dingy ungentlemanly business; it drops so much out of a man"; yet he was fated to pursue a vocation which in his own eyes was more accommodating and less perilous than that of a haberdasher or an attorney.

Accepting the vocation of a story-teller, however, and at his country's valuation, he was still left with one province where he could assert his independence and vindicate his conscience: the province of language. No matter how idle the tale he had to tell, he was resolved to tell it in words which might have graced the noblest themes. Here he was as nearly incorruptible as a popular entertainer could be. Yet style and content cannot be divorced, and his style suffered in two ways. It was too uniformly literary, and, his function being after all that of a pleasure-maker, it was too anxiously pleasing. Where it displeases us is by trying to please too much. If one compares it with the style of a contemporary of Stevenson, a writer whose utterance was just as consciously personal, it becomes light and secondary, in spite of all its genuine and laborious graces. The description in *The Master of Ballantrae* of the winter night in which the two brothers fight their duel is one of the finest passages in Stevenson before he found his full powers in *Weir of Hermiston*, and it may serve as a test.

> "I took the candlesticks and went before them (the brothers), steps that I would give my hand to recall; but a coward is a slave at the best; and even as I went, my teeth smote against each other in my mouth. It was as he had said: there was no breath stirring; a windless stricture of frost had bound the air; and as we went forth in the shine of the candles, the blackness was like a roof over our heads. Never a word was said; there was never a sound but the creaking of our steps along the frozen path. The cold of the night fell about me like a bucket of water; I shook as I went with more than terror; but my companions, bare-headed like myself, and fresh from the warm hall, appeared not even conscious of the change."

That is vivid and skilful in spite of the touches of affectation, the windless stricture and the smiting teeth. But set it beside a few sentences from Doughty's *Arabia Deserta*, and one feels at once the difference between a writer building up a pleasing romantic picture, and one treating of actual and displeasing things. It is a description of the great eruption of Vesuvius in 1872, and I have room only for a few sentences:

> "I approached the dreadful ferment, and watched that fiery pool heaving in the sides and welling over, and swimming in the midst as a fount of metal,—and marked how there was cooled in the air a film, like that floating web upon hot milk, a soft drossy

232

scum, which endured but for a moment,—in the next, with terrific blast as of a steam-gun, by the furious breaking in wind of the pent vapours rising from the infernal *magma* beneath, this pan was shot up sheetwise in the air, where, whirling as it rose with rushing sound, the slaggy sheet parted diversely, and I saw it slung out into many great and lesser shreds. The pumy writhen slags fell whissing again in the air, yet soft, from their often half-mile parabolas, the most were great as bricks, a few were huge crusts as flagstones. The pool-side spewed down a reeking gutter of lavas."

From such a comparison there is no escaping; Stevenson's phrases become mere flimsy decoration, and we see that the scene to which they lead up, the whole plot of the story of which that scene is the crisis, the characters, the setting, everything shrinks into decoration. Far the most of what Stevenson wrote withers in this extraordinary fashion. Then as though, like the hero of one of his stories, he had suddenly been transplanted into a new personality, he began when he was over forty to speak in the unaffected voice of a great writer. It is as though a film darkening his genius had suddenly been removed, so that we see in a flash all that he might have become.

The length of time during which this film continued to darken Stevenson's powers is the most melancholy riddle of all. That he should choose romantic themes was comprehensible enough, for he lived in a country where life was drably commercial or genteelly pious, where the diurnal round was unsweetened by culture, and where accordingly beauty and grace were habitually sought in the past and the strange. Habitually, for up to this time the Scottish novel had meant very largely the historical. Yet he had a more intelligent literary instinct than any of the other Scottish novelists. What made him continue for so long to avoid the real subject-matter waiting for him, which he ended by treating so superbly? His boyishness, his irresponsibility, his romanticism, these we can see were an escape; yet we do less than justice to him if we think they were an escape merely from the environment which he had known as a child and a youth. They were an escape from something far more terrible at the same time: the disease which threatened him so persistently, and which he fought with such genuine courage. One has the painful feeling, reading of the buried treasure which recurs so often in his stories, sometimes indeed quite irrelevantly, as though it were an obsession, that we are reading of the treasure of health which he sought for so desperately and never found. His malady indeed colours all his earlier work, both the good and the bad. It may even have been of positive use to him when he set out to draw his brilliant portraits of parsimonious types, such as Ebenezer Balfour in *Kidnapped*, for the compulsory discipline of the invalid, who must learn to dole out his strength daily as though it were an infinitely precious and irreplaceable substance, has points of resemblance with the solicitously cultivated obsession of the miser. Then there is the theme of disheritance, the subject both of *Kidnapped* and *The Master of Ballantrae*, and the one which perhaps adumbrates most pathetically Stevenson's long struggle for his lost heritage of health, for a life as free from sickness as that of his robust heroes. But though disease was the subject he knew most intimately, hardly ever in his stories is it directly introduced, so deep apparently was his need to ignore it if he was to go about his business. So it is only behind these flimsy and incongruous costume dramas that we can guess at the real, suffering Stevenson. And when at last the moment of clairvoyance came, and he wrote *Weir of Hermiston*, it was as though he dreaded the effort, and felt that he was exposing himself to a fatal peril. Having begun the book he left it aside almost for a year. "Then," says Sidney Colvin, "in the last weeks of his life, he attacked the task again, in a sudden heat of inspiration, and worked at it ardently and without interruption until the end came. No wonder if during these weeks he was sometimes aware of a tension of the spirit difficult to sustain. 'How can I keep this pitch?' he is reported to have said after finishing one of the chapters; and all the world knows how that frail organism in fact betrayed him in mid effort."

The difference between *Weir of Hermiston* and the other novels is simple and startling: the story is genuine, original and of the first rank from beginning to end. Everything is suddenly real. Take the following passage describing young Weir's feelings in church on a spring morning:

> "He could not follow the prayer, not even the heads of it. Brightnesses of azure, clouds of fragrance, a tinkle of falling water and singing birds, rose like exhalations from some

deeper, aboriginal memory, that was not his, but belonged to the flesh on his bones. His body remembered; and it seemed to him that his body was in no way gross, but ethereal and perishable like a strain of music; and he felt for it an exquisite tenderness as for a child, an innocent, full of beautiful instincts and destined to an early death. And he felt for old Torrance—of the many supplications, of the few days—a pity that was near to tears."

How tender and yet inflexible that is! It is not the style which we usually think of as Stevenson's. It is at once simple and full, delicate and noble, and without a trace of affectation. and it is the style in which, except for an occasional lapse in the first few chapters, *Weir of Hermiston* is written.

The whole story indeed has a noble gentleness and inflexibility. The figures exist in a clear dawn, and have the freshness of a morning race, where everyone without effort or distortion is a little above the human scale. All are so heroically complete, like natural objects, trees or rocks, that when the action casts them against each other we fear the injury to natures which in their power, if not always in their virtues, are so godlike. For all of them, even the Lord Justice-Clerk and the four brothers of Cauldstaneslap, rude as they are, embody something so precious and admirable, that it seems unbearable that the action should violate and perhaps destroy it. They differ from Hardy's characters, tragic in a lesser fashion, by their integral and active power. The dramatic conflict is more intense, the justice more impartial, the outcome more significant; for the outcome with Hardy was often, one feels, a foregone conclusion before the action began. Had it been finished *Weir of Hermiston* would have been something unique in fiction, a modern saga, a novel combining two elements which are almost always disjoined: a modern sensibility and a heroic spirit. It is a fragmentary monument not only to Stevenson's own unfulfilled powers, but to an unfulfilled possibility of modern literature. It is the one touchstone of his genuine status as a writer, and judging him by it, one can almost say that no other writer of his time showed evidence of equal powers.

So after the sentimental glorification of his contemporaries, and the neglect of his immediate successors, something of Stevenson still remains: a fragment of a masterpiece. The literary fop and the romantic story-teller were very largely make believe. For the greater part of his life Stevenson played at being a genius. This exasperated his successors, sober realists or busy amateur sociologists, who had no patience with such trifling. They could not know that the poseur playing at being a genius may chance after all to be a genius, and a genius quite unlike the mask which has deceived the world and perhaps himself. It is indeed an unlikely contingency, and the disguise was the most baffling that could have been found. And the disguise itself no doubt pointed to a hidden weakness. Is Stevenson's weakness completely explained in tracing it back to his heredity and early environment and the disease which he to fight so long? Or was there some personal flaw? Sidney Colvin has a very interesting description of Stevenson at the age of twenty-two in the preface to the *Vailima Letters*. "To know him was to recognize at once that here was a young genius of whom great things might be expected. A slender, boyish presence, with a graceful, somewhat fantastic bearing, and a singular power and attraction in the eyes and smile . . . a brilliant strain of humour and an unsleeping alertness and adroitness of the critical intelligence . . . in the formation of opinion and the conduct of life impatient, even to excess, of the conventional, the accepted, the trite . . . perceptions and emotions acute and vivid in the extreme . . . his judgments, whether founded on experience, reading, discussion, or caprice, not less fresh and personal . . . while to his ardent fancy the world was a theatre glowing with the lights and bustling with the accidents of romance. . . ." Too good to be true, one feels at once, too convincing to be real; it might be the portrait of a man of genius, or it might as well be that of a charming poseur exploiting his attraction. It is in fact both of these inextricably confused, and the author of *Treasure Island* and *The Dynamiters* is certainly there as that of *Weir of Hemiston*. It is as elusive as Stevenson's photographs, in which the expression seems continually to be on the point of changing, to be flying away before it can be caught; flying away perhaps to some place so absurdly childish or romantic that even its owner is not quite prepared to countenance it.

An Austrian writer who died a few years ago also had a long struggle with consumption, and also left in his writings a semi-fabulous account of his struggle. Franz Kafka was a far greater writer than Stevenson, and an incomparably greater mind, and his superiority is shown most clearly in the imaginative use he made of his tribulations. The hero of *The Castle* struggles like Stevenson's romantic heroes for the possession of hidden treasure; it is vouchsafed to him only at the moment of death. What he fights for, however, is not riches or fame, but the solution of the problem of life, and through that for redemption. The struggle is removed from its temporal ground; but it is not falsified, it is universalized. It is the starting point from which begins Kafka's inquiry into the problem of destiny. Stevenson had courage in abundance, but he had not the courage which turns the knife in one's own wound to investigate it, to discover what it means, or how it can be squared with divine and human ordination. He tried to forget it, and only a moral pedant could condemn him for doing so. But the difficulty about forgetting is that one can rarely forget altogether, and he only succeeded in doing so when near the end of his life a great theme took absolute possession of him. His fate, curiously enough, was the same as that of the hero of *The Castle*; after circuitous wanderings for twenty years he found his mark almost too late.

29

The Real R.L.S*

This is an important book. It dissipates for the first time several elaborately discreditable stories which certain of his biographers gathered round Stevenson's name. It advances evidence where there was mere supposition. The full evidence, it is true, was not available until a few years ago: the correspondence with Henley, and part of the letters to Mrs. Sitwell. Mr. Furnas is fortunate in having been able to consult this material so long inaccessible; but he deserves the highest praise for the manner in which he has used it.

Some of the results of his use of the material are really surprising. There is the case of Claire, in whose shadowy existence biographers found "hints of a love tragedy of intense passion and suffering acted in Edinburgh in the opening years of Stevenson's manhood." According to one piece of evidence, drawn by a medium from the spirit world, she was "a blacksmith's daughter . . . in her teens, a beautiful fair-haired lassie." Subsequent biographers, both easy and conscientious, adopted this mysterious figure, and argued busily about her. It seemed she was not fair but dark, not innocent but only too experienced, not Lowland even but Highland. Mr. Furnas now proves from some unpublished letters of Stevenson to Mrs. Sitwell that Claire was a character in a novel which he was never able to finish, and that when he wrote, "Of course I am

* (Review of *Voyage to Windward* by J.C. Furnas), *The Observer*, No. 8416 (21 September 1952), p.9.

not going on with Claire" (a sentence which has brought him a reputation for callousness), he was merely in the middle of a literary difficulty.

The legend of Stevenson's early love affair is not the only one which melts away under scrutiny. One biographer asserted that Mrs. Sitwell was the real Claire; yet Mrs. Sitwell's relations with Stevenson now turn out to be quite blameless. The quarrel with Henley was plainly caused by Henley's jealousy and dislike of Stevenson's wife, and it was expressed in such a nauseating mixture of insinuation, bullying and fawning that Stevenson had no choice but to break with him. Mr. Furnas does not take sides in these controversies; he states the facts, lets them speak for themselves, and makes us heartily thankful for an honest biographer.

To have cleared away so many false but persistent stories would itself make this an indispensable book for students of Stevenson, but it might not have made it a good biography. Actually it is one of the most interesting biographies that have appeared for a long time. The reader may be surprised at first by an unusually informal style sometimes falling into oddity; yet it is full of character, the style of a man who sticks to his own idiosyncrasy. Mr. Furnas is continuously alive and responsive; he enters into each phase of Stevenson's life with direct sympathy, as if at each stage he were contemporary: an unusual gift. But though he is responsive he is not uncritical; he likes his subject with the discriminating liking of an old and tried friend. His knowledge of the South Seas and Samoa makes it possible for him to follow Stevenson, as an amicable travelling companion, to the end.

The portrait of Stevenson in this book is vivid and lifelike and resembles only in superficial points the portrait to which we are accustomed. It would be hard to formulate the general impression, but one cannot help feeling that in spite of Stevenson's impetuous intimacies, he was a man difficult to know. In his letters he seems to speak from the heart, but the charm which he could neither discard nor control comes between him and plain and direct utterance. That charm was so obvious and natural that it captivated Henry James as well as Henley, and extended itself equally over the discriminating and the undiscriminating, the good and the bad, the young and the old. It was his essential quality. He had others more reliable, courage above all. But the charm was infused so strongly into all his responses to life that they became set and stylised before their time. One can see this transmutation in his letters, above all in his stories.

Perhaps the charm came from his perennial youthfulness, which he carried with a sort of apologetic grace. Mr. Furnas notes that after establishing himself in Samoa he assumed at last a belated maturity. This may help to explain the difference between the greatness of *Weir of Hermiston*, which he never lived to finish, and the playboy attraction of a story like *Kidnapped*. He died while he was still young, at the moment of his greatest promise.

30

George Douglas*

A little over two decades ago, *The House with the Green Shutters*, a novel by a young Scots writer, George Douglas, attracted the attention of the critics. It was in reality one of the great novels in the English language. While the sensation caused by his book had not yet subsided, an announcement appeared in the journals that the author, still not much over twenty, had died in tragic circumstances. Hardly anything was said at that time about his brief life, and very little has been said to this day, out of a regard for his misfortunes which, mistaken or not, one must respect. We know now that he was the illegitimate son of a Scots farm servant girl; that he was educated at his village school and, on account of his precocity of talent, sent later to Glasgow University; and that he died after having written his first novel. That work, full of genius and style, is still read and remembered by people who appreciate imaginative literature; but for a decade now I have not seen it mentioned in any review. Yet in solidity, in form, above all in imaginative power, it is easily greater than anything that has been achieved since, either by the reputations (a little aging) of Mr. Conrad and Mr. Galsworthy, or by later writers such as Mr. Lawrence and Mr. Joyce whom no one can avoid the obsession of taking too seriously. Of Douglas it may be said that the only gift he lacked in comparison with his contemporaries was that of becoming the rage; his other talents were of the kind which are given only

* *Freeman*, VII (4 April 1923), pp. 80-3.

to great writers. The novel which *The House with the Green Shutters* resembles most is *Wuthering Heights*, and if Douglas was inferior to Emily Brontë in pure imagination, in the capacity to create a world of art which is real and yet is not the world of reality as we see it, he was her superior in many ways: in a power of visualization not like hers, wild and romantic, but exact and solid; in a ripe knowledge, marvelous for his years, of the motives which determine human conduct; in a sense of life which might without exaggeration be compared with that of Scott; and in an architectural completeness which in achieving harmony does not become artificial. Every quality in his novel was genuine and was great, and such as one might have predicted to weather all the accidents of time. Yet, after twenty years, the book has all the appearance of having come to grief. The chance which robbed Douglas of life after he had written his first book, also robbed that work for the ensuing decade of the notice which was its due. Had the author lived to write a few successors to this novel, these, even had they been mediocre, would have assured it of fame by keeping the author in the central regard of the public.

The House with the Green Shutters is, like most first novels in our own time, an autobiographical novel. It is partly the record of the unalleviated life of young John Gourlay (an imaginative portrait of the author), and partly the story of the downfall of the Gourlay family and of the symbol of its pride, the house with the green shutters. These two themes are woven into one, giving the book a unity and an accumulating movement towards disaster. The elder John Gourlay, the chief figure in the book, is one of those Scotsmen of little intellect, brutal will and contemptuous absence of pity who can be found in positions from the highest to the lowest, in Scotland and all over the world. He is stupid, slow of speech, relentless towards his inferiors, without fear of his superiors, giving and taking no quarter; and he is the richest man in the little town of Barbie, where all the small people hate him on account of his wealth, his insolence and his stupidity. Denied by the dullness of his parts, and perhaps by his honesty, the posts of honor which his social position should have gained him (he could not even hope to become the Chairman of the Gasworks!), he builds the house with the green shutters, the most prominent house in Barbie, "cockit up there on the brae", as a symbol of his power and superiority. "Every time he looked at the place he had a sense of triumph over what he knew in his bones to be an adverse public opinion. There was anger in his pleasure, and the pleasure that is mixed with anger often gives the keenest thrill. It is the delight of triumph in spite of opposition. Gourlay's house was a material expression of that delight, stood for it in stone and line." He was always embellishing it, always adding to it, and every improvement "had for its secret motive a more or less vague desire to score off his rivals. '*That'll* be a slap in the face to the Provost!'" he smiled, when he planted his great mound of shrubs. 'There's noathing like *that* about the Provost's!'" The Provost, the Deacon, and all the other great little men who suffer under Gourlay's power and indifference, are in time corrupted by their hatred towards him and their inability to give it effect. "But, oh no, not he; he was the big man; he never gave a body a chance! Or if you did venture a bit jibe when you met him, he glowered you off the face of the earth with thae black een of his. Oh, how they longed to get at him! It was not the least of the evils caused by Gourlay's black pride that it perverted a dozen characters. The 'bodies' of Barbie may have been decent enough men in their own way, but against him their malevolence was monstrous." These "bodies" act throughout the book as a malignant chorus to Gourlay's drama, acrid and unavailing at the beginning, when he is at the height of his power, but rising in sordid triumph as he sinks beneath the blows of a new competitor in the town, a man more clever but more ignoble, on the whole, than himself. Gourlay falls in the end through an inability to adapt himself to the changes which come with the arrival of the railway at Barbie; through the fecklessness of his wife, "a long, thin, trollop of a woman with a long, thin, scraggy neck, seated by the slatternly table, and busy with a frowsy, paper-covered novel"; and the failure of his son, a suffering creature, insolent in prosperity and abject in adversity. These causes ultimately bring about the downfall of the house of the green shutters and the death of all the Gourlays by violent means.

A fatality lies on young Gourlay from his birth; the shapes and colours of things are so intensely apprehended by him that they bring him a personal terror before nature and life. "With intellect little or none," the author says briefly, "he had a vast, sensational experience"; and that is the cause of his apparent cowardice, his incapacity to face the world. He was born in circumstances of unusual terror. I quote the passage, both as indicating the artistic *motif* for young Gourlay's life, and as an example of Douglas's exact and vivid powers of description.

> Ye mind what an awful day it was (he makes one of the characters say), the thunder roared as if the heavens were tumbling on the world, and the lichtnin' sent the trees daudin' on the roads, and folk hid below their beds and prayed—they thocht it was the Judgment! But Gourlay rammed his black stepper in the shafts, and drave like the devil o' hell to Skeighan Drone, where there was a young doctor. The lad was feared to come, but Gourlay swore by God that he should, and he garred him. In a' the country-side driving like his that day was never kenned or heard tell o': they were back within the hour! I saw them gallop up the Main Street' lichtnin' struck the ground before them; the young doctor covered his face wi' his hands, and the horse nickered wi' fear and tried to wheel, but Gourlay stood up in the gig and lashed him on through the fire.

The mother was never herself again; the boy was born weakly and fretful, and so afraid of the anger of nature that even when he was grown up a thunderstorm sent him hysterical with terror. A storm broke one summer afternoon when he was in a little wayside station.

> A blue-black moistness lay heavy on the cowering earth. The rain came—a few drops at first, sullen, as if loath to come, that splashed on the pavement wide as a crown piece; then a white rush of slanting spears. A great blob shot in through the window, open at the top, and spat wide on Gourlay's cheek. It was lukewarm. He started violently—that warmth on his cheek brought the terror so near. . . . "The heavens are opening and shutting like a man's eye (he cried as the lightning came and went), Oh, it's a terrible thing the world!"

An absolute clearness of vision into the forms of nature, with a total inability to do anything with it: that is the tragedy of young Gourlay.

If this portrait is autobiographical, as it is almost certainly, it is surely one of the strangest pieces of self-revelation ever written. Such self-loathing combined with such clearness of knowledge and delineation, such a masterly holding of oneself up to contempt, a contempt felt first and led by oneself, have an unusualness that approaches unnaturalness. One can not look upon the portrait with pity, for the mood of the author kills a sentiment which to him, one feels, would have appeared facile. Young Gourlay suffers from beginning to end, yet his sufferings do not awaken compassion in the author, but a mood which one can only call disgust. The human race was disgusting to Douglas as it was to Swift, and its sufferings had generally something ridiculous or mean in them which made them only another circumstance of disgust added to the sum. It was to Douglas, one feels, a metaphysical indignity that the people whom he delineated in *The House with the Green Shutters* should exist; and his novel came clean out of a burning negation of life as he knew it, and with most intensity, therefore, out of a negation of his own being. In this negation there was nothing consoling, no ease from the fact that one had existed, and that in existing one had been vain, vulgar and unreal, as the majority of the human race are. The thing, accordingly, which obsessed him most strongly was not vice or suffering, but the disfiguring touch of vulgarity which he always found upon them. In his portrait of young Gourlay, he revealed this ineluctable vulgarity of existence relentlessly; but inwardly he was appalled by it. This much is sure: only a spirit of the most fine fastidiousness could have apprehended vulgarity so vividly and have hated it so extravagantly. The cowardice of the world, the good sense of the average sensual man, may easily see in such an excess of sensitiveness something pathological; but any one who detaches himself from the conspiracy of mankind will scarcely deny that Douglas spoke the truth. And truths such as his are not profitless; they are, on the contrary, in the highest degree salutary for us, who usually have no very strong sense of the unsatisfactoriness of our existence as we live it. Douglas saw, it is true, the ignobility of life too constantly, too exclusively. Not one or two, but all of his characters are betrayed into some meanness which we feel is ridiculous, into some movement of the body or of the mind which recalls faintly the gestures of the lower animals. But these perceptions gave Douglas no satisfaction; they were, on the contrary, the obession and the torment of a disappointed spirit to whom human life and the

245

existence of this world were not enough.

There is a kind of imagination which manifests itself in the vivid realization of great scenes; and there is another kind, higher, indeed the highest, which is shown in the unremitting grasp of the passions and conflicts of the characters in a work, from the beginning to the end. Douglas possessed the latter in a high degree; but he possessed the former in a degree greater than any one else since Emily Brontë. There are places in *The House with the Green Shutters* where the conflict between the two wills is held for twenty pages with that intensity of imagination and greatness of truth, which, though common in great literature, always astonish us. The last scene between Gourlay and his son, which ends, because there is no other issue for it, with the murder of the father, is too long to quote. It is one of the greatest scenes in literature. In the realization of the immediacy of the enmity between father and son there is nothing to set beside it; and in this direction tragedy could go no farther. I must content myself with transcribing one or two pasages less great than this, among the many in the book. After the murder, young Gourlay is pursued by the hallucination that his father's eyes are following him. He soaks his mind in drink and locks himself up in the stable.

> An hour later he woke from a terrible dream, flinging his arms up to ward off a face that had been pressing on his own. Were the eyes that had burnt his brain still glaring above him? He looked about him in drunken wonder. From a sky-window a shaft of golden light came slanting into the loose-box, living with yellow motes in the dimness. The world seemed dead; he was alone in the silent building, and from without there was no sound. Then a panic terror flashed in his mind that those eyes had actually been here—and were here with him still—where he was locked up with them alone. He strained his eyeballs in a horrified stare at vacancy. Then he shut them in terror for why should he look? If he looked the eyes might burn on him out of nothingness. The innocent air had become his enemy—pregnant with unseen terrors to glare at him. To breathe it stifled him; each draught of it was full of menace. With a shrill cry he dashed at the door, and felt in the clutch of his ghastly enemy when he failed to open it at once, breaking his nails on the baffling lock. He mowed and chattered and stamped, and tore at the lock, frustrate in fear. At last he was free! He broke into the kitchen, where his mother sat

weeping. She raised her eyes to see a disheveled thing, with bits of straw scattered on his clothes and hair.

"Mother!" he screamed, "mother!" and stopped suddenly, his starting eyes seeming to follow something in the room.

"What are ye glowering at, John?" she wailed.

"Thae damned een," he said slowly, "they're burning my soul! Look, look!" he cried, clutching her thin wrist, "see there, there—coming round by the dresser! A-ah!" he screamed, in hoarse execration. "Would ye, then?" and he hurled a great jug from the table at the pursuing unseen.

The jug struck the yellow face of the clock and the glass jangled to the floor.

Mrs. Gourlay raised her arms, like a gaunt sibyl, and spoke to her Maker quietly, as if he were a man before her in the room. "Ruin and murder," she said slowly, "and madness; and death at my nipple like a child! When will Ye be satisfied?"

This passage, beginning in realistic analysis, rises gradually until it attains in the end a kind of poetry which is at the same time a simple statement of the literal truth; "death at the nipple like a child" being a cancer contracted long before from a blow given by the husband. This one stroke of intense imagination, in which the mother, after having suffered blindly for so long, realizes in a moment, and in simple, universal terms, all that has befallen her; and emerges, not on the plane of ordinary living but on that of aesthetic contemplation, where her sorrows seem to be impersonal, belonging to her and yet not belonging to her, is one of those signs by which one can tell a writer of great endowment from one of secondary power. Only genius could have realized that situation; and Coleridge in his analysis of imagination would have admitted it as a legitimate example. In his evocation of states such as this, which go to the very limits of human endurance, Douglas is wonderfully sure; and his scenes are full of mastery and vigour as well as of horror. He had the capacity to let himself go, and to let the passions of his characters stand naked before us on the page, as if they had no control over themselves and no choice but to do so.

But his genius was not always on the stretch; his gifts were too solid to manifest themselves in one direction only. He had a capacity not unlike Carlyle's for the vivid phrase. One of his Scotsmen coming back from Paris describes the incense in Notre Dame as "burning stink". Old Gourlay "had a chest like the heave of a hill". After Templandmuir had insulted him and walked away in the darkness, "his blood rocked him where he stood." Logan, the middle-aged tippler who loved the society of youths, "the slow, sly, cosy man, with a sideward laugh in his eye, a humid gleam" was attracted to young Gourlay on their first meeting in Edinburgh. "He sat smiling in creeshy benevolence, beaming on Gourlay, but saying nothing." It is possible that only a Scotsman, who knows the nuances of the adjective, can grasp all the virtues of that inimitable and ignoble picture. Such minor triumphs as these illustrate perhaps better than his great scenes the most remarkable of young Douglas's qualities; his ability to render confidently and unerringly, with hardly one uncertain touch, whatever his imagination attempted; and his imagination rose to the highest themes.

The House with the Green Shutters is an autobiographical novel, but it is autobiographical as *Roderick Random* and *David Copperfield* are autobiographical; that is, with a true detachment, a true measure, and an immense realization not only of the chief figure, but of the life which surrounded him, giving to the portrayal that universality and justice which we demand from art. It is not, like the best example in the other genre, Mr. Joyce's *Portrait of the Artist as a Young Man* (a work accomplished and sometimes, indeed, beautiful), a full-length picture of the writer himself seen from within, and of the world only through a sort of secondary vision, as it was observed or felt by the hero; but a vision of life with all the figures in which the author identifies himself by the magnanimity of imagination, in that renunciation which is the beginning of art. Mr. Joyce's book, to use a convenient philosophical term, is subjective merely, while Douglas's is objective as well; and this objectivity it is which by its presence distinguishes a true work of art from one which is only partially realized, and by its greater power and soundness distinguishes what we call classical art from the art which is generally termed romantic. The characteristic of classical art is that it is so securely objective that whatever circumstance of grief, of turpitude or of horror it may describe, it raises no echo in our ordinary subjective emotions, and is entirely incapable of corrupting us. The characteristic of romantic art is that, in giving us a picture of the world which is indeed aesthetic, it moves these emotions at the same time, and moves them pathetically and agreeably. But the characteristic of Mr. Joyce's art is, one must say, that it moves these emotions almost exclusively, and that the aesthetic picture which it leaves is in the last degree fragmentary and unsatisfying. In aspiration, in temper, in his view of life, Douglas was classical, but his classicism was plucked with "forced fingers rude"; and to detach himself from his characters he had to employ a coldness which was almost contemptuous, a harshness so grudging that it is a blot on the book. A spirit of unremitting calculation which, even when he has revealed the worst weaknesses of his characters, makes him go a little farther and discover a more abysmal meanness, gives his book a sense of terrible intimacy, where we feel that the last bounds of decency have been passed, and it is painful to look. Nevertheless we are persuaded in spite of our distaste; Douglas's pen, when it is most savage, is solid and just; and his art convinces us, as classical art does.

Yet *The House with the Green Shutters*, in spite of the greatness and solidity of its qualities, does not strike one as expressing fully the genius of Douglas. It has truth, imagination, style, architecture; and that confidence which, in a man of Douglas's powers of mind, could come only from a sense of his own genius. All his characters are seen with undeviating objectivity, with deliberate justice; yet there is something strained in his justice, and that is perhaps his chief fault. His objectivity was not a thing which had ripened of itself and fallen into his lap; he seized upon it violently, tearing himself, seeing that it was himself, when he tore it from experience. There is no serenity, therefore, in his detachment, but a constant separating struggle, which by its hardness imparts to his characters something hateful, the reflection of the deliberate enmity he had to practice to detach himself from them. In spite of his magnanimity, or rather because of it, and because it was attained with such effort, the mark of his reprobation lies on every one of his characters. As he is without serenity, so he is without pity; and his picture is sometimes unbearably grim and hateful. Yet when his imagination was freed by a great scene, and he was delivered for a moment from the struggle to remain aloof, and was carried into the spaces of art with all his faculties

249

consenting, he was indeed a great writer.

Life was hardly kind to him once from his birth, and was most harsh of all in leaving him when fame and enjoyment of his unfolding genius seemed to lie before him. but the qualities of his genius were so authentic, so solid, and so clearly not in their full maturity when he wrote his first book, that, with better fortune than he had been accustomed to, he must have lived to be the greatest writer of our time.

31

Lewis Grassic Gibbon: An Appreciation*

The world in general, or that part of it which is interested in good literature, is regretting the passing of Lewis Grassic Gibbon: those who knew him as Leslie Mitchell are mourning the deeper loss of a friend. I met him first only about two years ago, but I soon came to know him intimately—and one could not know him at all if one did not know him intimately: in his personal relationships as in his ideas and his expression of them he was as clear as the day, and he allowed no compromise to cloud friendship. Knowing him so well, I find it very difficult to judge him either as an anthropologist or as a writer. His anthropological ideas certainly meant a great deal to him, and they were founded on an extensive and exact knowledge of human history. He believed, with Professor Elliot Smith, that the legend of a golden age preceding the recorded history of mankind was founded on truth; that man was inherently good; and that his vices were caused by faults implicit in the succession of civilisations which rose from the cradle of them all, that is, ancient Egypt. This was a theory which appealed very strongly to me, as helping to explain the dream of an Eden which mankind has nursed so stubbornly through the darkest ages, and to justify the hope of a better future age which has inspired so many movements, both religious and secular, up to modern Socialism. We had many arguments over the subject nevertheless, in spite of our agreement; for we both liked

* _Scottish Standard_, I (March 1935), pp. 23-4.

argument, and took pleasure in seeing where an idea would lead if it were pushed far enough. The more extravagant the conclusions the better we were pleased. The last time I met Leslie Mitchell, I remember that he, George Malcolm Thomson and I started an imaginary battle which began in 1314 on the field of Bannockburn and ended in Peru somewhere in the middle of the nineteenth century. How we managed the complicated strategy I have forgotten by now—it was both a land battle and a sea battle—but I think that John Knox, whom Leslie suddenly decided to stick up for, came into it somewhere or other. Leslie Mitchell had this gift of unfettered extravagance in conversation which I imagine is given only to men who disinterestedly pursue great impersonal aims, when all thought of personal advantage is lost. He would gladly argue on any side, simply to give some unlikely idea a chance and see how it worked out. Yet he had, at the same time, a passionate devotion to such things as truth, justice and freedom, and a belief in their ultimate victory that nothing could shake. He was firmly convinced that man once lived a life of innocence and happiness; but all his impetuous energy was concentrated on drawing the vital conclusion from this, which was that by breaking the bonds imprisoning him man can so live again. This, I think, was Leslie Mitchell's deepest faith; and it can be discerned by any understanding reader in his novels no less than in his works on anthropology. Here he was on the side of Rousseau and Shelley. Obtuse people have detected a sordid view of life in his Scottish trilogy: actually the ideal of humanity that he upheld in all his books was an unwaveringly high and noble one.

A Scots Quhair will probably stand as his most remarkable book. It reflects more adequately than any of his others the qualities one felt in him as a man: his impetuous passion, his scorn of pretence, his endless curiosity about and sympathy for human life in its diverse forms, his Rabelaisian humour, his indignation at injustice, and his faith that if men were only freed from the bonds that make them what they are they would be worthy of respect and admiration. *A Scots Quhair* is more than a mere description of life in Scotland in the country, the small town and the city; and readers who blame it for not coming up or down to their idea of what such a description should be are merely guilty of misunderstanding. For the book is also a sort of testament of Leslie Mitchell's faith in humanity and of his love for his country, a love mingled with much disappointment and even anger certainly, but at bottom far deeper than the love of those who say soft and flattering things.

Leslie Mitchell was only thirty-five when he died. For a man of that age his achievement was truly remarkable; but nobody who knew him doubted that it would have been far surpassed by what he had it in him still to do. His mind was so adventurous and so unpredictable that it would have been bound to surprise even those who thought that they were familiar with it; and his energy was such that one could not imagine even old age exhausting its infinite variety. He had fought with hardship most of his life; and it seemed to everybody that he had almost reached a position where he could at last sit down and produce the work that was in him when death came. What his loss is to Scottish literature is past computation. He has left a few books which will continue to be read, and to his friends an inspiring memory. The qualities that stand out most clearly now that I look back on him are his boundless generosity; his disinterested passion for the thing that seemed to him most worth striving for, that is a society where men and women could live in freedom; his almost impatient intellectual curiosity; and his radiant personal charm.

32

Readers and Writers*

How little we know of contemporary literature! By a series of happy accidents I came recently into possession of a remarkable book. It was published this year; it is full of unusual literary virtues; yet in none of the literary reviews have I seen a single mention of it. It might have been printed in Central Africa and distributed among natives who could not read, for all I might have known a few weeks ago; and, like most people who write about books, I watch with vigilance, which is somewhat like despair, over those customary notices which tell one so little unless one reads between the lines. I reflected that there might well be a dozen or more other volumes worth reading lost in the hurry of the publishing seasons, until I began to realise that the present volume had had less than the usual chance, and a preliminary send-off which explained convincingly its obscurity. Its author does not reside in London, and, moreover, he is his own publisher.

The book is entitled *Annals of the Five Senses*; its author is Mr. C.M. Grieve; and it may be obtained from him, at 16, Links Avenue, Montrose, for 7s. 6d. It is, I believe, Mr. Grieve's first published work, and it is not only accomplished in style, but in almost every way original and unusual. It gives one an impression of obstinate and self-distilled novelty which is rare in present-day literature. It is not original in the sense that it

* [Review of *Annals of the Five Senses* by C.M. Grieve], *New Age, XXXIV* (15 November 1923), pp. 32-3.

contains fresh and powerful ideas, or provides a striking form for old ones. It does neither of these things; but in its approach to ideas and to life in general, it has an originality so arresting that one feels it as somehow unusual, almost foreign. It is as if an alien were writing in English without attempting to be English in anything but his language. Now this has not been very often done. Stevenson did not do it, although in essentials he was as unlike an Englishman as possible; nor has Mr. Conrad done it, Mr. Conrad, who has almost succeeded in being more English than the English themselves. Mr. James Joyce has perhaps succeeded better than anyone else; and in a something exotic and almost excessively accomplished in his style, Mr. Grieve is not unlike Mr. Joyce; and I should say that, except Mr. Joyce, nobdy at present is writing more resourceful English prose. Mr. Grieve is a Scot; that is, he is more intellectually subtle and on the whole less sane than the English who write English. Like Mr. Joyce he takes a delight in the subtle windings of the intellect for their own sake, and, like Mr. Joyce again, that delight is in him partly sensuous. This, which must make the book appear foreign to English readers, is part of its originality. It could only have been written by a Scotsman, and one of a type quite unguessed at by other peoples.

What that type is I can best define by enumerating some of the qualities of the book. It is a book of curious reflection and speculation, with an enjoying eye for things which are odd and apparently exceptional, and a disposition to find in these the real significance, and real riches, of life. To Mr. Grieve, and to the type of Scotsman whom he has brought into literature, there is infinitely more to be found in the by-ways of life and thought than on the main thoroughfare. He is interested not in the mean, nor in that kind of violent and obvious exception which is so often a reversed reflection of the mean, but in the natural, involuntary aberration where life gives itself away without knowing it. The more imperceptible this aberration is the better it is for Scotsmen of Mr. Grieve's type; and if it should happen to have two faces, and in deviating from the rule appear at the same time to conform to it, then it is perfect and satisfies completely the subtle Scots mind. For the source of this curious, and as it appears, living and fruitful cast of thought, one has not to search far, though one must search much, in Scotland. It is

255

the intellectual complement, infrequently present in fact, of Scots republicanism, of the Scottish disposition to look always for the man behind the title or the function, and to see human nature wherever humanity is, and in whatever strange disguises it may present itself. The excessive pleasure which Scotsmen get from Rabelaisian anecdotes, especially if they implicate the aristocracy or the church, is one aspect of this disposition of mind. Mr. Grieve is not Rabelaisian, save in the sense that he has a keen enjoyment of the humanity behind, and in, a thought or action; but I fancy that his attitude has nevertheless frankly Rabelaisian implications. He is full of curious observations and recondite quotations, to all of which he gives significance by making us feel the weight of human nature behind them. His book does not fall into any category. The form is neither story, nor essay, nor monologue; but it is nevertheless a form, and one admirably suited to the content. In spite of its youth, its undisguised immaturity, and its too persistent intellectualism, it is unusually packed with literary virtues, and its style is, save for occasional lapses into virtuosity, a delight to anyone who can appreciate the niceties of writing.

I must let Mr. Grieve's style speak for itself, although in a book so closely packed it is difficult to detach a passage for quotation. I make no pretence, that the following is a passage in any proper sense; and I have detached it simply as an example of Mr. Grieve's manner of writing, the main virtues of which seem to be exactness and elegance:

> "Why a man should be set off on a particular line of thought he could account for easily, and the methods in which particular aspects of a case presented themselves to such and such a mind he was able to realise in the most meticulous photographic fashion, but why they should do so was a perpetual mystery upon which he could not secure the faintest light. He could find no centre of motivation and rebelled at times against this spring slavery. He likened himself to a lighted circle, a camp-fire, into which came all manner of waifs and strays from the surrounding imponderable night. Deviously and incessantly, through many a mood which was sheerly pathalogical, in many an excursion which took him well over the recognised borders of sanity, he pursued his investigations. Still, all these mazy, meticulated divagations were in his mind only what insect life in the world as

256

we see it, ubiquitous, but infinitesimal. Another obscure ray he knew of which was fused in the broad light of his thought, and with the properties of which a tiny specialist-cell in his brain was always experimenting, emanating from his subtle realisation that beyond the individual mind of each man was a collective mind, quite different in its psychology, directed he could not imagine how, or to what ends, employing the symbols of religious systems, world politics and racial instincts. The little specialist was able to use this pretty much as a man uses electricity or radium. The consequence was that he was enabled, indefinably but quite definitely, to trace the thin line of his own mentality through all the incalculable fabric of the thought of humanity. This gave him latitude and longitude on the oceans of speculation."

This is Mr. Grieve at his most abstract and difficult, and it seems to me that there he is best. When his subject-matter is too easy his style does not sink naturally, as it should; and he then takes refuge in virtuosity. It is his chief temptation, and it leads him into such things as "nor was there any element of perturbation or torment in his mutable face." But in the next sentence he is very fortunate with "His eyes were happy and active as birds on a summer's morning, and his pipe was drawing evenly." There are faults and to spare in the book, as I have tried to show; but as an achievement in style it deserves the attention of every one still capable of maintaining attitude of expectancy twards contemporary literature, and I heartily recommend it to them.

33

To Circumjack Cencrastus *

The author of this poem is, I think, the most considerable Scottish poet since Burns; but for two reasons he has not so far won the recognition in England, nor the popular name in Scotland, which Burns secured very soon after the publication of the Kilmarnock edition. The first is that he writes in a Scots which, while like Burns' an artificial literary language, is far less watered down with English; and the second is that in his later poetry he deals with somewhat abstruse themes. His first two volumes, *Sangschaw* and *Pennywheep*, were collections of lyrics in which he used a synthetic Scots formed out of words and idioms taken from the Makars and such modern Scots dialects as suited his purpose. In his next volume, *A Drunk Man looks at the Thistle*, a long poem of some 3,000 lines, this language had become a natural medium with little or no trace of its artificial origin, a language capable of great poetic as well as broad humorous effects. "Hugh M'Diarmid" writes it now with the ease of one brought up in it, and the freedom of one continually forming and modifying his vehicle, The result is a poetic speech which in freshness and daring is, I think, quite unique to-day.

A new or a renewed language brings with it a new world of feeling and thought; and the intellectual fancies in *To Circumjack Cencrastus* could never have been put into contemporary English, for the shades of meaning in its speech come from

* [Review of *To Circumjack Cencrastus* by Hugh MacDiarmid], *Criterion*, X (April 1923, pp. 516-20.

different psychological roots. But neither could they have been put into Scots as it was written before "Hugh M'Diarmid" fashioned his new speech, for ever since Burns Scottish vernacular poetry has been local, treating only a few humble and conventional themes; the poverty of its vocabulary, indeed, making it incapable of anything more. Consequently, in the present poem we see a modern poet undertaking the task of treating for the first time in his own language the world of modern life and thought; of rendering that world with all the peculiar shades of emphasis which the spirit of his nation and his language imposed upon him.

The world of modern knowledge is too provisional and too vast, as I think was demonstrated in Robert Bridges' *Testament,* to be treated in the old systematic way; and in both his long poems "Hugh M'Diarmid" employs a more indirect method. He takes a symbol and pours his mind into it. In the present poem his symbol is the great curly serpent Cencrastus, the symbol of the thing which the mind always pursues and always falls short of; and his attack is a sort of catch-as-catch-can, resulting in a series of abortive attempts, reverses, modified successes, arguments with himself and his antagonist; in short, a confrontation of himself and his enemy, sometimes wildly humorous, sometimes serious; the whole making by oblique routes to a clearer apprehension of the ways of Cencrastus and a recognition of the primacy of the reason which is employed in discovering them. The poem begins with a long invocation whose refrain is

There is nae movement in the warld like yours.

Then it sweeps in everything, great or small, which might throw light on that movement: Scotland and Gaelic poetry (these being the author's most immediate pre-occupations), Professor Einstein and relativity, Rainer Maria Rilke and Sir Harry Lauder, the author's private affairs, politics and religion, scenes from low life, and speculations on the nature of reality. The scope of the poem is encylopaedic, but its arrangement is deliberately grotesque, or explicable only by a passage such as the following:

Vain is the Image of Leviathan
And vain the image o'reflectit throes,

259

For you rin coonter to the rhythms o' thocht,
Wrenched oot o' recognition a' words fail
To haud you, alien to the human mind,
Yet in your ain good time you suddenly slip,
Nae man kens hoo, into the simplest phrase,
While a' the diction'ry rejoices like
The hen that saw its ugly ducklin' come
                    Safe to the shore again.

An encyclopaedia sometimes rejoicing, sometimes in labour, sometimes topsy-turvy: this is the object of the author's attack, and he deals with this heterogeneous mass of material in a variety of ways: by speculation, satire, parody, soliloquy, rhapsody. Yet the poem remains completely in character throughout, and is obviously the full expression of an individual mind.

Scottish poetry at its best has never run to sweetness or magnificence like English, but to a sort of wild play with imagination and technique, coming from an excess of energy which expends itself both recklessly and surely. It is seen at its most characteristic in Dunbar, the greatest craftsman in Scottish poetry; but it is seen in Burns too, though he was only an apprentice in his art compared with the older poet. It is displayed in Dunbar's almost endless and yet effortless surplus of internal rhymes, his "showing-off", and in such grotesque fantasies as "The Seven Deidly Sins" with their wild but extremely skilful mixture of the coarse and the terrible. This kind of poetry by a natural twist, a "thrawnness", combines the most violently opposed elements out of an intellectual relish in the contrast. "Hugh M'Diarmid's" poetry is of this kind; for though there are passages in the present volume where he rises to magnificence, they are always broken into by some deliberate incongruity reminding us that he is simultaneously dealing with the greatest and the meanest things. To show this, however, I should need to quote at greater length than is possible here; yet this quality is the mainspring of all the transitions and contrasts which make the poem so various and so continuously interesting. His wit is more quotable, as when he finds the brief title of "the apprentice deid" for the living, and describes an emotion of relief by the lines

260

> And felt as gin Squire's poem had passed
> And let me see the Mune again,

and sees a vision of Sir Robert Horne being borne down
Sauchiehall Street in Glasgow,

> Lum hat and spats a' complete,

in the mouth of the Scottish lion, which has come out of the flag:
a half-heraldic picture not unworthy of Dunbar himself.

"Hugh M'Diarmid's" more serious passages are too long for
quotation; unfortunately, for it is in them that the extent of his
powers is displayed. He has, I think, in greater measure than
any other poet to-day, the impetuous force which sweeps the
reader away on long and rapid flights. But he has also a great
skill in descending, and in keeping our minds occupied until he
is ready for another ascent; for his invention never seems in
danger of flagging, nor the great variety of measures he uses
look like coming to an end. There are careless lines in this long
poem, but there is scarcely one which does not give the
delightful shock of originality. A poem so long, so various, and
so sustained as this, written on such a theme, could only have
been written by a man of poetic genius.

To Circumjack Cencrastus is in Scots, but I imagine it should
give no very great difficulty to an English reader. It is a pity that
the author has not provided a small glossary, for then there
need not have been any difficulty at all. But I shall quote one of
the harder passages, merely to show that, even when some of
the words are strange to him, the reader can gather from their
sound the atmosphere and mood the author wished to convey:

> Here in the hauf light waitin' till the clock
> Chops: while the winnock
> Hauds me as a serpent hauds a rabbit
> Afore it's time to grab it
> A serpent faded to a shadow
> In the stelled een its een ha'e haud o',
> Here in the daurk, while frozen
> Scurl on Life's plumm the lozen
> Skimmers—or goams in upon me
> Wan as Dostoevski
> Glowered through a wudden dream to find
> Stavrogin in the corners o' his mind,
> Or I haud it, a 'prentice snake, and gar

261

Heaven dwine to a haunfu'r haar,
Or am like cheengeless deeps aneth
To' sea or sunshine, life or death,
Chequer the tap; or like Stavrogin
Joukin' his author wi' a still subtler grin. . . .

I have to break off here; but this is a good example of the daring
and vitality of "Hugh M'Diarmid's" language, and as it is very
much more difficult than nine-tenths of the poem, I hope that
the English reader will see that he need not fear the book, and
that to attempt it will repay him.

262

34

A New Scottish Novelist *

The author of this book has very remarkable gifts. He is, first of all, a born writer; he uses words sensitively, forcibly and exactly, and at times with great poetic power. His observation of character and physiognomy is extraordinarily subtle, his rendering of half-conscious feelings and sensations full of definition. He has the very rare ability to create characters completely, from the crown of their heads to the soles of their feet, so that they give an illusion of almost physical reality; and he can evoke a scene just as solidly. He has humour, passion, sincerity, and an extremely effective turn for satire. Yet though *The Albannach* is a brilliant performance, and should receive an unequivocal welcome from a country not remarkable for brilliant performances in literature, it has too many faults to be satisfying, the worst of these being that it has really no effective construction.

This may be partly due to the fact that it is an autobiographical novel. For one of the faults of the autobiographical novel is that it is apt to end inconclusively, like Lawrence's *Sons and Lovers*, for example, and Joyce's *Portrait of the Artist as a Young Man*. The author is presented with the problem of breaking off his story of one human life at some point, and there is no point conceivable by him (except death, which would involve a sort of vicarious suicide) that is decisive enough to serve as the final conclusion of a work of art. Lawrence ends *Sons and Lovers* with his hero's

---

* [Review of *The Albannach* by Fionn MacColla], *The Modern Scott*, III
  (August 1932), pp. 166-67.

resolve to lead a different life; Joyce ends the *Portrait* with Stephen's dedication to literature. But the end is not really an end, but a beginning, the beginning of a dispensation which we are asked to assume will be better than the former one; and that assumption is never capable of convincing us, for no matter how sincere aspiration and resolution may be, we know that life goes on. "Fionn MacColla" has also rounded off his story by a device of this kind; the hero, having sunk into drunken apathy, is rescued by an idea which he sees springing up round him, the idea of nationalism. But to end on that note is to plunge us into the midst of the ordinary illusions of life, to deliver us up to their undifferentiated blind force after we have been living in a world in which they were merely objects of contemplation.

The construction of the book is unconvincing, then, and the conclusion false. there is also an occasional weakness in characterization; the figure of the kindly Glasgow priest is the worst example. But having said this one must return again to the virtues of a very remarkable book. It contains a whole gallery of portraits of an almost startling life-likeness. The father and mother of Murdo, the hero, are the best in that gallery; but the Highland minister with his unction, his gluttony and his lecherous little eyes is almost as good, and the various deracinated Highlanders whom Murdo encounters in Glasgow are completely convincing, though outlined with a few strokes. To come to the various scenes, the funeral of John the Elder is the best I have read in a literature well packed with funerals. The description of the row in the Glasgow café is also extremely vivid. But the passage that shows best the author's extraordinary power and sincerity of imagination is the one describing his half-mad terror in Glasgow after discovering that he was physically tainted. One may legitimately complain that here the author does not explain adequately the nature of the pollution (he is frank enough elsewhere, as is right); but the description of Murdo's state of mind is nevertheless the work of a writer of first-rate powers. These powers are undisciplined as yet, which is natural enough, seeing that this is a first novel; but they are unquestionably there, they make the reading of this book an exciting experience, and they are sufficiently extraordinary to make one wonder whether in "Fionn Mac Colla" there may not be the making of a writer of first class.

35

A Mature Book: The Quality of *The Serpent**

The quality which impressed me most in Mr. Neil M. Gunn's latest novel *The Serpent* (London: Faber 8s. 6d.) is its maturity. In writers of true imagination a typical development can be traced. At the beginning we find vivid flashes of insight into this or that province of experience; at a later stage, the writer's work appears to change, the kind of illumination we had grown accustomed to expect from it disappears, to be replaced by a different kind; later a semblance of indecisiveness is produced by the writer's struggle to use in one book all the potentialities of imagination which he has employed in different books at different times; and finally maturity comes of itself, and all the powers of his imagination fall into place and exert themselves naturally and as if spontaneously. I do not say that this is a description of Neil Gunn's development in particular; it is rather a general graph, applicable to the work of many writers, and particularly to those who have remained true to the needs of their genius. At any rate, *The Serpent* is a mature book, in this sense that we can see in it the free deployment and use of a mind of rare insight. The effect of imaginative maturity is to make you feel that everything you are shown is in its proper place and on its true scale. This is the effect produced by Neil Gunn's latest story.

That does not mean, of course, that it is made up of a given

* [Review of *The Serpent* by Neil M. Gunn], *Scots Magazine*, No. 39 (August 1934), pp. 382-84.

number of harmonious elements; the harmony resides in the total effect, but the material out of which it is woven is conflict, disaster, loss, betrayal, and on occasion supernatural horror. The harmony is not achieved by softening or disguising any of these things, but rather by making each ring out with its true note.

I do not intend to give a summary of the story, for the story would not be contained in the summary. It is the story of one man's life in the Highlands, with brief break in Glasgow, at the end of the Victorian Age, when Socialism was in its early idealistic phase. The unity of the story is the unity of one man's experience as seen by himself shortly before his death, when the pattern has already woven itself, and by turning round he can see it spread out before him. If you ask what the meaning of the pattern is, the only reply is that the pattern is the meaning, and the meaning the pattern; you cannot separate them, and put one here and the other there. With this I come back again to the sense of harmony the story produces; it is a kind of completeness; the saying of something, which is much more than the explaining of something. There are two things said (not explained) in the book with special power: the hero's love story, and his conflict with his father. Both these are beyond praise. But it is the story itself, in its harmony and completeness, that is the remarkable achievement. One is proud to think it belongs to Scottish literature.

Index

267